**RESCUED BY**

UPGRADING
YOUR PC
THIRD EDITION

Kris Jamsa, Ph.D., MBA

JAMSA
P·R·E·S·S
...a computer user's best friend®

Published by
Jamsa Press
3301 Allen Parkway
Houston, TX 77019
U.S.A.

http://www.jamsapress.com

For information about the translation or distribution of any Jamsa Press book, please write to Jamsa Press at the address listed above.

Rescued by Upgrading Your PC, Third Edition

Printed in the United States of America.
98765432

ISBN 1-884133-64-9

Performance Manager	*Technical Advisor*	*Proofer*
Kong Cheung	Phil Schmauder	Jeanne K. Smith
Copy Editor	*Cover Photograph*	*Technical Editor*
Rosemary Pasco	O'Gara/Bissell	Phil Schmauder
Composition	*Illustrators*	*Cover Design*
New Vision Media	Jeff Wolfley & Associates	Debbie Jamsa
	Marrianne Helm	
Indexer	Colin Hayes	
Kong Cheung		

Jamsa Press is an imprint of Gulf Publishing Company:

Gulf Publishing Company
Book Division
P.O. Box 2608
Houston, TX 77252-2608
U.S.A.

http://www.gulfpub.com

Contents

continued on the following page

continued from the previous page

Section One

GETTING STARTED WITH PC UPGRADES

Since you have picked this book up, it is reasonable to assume that you may be wondering if you can really upgrade your own PC. The lessons in this section not only show you that you can perform upgrades yourself, they also get you started. In fact, before you finish Lesson 1, you will have performed your first PC upgrade! By the time you finish Lesson 2, you will be able to open your system unit and identify the key components. So, put your fears aside and get started. As you will find, upgrading your PC is very easy. This section's lessons include:

Lesson 1 *Getting Past Your Fears (You Can Do This)*

Lesson 2 *Opening Your PC's System Unit*

Lesson 3 *Understanding Your Computer's Ports*

Lesson 4 *Understanding the PC's Expansion Slots*

Lesson 5 *Working with Boards and Chips*

Lesson 6 *Understanding Your Computer's CMOS Memory*

Lesson 7 *Replacing Your PC's CMOS Battery*

Lesson 1

Getting Past Your Fears (You Can Do This)

If you own or work with a computer, the reality is that your computer is already obsolete. Computer technology changes so fast that by the time you unpack a new computer, faster and more powerful systems are available. The good news, however, is that if your computer lets you perform your work, you can relax. The lessons presented throughout this book will show you several ways you can improve your existing computer's performance without spending a dime! In addition, you will learn fast and inexpensive hardware upgrades you can perform yourself to improve your system's speed without spending a bundle.

There are several new capabilities sweeping computer communities that include multimedia, computer-based faxes, and online access to the information superhighway. To make the most of your computer, you will eventually need a CD-ROM drive, a sound card, a fax/modem, and more memory. By following the step-by-step instructions presented throughout this book, you can easily perform these key upgrades yourself, saving a bundle.

You do not have to be a computer genius to perform the upgrades this book presents. In fact, you do not even have to like your computer. By working a lesson at a time, you will find that performing most upgrades is easy. In fact, after you have one or two upgrades under your belt, you will find your PC much less frightening. Also, when you experience the increased productivity that follows an upgrade, you will wonder how you ever got along without it. This lesson helps you "break the ice," letting you understand that, regardless of your level of expertise, you can perform computer upgrades yourself. By the time you finish this lesson, you will understand the following key concepts:

- What it means to upgrade your PC
- Why you will need to upgrade your PC
- When upgrading is not cost effective
- Steps you need to take before you begin an upgrade
- How upgrading your PC affects your warranties and registrations
- Common tools of the trade
- Performing your first upgrade is as easy as plugging in a hair dryer

The best way to get started is to begin. So, let's begin.

WHAT IT MEANS TO UPGRADE YOUR PC

Ask ten different users what it means to upgrade a PC, and you will probably get ten different answers. Everyone has a different view of upgrading a PC, based on their current needs. To the user who is getting started with multimedia, upgrading a PC might mean adding a CD-ROM drive and sound card. Likewise, to a traveling salesperson, upgrading a PC might mean adding a fax/modem. Finally, to a computer programmer, upgrading a PC might mean installing a new Pentium processor.

Upgrading your PC is simply the process of installing new hardware or software that improves your computer's ability to serve your needs. This book examines several different ways you can upgrade your PC. In some cases, the upgrade will require new hardware. In other cases, you might need to install new software. Finally, there will be some cases when you simply need to put your existing software to better use.

UPGRADING PC SOFTWARE

One of the most important PC upgrades you need to know how to perform is how to install or upgrade software. Just as many users do not feel comfortable with their PC's hardware, many feel even less comfortable with software—the programs your computer runs. As a result, many users still run old software because it "meets their needs" and because they have never performed a software upgrade.

In Lesson 31, "Installing New Software" you will learn how to perform software upgrades. As you will learn, installing software programs is very easy—software manufacturers work hard to make it easy. Like hardware upgrades, after you install one or more software programs, you will become very comfortable with the process. As a result, you will no longer be dependent on someone else upgrading your software for you!

IT IS HARD TO HURT YOUR PC

Many users hesitate to upgrade their PC because they are afraid of "breaking it." As it turns out, it is harder to damage your PC than you might guess. If you follow the steps presented in this book, you will not hurt your PC. So, treat your system with care, but do not be afraid to perform the operations this book's lessons present. In that same light, however, if something is not broken, do not fix it. Until you have more experience with PC upgrades, do not experiment.

WHEN YOU SHOULD UPGRADE YOUR PC

PC upgrades help you maximize your existing computer's capabilities. In some cases, you will upgrade your PC to improve its performance. In other cases, your upgrade will add new capabilities, such as a CD-ROM drive, sound card, or fax/modem.

Companies, such as Microsoft, release software upgrades for one of two reasons. First, some upgrades simply fix errors (called *bugs*) that were present in the previous versions. Normally, software manufacturers will offer such upgrades for free or for a very nominal price. Second, major software upgrades add new features to the software program. As a rule, you should normally upgrade your software to the latest version.

If you want to upgrade your PC to improve your system performance, you must first identify your computer's *bottlenecks* (the devices that slow down your PC). Use the following symptom list to determine where you should focus your initial upgrade efforts:

1. Programs start slowly after you double-click your mouse on a program icon within Windows—see Lesson 36, "Defragmenting Your Hard Disk," that discusses defragmenting your disk.

2. You experience considerable delays when switching from one program to another within Windows—see Lesson 37, "Fine-Tuning Windows Memory Use," on Windows memory management.

3. You are constantly struggling due to insufficient disk space—first see Lesson 39, "Cleaning Up Your Existing Disk Space," and then turn to Lesson 34, "Doubling Your Disk's Storage Capacity," that examines compressing your hard disk.

4. Your monitor's sharpness does not match that of another computer—see Lesson 19, "Upgrading Your Monitor," and Lesson 20, "Upgrading Your Video Card."

5. You experience delays when a program reads or writes to a file—see Lesson 32, "Improving Performance with a Disk Cache."

6. Your system does not start—see Lesson 42, "Basic Troubleshooting Tips."

7. You run two or more programs within Windows on a regular basis—see Lesson 12, "Adding Memory to Your PC."

UPGRADING DOES NOT MEAN REPAIR

Sometimes you will have a choice as to when you perform your upgrades. At other times, you will turn on your computer and . . . nothing. When your computer fails to start or when a hardware device stops working, you'll need to determine the cause. In Lesson 42, you will learn how to troubleshoot the most common PC problems. After you identify the source of an error, you will need to determine how best to correct it. With hardware costs constantly decreasing, you will normally find it less expensive to replace, rather than repair, hardware. In fact, by following the lessons presented in this book, you can perform many such replacements yourself. Unless you happen to be a hardware technician, you will not be able to repair most PC hardware devices.

WHEN UPGRADING IS NOT COST EFFECTIVE

Just as computer capabilities constantly change, so too do computer prices. So, there will be many times when you must weigh the cost differences between upgrading your existing hardware and simply purchasing a new system. For example, before you add multimedia capabilities, you need to determine whether your current system can handle multimedia applications. As a general rule, if your computer is less than two years old and you simply want to improve your existing capabilities, you should upgrade. For example, if you use your computer to perform word processing, you can normally improve your system's performance by adding memory (see Lesson 12), fine-tuning Windows disk-caching software (see Lesson 33), or by defragmenting your disk (see Lesson 36).

Note: *Most PC hardware, such as the processor, memory, and disk drives, doubles in speed or storage capacity every 18 months. So, if your PC is more than two years old, you should consider purchasing a new system.*

If you are adding new capabilities, however, you need to decide whether the upgrade is cost effective or whether you should purchase a newer system. As a general rule, if your upgrade exceeds $300, you should evaluate a new system purchase. For example, adding a $150 fax/modem to your computer can greatly increase your existing computer's capabilities. However, if you are considering a multimedia upgrade kit that includes a CD-ROM and a sound card, you might not be satisfied with your existing computer's performance. How should you decide when to upgrade or replace your PC? In general, when you shop for new hardware, ask the salesperson how a computer's type (such as a 386 or 486) affects the device's performance. In the case of a fax/modem, for example, your computer type will have no impact. For a multimedia upgrade, however, the faster your PC, the greater its multimedia capabilities.

BEFORE YOU REPLACE YOUR COMPUTER

Before you decide to replace your computer, make sure that you have "fine-tuned" your PC's existing capabilities. Specifically, make sure that you have performed the following operations:

1. Defragmented your hard disk, as discussed in Lesson 34, "Defragmenting Your Hard Disk."

2. Fine-tuned Windows disk-caching software, as discussed in Lesson 31, "Improving Disk Performance with a Disk Cache."

3. Fine-tuned Windows settings, as discussed in Lesson 37, "Fine-Tuning Windows Memory Use."

4. Maximized your existing disk space, as discussed in Lesson 39, "Cleaning Up Your Existing Disk Space."

5. Doubled your computer's current disk space, as discussed in Lesson 34, "Doubling Your Disk's Storage Capacity."

6. Installed the most recent version of your software programs, as discussed in Lesson 32, "Installing New Software."

To maintain maximum PC performance, you might need to tweak several of these settings on a regular basis.

BEFORE YOU GET STARTED

After you perform one or two hardware upgrades, you will feel comfortable with the upgrade process. Thus, when you perform subsequent upgrades, you may be in a hurry to get started. Put aside your desire to get started and take time to create a good working environment. To begin, make sure you are working in a well-lit area. When you install different hardware boards, you might need to change small on-board switches. If you cannot see the switches, you might end up spending a great deal of time trying to troubleshoot why the board does not work. In addition, you will want room to spread out your computer pieces. Likewise, make sure you have the proper tools of the trade, as discussed next.

TOOLS OF THE TRADE

Before you perform any of the upgrades presented in this book, you should spend a few dollars to get the right set of tools. Almost any computer store will sell a computer tool kit for less than $20. Purchase such a kit and place it in the drawer next to your computer. Should you ever need to perform an upgrade, you will have all the tools you need.

In addition, locate several empty pill containers. When you later perform an upgrade, you can place the screws you remove into related pill containers. By taking time to organize screws in this way, you will save considerable time you might otherwise spend looking for lost screws.

CHASSIS   OTHER

PERFORMING YOUR FIRST UPGRADE

Your first hardware upgrade is one of the most important upgrades you will ever perform and also the easiest. If your computer is not currently plugged into a surge suppresser, put down this book and run to the computer store! A surge suppresser protects your computer from electrical surges that travel down power lines, normally as the result of lightning. In short, the surge suppresser prevents the power surge from reaching your computer's hardware.

Suppresser

Outlet Suppresser   Chassis Suppresser

Although their sizes and shapes may differ, there are two primary surge suppresser types. The first surge suppresser plugs directly into the wall outlet. The second suppresser type typically sits beneath your monitor or PC.

The advantage of this second suppresser type is that it typically includes on/off switches for each plug, letting you control each hardware device.

To install a surge suppresser, perform these steps:

1. Exit all running programs and turn off your computer.

2. Unplug your computer and other devices, such as your monitor and printer.

3. Plug in your surge suppresser.

4. Plug your computer and other devices into the surge suppresser.

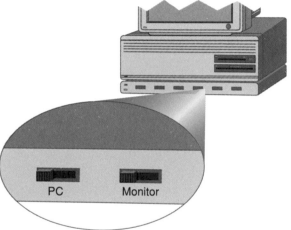

After you install your surge suppresser, you may be able to turn your computer on or off either using the computer's on/off switch, or the on/off switch found on the surge suppresser.

WHAT TO LOOK FOR WHEN BUYING A SURGE SUPPRESSER

As you shop, you may find several different surge suppressers whose prices vary considerably. Before you choose a suppresser, consider the following capabilities:

1. Is the surge suppresser Underwriters Laboratories (UL) approved?

2. Make sure the device is a surge suppresser, and not simply a power strip that merely provides more power outlets but no surge protection.

3. Does the surge suppresser provide on/off switches that let you control each outlet? Do you need such support?

4. Does the surge suppresser support modem phone lines? Remember, phone lines, too, are susceptible to carrying electrical spikes.

Note: If you travel with a laptop computer, you should purchase a small surge suppresser that you can take with you. In this way, you protect your computer resources while on the road.

A Word on MS-DOS and Windows 3.1

If you are concerned about productivity and you are still running Windows 3.1 on an MS-DOS-based PC, you should consider replacing as opposed to upgrading your PC. Over the past few years, PCs have become quite affordable, and for the price you would pay to upgrade each of your system components, you would be better served simply to purchase a new PC. Although many users feel that their older systems still meet their needs, in almost all cases, users will receive significant peformance benefits by moving to a higher performance PC. For those users who still plan to upgrade their MS-DOS-based system one piece at a time, this book will examine some key related topics.

Shutting Down Windows

Throughout this book's lessons, you must periodically shutdown Windows. To shutdown Windows, perform these steps:

1. Click your mouse on the Start button. Windows, in turn, will display the Start menu.

2. Within the Start menu, select the Shut Down option. Windows will display the Shut Down Windows dialog box.

3. Within the Shut Down Windows dialog box, click your mouse on the Shut down button and then choose OK.

Depending on the programs you run, you may find that you can improve your system performance by restarting your system once a day, such as first thing in the morning. To restart your system, you to do not have to power off your PC. Instead, you simply restart Windows by performing these steps:

1. Click your mouse on the Start button. Windows, in turn, will display the Start menu.

2. Within the Start menu, select the Shut Down option. Windows will display the Shut Down Windows dialog box.

3. Within the Shut Down Windows dialog box, click your mouse on the Restart button and then choose OK.

Understanding Warranties and Registration

Many users hesitate to perform hardware upgrades because they are concerned about damaging their computer or violating their computer's warranty in some way. If you follow the steps presented in this book, you will not damage your computer's hardware. Likewise, computer upgrades are a common occurrence. PC manufacturers sell computers with the knowledge that users will need to install new hardware boards over the PC's lifetime. By installing standard PC components, such as those discussed in this book, you should not violate your PC's warranty. Note, however, you should never open some high-voltage PC components, such as your monitor and power supply. Such hardware devices normally contain a warning message that tells you not to open it. Opening such a device will very likely violate the device's warranty and might place you in danger. When you purchase new hardware or software, the package will normally contain a registration card. Always take time to fill out and return such cards. Manufacturers use the card to make you aware of new products and upgrades. In addition, some manufacturers may require receipt of the card before they will provide you with technical support.

WHAT YOU MUST KNOW

Users can upgrade almost every PC in one way or another. As long as your computer meets your current needs, do not become obsessed with upgrading. However, by improving your computer's performance, you will very likely improve your own productivity. In the past, users had to determine when they could afford to upgrade their computer. In the future, you will need to decide when you can no longer afford *not* to upgrade. In Lesson 2, "Opening Your PC's System Unit," you are going to open up your PC and get to know several different pieces. Before you continue with Lesson 2, however, make sure that you understand the following key concepts:

- ✓ In the simplest sense, upgrading your PC is simply the process of using new hardware and software to get the most from your existing PC.

- ✓ Users often upgrade PCs to add new capabilities or to improve their system's performance. If you plan to add new hardware to improve your system performance, first identify bottlenecks within your computer.

- ✓ With the cost of computer hardware constantly decreasing, there may be times when it is more cost effective to invest in a new system than to upgrade an older system. When you plan to invest more than $300 on a hardware upgrade, consider buying a new PC.

- ✓ Before you perform a hardware upgrade, make sure that you have a well-lit work space, a tool kit, and containers to hold screws you might remove from your system.

- ✓ PC manufacturers expect you to add new hardware boards to your system. Thus, you will not violate your computer's warranty by adding a fax/modem or sound card to your PC.

- ✓ Having the correct tools can simplify most PC upgrade operations. Before you perform an upgrade, purchase a tool set from your computer retailer.

- ✓ If your computer is not currently plugged into a surge suppresser, make the installation and use of a surge suppresser your first computer upgrade.

Lesson 2

Opening Your PC's System Unit

Your PC's system unit houses your computer's disk drives, memory, central processing unit (CPU), motherboard, and other hardware boards, such as a modem or sound card. When you perform hardware upgrades, you normally must open up your system unit. For most users, opening the system unit for the first time can be quite intimidating. However, after you look around inside the system unit once or twice, you will find the process quite straightforward.

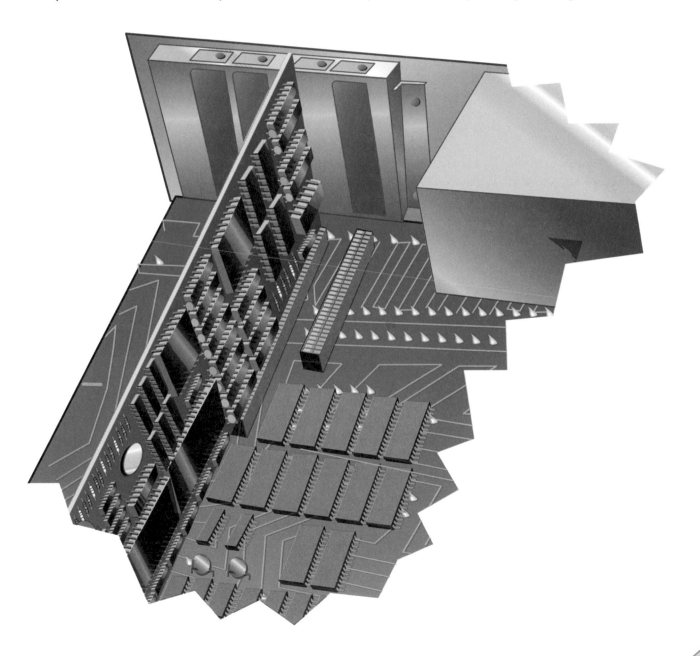

To help you become comfortable with opening your system unit, this lesson walks you through the steps you must perform. Before you get started, relax. By following the steps this lesson presents, you cannot hurt your system. By the time you finish this lesson, you will understand the following key concepts:

- Your system unit houses the PC's disk drives, central processing unit (CPU), memory, and other hardware devices.

- Regardless of your PC type, the system unit contents are the same.

- Before you open your system unit, you should turn off your PC and unplug your system.

- To open your system unit, you simply remove the screws that hold on the unit's cover and then remove the cover.

WHAT YOU WILL NEED

Before you get started with this lesson, make sure that you have the following readily available:

1. A PC tool kit with a screwdriver
2. A container within which you can place the chassis screws
3. A well-lit workspace with room for you to place the chassis

Note: *Never open up your system unit with the computer's power on. By working with the PC's power on, you not only risk damage to your system components, but you also put yourself at risk of an electric shock. In addition, you should unplug your system to further reduce your risks.*

OPENING YOUR SYSTEM UNIT

If you examine the back of your PC, you should find several screws that connect the system-unit cover to the chassis. Using a screwdriver, remove these screws. Place the screws into a container you can later locate.

Note: *To remove the system unit cover, you normally only remove the screws that are found on the outer edge of the system unit chassis.*

Next, gently slide off the PC cover. Be careful; the PC's system unit contains many cables. As you slide off the cover, make sure the cover does not hang up on one of the cables. In other words, if the cover does not easily come off, do not force it. After you remove the cover, place it to the side of your computer.

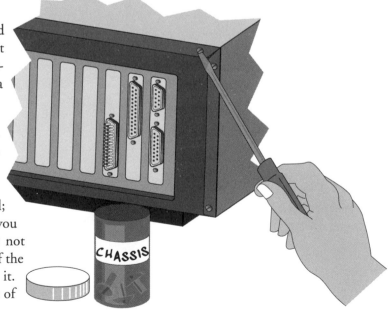

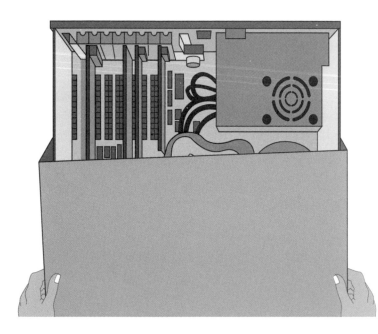

Note: As you slide the system unit cover off the PC, be very careful not to pull or stretch any of the PC cables.

Note: Before you touch anything else, make sure that you touch the outside of your system unit chassis to ground yourself. In this way, you will greatly reduce the possibility of static electricity damaging one of your computer's internal cards or chips. You may want to purchase a clip that grounds your computer while you work. In this way, you reduce the chance of static "zapping" your chips! For information on purchasing such a ground, see your computer retailer.

WHAT YOU WILL SEE

Whether you are using a tower or desktop PC, the components you will find within a system unit are the same. Before you continue, take time to identify the key components discussed next.

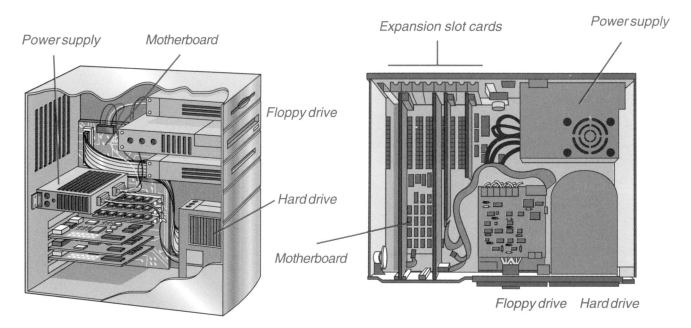

RECOGNIZING THE MOTHERBOARD

Your computer's *motherboard* is the large flat electronic board that contains the majority of your computer's chips. In particular, the motherboard contains the central processing unit (or CPU), the computer's electronic brain. When you hear users talk about their 486 or their Pentium, the users are talking about their PC's CPU. Lesson 10, "Upgrading Your Processor," examines the processor in detail. The motherboard also contains the PC's memory, which users refer to random-access memory or RAM. Before a computer program (software) can run, the program must reside within the computer's electronic memory. If you make extensive use of Windows, you can normally improve your system's performance by adding more memory. Lesson 12, "Adding Memory to Your PC," examines PC memory in detail.

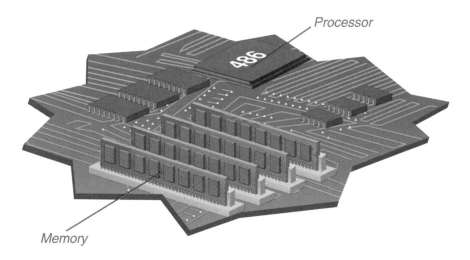

Processor

Memory

Of your computer's components, you need to treat the motherboard with the most care (it is normally the most expensive component). Although experienced users occasionally replace their computer's motherboard, such operations are best left to the experts and will not be covered within this book's lessons.

RECOGNIZING THE POWER SUPPLY

Your computer is an electronic device whose different parts work based on the presence or absence of electrical signals. When you plug your computer into your AC (alternating current on which your house runs) wall outlet, you actually plug in your computer's power supply. The power supply, in turn, turns the alternating current into the direct (one-way) current that your computer can use, and disseminates this power to the rest of your computer. When electronic signals travel through your computer, the signals generate heat. The power supply contains a fan that helps cool the PC. As you position your PC on or next to your desk, make sure you leave sufficient space between your PC and other objects (such as your desk or the wall) for the fan to vent.

RECOGNIZING HARD AND FLOPPY DISKS

To store information from one session to another, you must record the information on a disk. If you look closely at a floppy drive inside your system unit, you may find that you can see a floppy disk within the floppy drive. In contrast, the hard disk is completely enclosed, hiding its storage media. Both hard and floppy disk drives connect to the power supply. Likewise, most disks will have ribbon cables that connect the disk to the computer's motherboard or to a special hardware card called the *disk controller*.

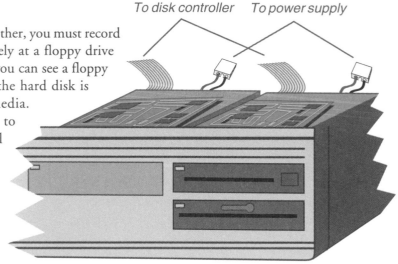

To disk controller   To power supply

RECOGNIZING THE EXPANSION SLOTS

Throughout this book, you will learn ways to add different hardware components, such as a modem or sound card, to your PC. When you install a new hardware board, you will insert the board into one of the PC's expansion slots. Lesson 4, "Understanding the PC's Expansion Slots," examines expansion slots in detail.

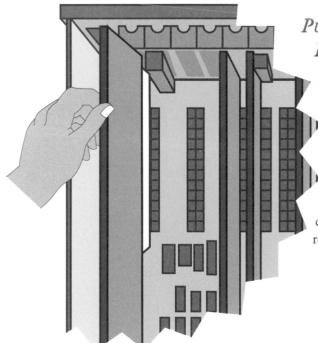

PUTTING YOUR SYSTEM UNIT BACK TOGETHER

After you have viewed your PC's inner components, you must replace your PC's cover. To do so, simply slide the cover back on to the PC. As before, take care not to damage any of the PC's ribbon cables. Next, replace the screws that secure the cover to the PC.

Throughout this book, you must take your PC's cover off to install different hardware components. In such cases, simply follow the steps this lesson presents to remove and later replace your system-unit cover.

WHAT YOU MUST KNOW

As you perform different upgrade operations, you will need to open your system unit. In this lesson, you may have opened your computer for the first time. With this experience under your belt, you are now well on your way. In Lesson 3, "Understanding Your Computer's Ports," you will learn more about your computer's ports, which let you connect printers, mice, and other devices. Before you continue with Lesson 3, however, make sure you have learned the following key concepts:

✓ Your PC's system unit houses your computer's disk drives, memory, central processing unit (CPU), motherboard, and other hardware boards, such as a modem or sound card.

✓ When you perform hardware upgrades, you will normally open up your system unit. After you do so once or twice, you will find that process quite straightforward.

✓ Whether you have a desktop or tower PC, the system unit contents are the same.

✓ Never open your system unit with your PC's power on or your PC plugged in.

✓ To open your system unit, you simply need to remove the screws that hold on the unit's cover. As you remove, and when you later replace the system cover, take care not to damage cables within the system unit.

Lesson 3

Understanding Your Computer's Ports

When you connect other devices, such as a printer, to your computer, you connect a cable from the device to a *port* (a connector) that appears on the back of your computer. Depending on the device, the type of cable you use to connect the device to your PC will differ. In this lesson, you will learn how to identify common port types quickly. By the time you complete this lesson, you will understand the following key concepts:

- You connect devices, such as your monitor, to your computer's ports, which you will find at the back of your PC's system unit.

- Ports and cables use male or female connectors which control whether a port plugs into a cable or the cable plugs into the port.

- Every PC uses several common port types which you can identify quickly by counting the port's pins and by knowing the port's gender (male or female).

- By installing a hardware card within your PC, you can add ports to your computer.

When you add hardware, you need to determine whether your computer will need additional ports. Thus, it is very important that you be able to recognize common port types.

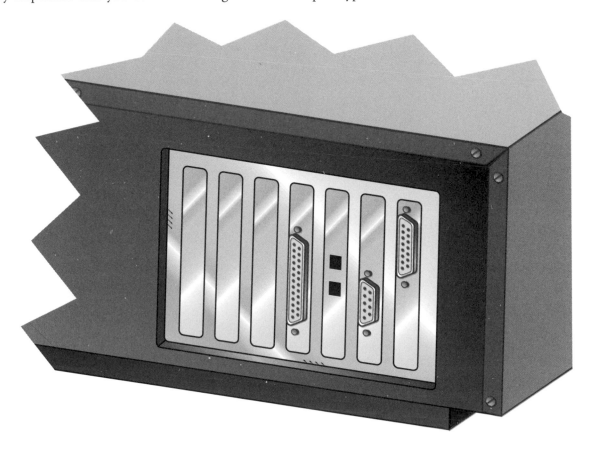

FINDING YOUR COMPUTER'S PORTS

A port is a connector that lets you attach a device to your PC. Ports let you connect devices such as a monitor, a mouse, a printer, or even a keyboard. If you examine the back of your PC, you will find several different ports. As you will learn, most PCs contain several common port types.

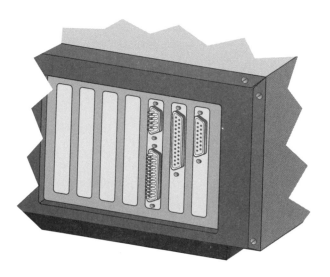

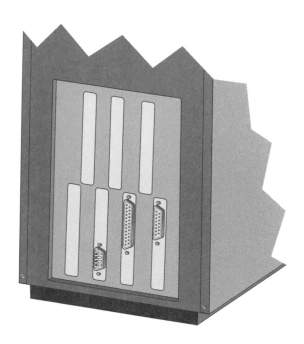

UNDERSTANDING MALE AND FEMALE PORTS

If you examine your PC's ports, you will note that some ports are designed to plug into a cable, while others are designed for a cable to be plugged into the port. Ports and cables, therefore, are classified as *male* or *female*, based on whether they plug in or are plugged into. A male cable or connector contains visible pins that plug in.

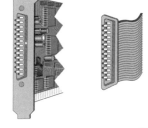

A female cable or connector, on the other hand, does not have such pins.

When you purchase a cable for a device, you must examine your port type to ensure that you buy the correct cable (male or female). If you have a female port, buy a male cable. Likewise, for a male port, buy a female cable. To help you connect a cable to a port, ports and cables are shaped to ensure that you plug in the cable correctly.

Users often describe ports based on the number of pins the port supports. For example, common port types include 9-pin and 25-pin ports. When you shop for cables, or talk to a company's technical support staff, you may have to describe a port or cable. In such cases, you must know the port's gender (male or female) and the number of pins the port supports, such as a 25-pin male port.

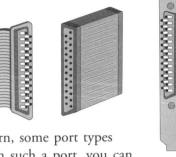

Using a Gender Changer

When you purchase a cable, you should purchase a male cable for a female port and a female cable for a male port. Should you purchase the wrong cable type, you can change a cable or port's gender using a *gender changer*. In other words, using a gender changer you can change a male cable into a female or vice versa.

Later in this lesson, you will learn how to recognize common PC port types. It is important that you understand the common port types. As you will learn, some port types look very similar, differing only by gender. If you use a gender changer with such a port, you can confuse the port's purpose.

Recognizing Common Port Types

PCs contain several common port types. This section examines several of these port types. Take time to compare the ports presented in this lesson to those found on the back of your PC. In fact, you might want to label your ports to help you later recall each port's purpose.

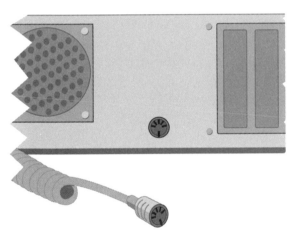

Recognizing the Keyboard Port

Like other hardware devices, you connect your keyboard to your computer through a port. Also, like most cables, you must align the keyboard cable pins with the port openings before you can connect the cable. Take time now to power off your computer (unpredictable results are possible if you leave the power on while plugging and unplugging the keyboard cable) and unplug your keyboard. Examine the cable and port. Align the cable's pins to the port and plug in the cable. Lesson 26, "Upgrading Your Keyboard," examines keyboards in detail.

Recognizing the Monitor Port

Depending on your monitor type, your monitor will connect to either a 9- or 15-pin port. If you are using an older EGA monitor, your monitor will connect to a 9-pin port. If you are using a VGA or SVGA monitor, on the other hand, your monitor will connect to a 15-pin port. Lesson 19, "Upgrading Your Monitor," examines monitors in detail.

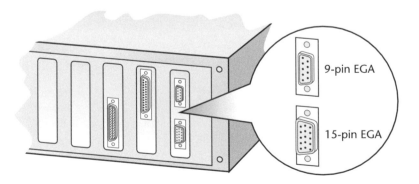

9-pin EGA

15-pin EGA

RECOGNIZING THE PRINTER PORT

You can connect a printer to either a parallel or serial port. *Parallel* ports are so named because they transmit data eight bits (binary digits) at a time, over eight wires. Because they transmit data eight bits at a time, parallel devices are much faster than their *serial* counterparts, which send all data through one wire in a *series*. PCs can support up to three parallel ports, named LPT1, LPT2, and LPT3. Parallel ports use a 25-pin female connector. Lesson 25, "Upgrading Your Printer," examines printers in detail. As you will learn throughout this book's lessons, you can also connect a Zip drive or some modems to the PC's parallel port.

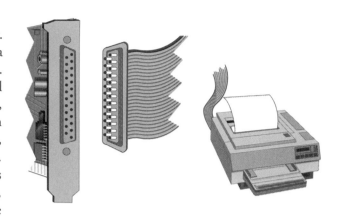

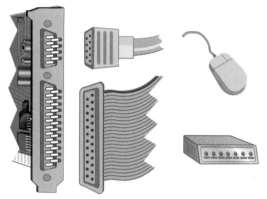

RECOGNIZING THE SERIAL PORT

You normally use serial ports to connect devices such as a modem, mouse, or joystock (that you will use with a computer game). Because parallel ports are faster, most users connect their printers to parallel ports. Serial ports transmit and receive data one bit at a time. PCs can support up to four serial ports, named COM1, COM2, COM3, and COM4. However, most PCs only use two serial ports. Serial ports can be either 9- or 25-pin ports. In either case, the serial port uses a male connector. If your PC only has a 25-pin serial port, but you have a 9-pin serial device, you can purchase an adapter that converts the 25-pin connector to a 9-pin connector and vice versa.

RECOGNIZING THE MOUSE PORT

As you will learn in Lesson 23, "Upgrading Your Mouse," you can connect a mouse to a serial port, a bus mouse adapter, or a special proprietary port. Serial mice normally use a 9-pin serial female connector. A bus mouse and proprietary mouse both use small connectors that look like a small version of your keyboard cable.

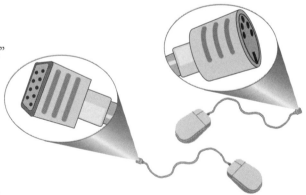

RECOGNIZING THE SCSI PORT

In Lesson 14, "Installing a SCSI Adapter," you will learn that a SCSI adapter provides you with a way to connect up to 7 high-speed devices, such as a hard disk, CD-ROM, or tape drive. SCSI connectors normally use a 50-pin connector. When you connect SCSI devices, you connect one device to the SCSI adapter, and then connect other devices to each other, building a chain of devices.

RECOGNIZING A UNIVERSAL SERIAL BUS PORT

In Lesson 28, "Using a Universal Serial Bus (USB)," you will learn that many new desktop and notebook PCs support a new bus called the universal serial bus to which you can connnect devices such as scanner, answering machines, a mouse, and much more. As you will learn, you can connect a single device to your PC's universal serial bus, or you can connect the a hub to the port to which you can then attach serveral devices or additional hubs. Using a universal serial bus, you can attach up to 127 devices to your PC.

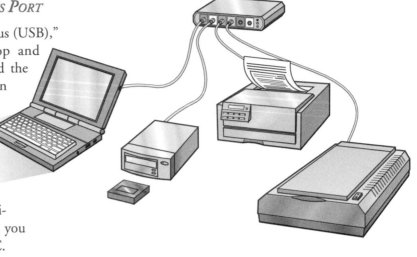

LOCATING PORTS ON A NOTEBOOK PC

If you are using a notebook PC, your system will have many of the ports this lesson discusses. To locate your notebook PC's ports, open the plastic cover that you will find on the back of your PC. If you require a SCSI adapter, you can purchase a PC-MCIA-based SCSI adapter, as discussed in Lesson 14.

HOW TO ADD PORTS TO YOUR COMPUTER

As you have learned, most PCs contain at least one serial port and one parallel port. Depending on the hardware you attach to your computer, there may be times when you need to add a new port. To add a port to your computer, you install a hardware board within your PC. Before you install the second hardware board, you will need to change settings on the board that let the PC distinguish one similar board from another. Lesson 9 discusses the steps you must perform to change hardware settings.

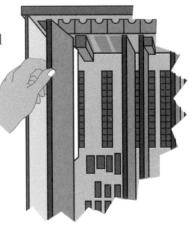

WHAT YOU MUST KNOW

When you connect other devices, such as a printer, to your computer, you connect a cable from the device to a port that appears on the back of your computer. Depending on the device, the type of cable you use to connect the device to your PC will differ. In this lesson, you learned how to identify common port types quickly.

In Lesson 4, you will examine your PC's expansion slots, which let you install hardware cards into your PC system unit. Before you continue with Lesson 4, however, make sure that you understand the following key concepts:

✓ If you examine the back of your computer, you will find the PC ports, which let you connect devices to the computer.

✓ Cables and port connectors are classified as male or female, based on whether the cable plugs in or is plugged into. Male cables and connectors have pins that plug into a female receptacle.

✓ When you describe a port connector or cable, you specify the gender (male or female) and the number of pins.

✓ If you inadvertently purchase the wrong cable type, you can use a gender changer to change a male connector to a female and vice versa.

✓ Regardless of your PC type, you will normally find at least one parallel and one serial port. Parallel ports are 25-pin female connectors. Serial ports are male connectors and can be 9- or 25-pin ports.

Lesson 4

Understanding the PC's Expansion Slots

When you install a hardware card, such as an internal modem into your PC, you insert the card into an *expansion slot*, which consists of a *slot opening* in the system-unit chassis and a *slot socket* on the motherboard. At first glance, you might think that one slot is the same as another. However, as you will learn in this lesson, that is not always the case.

This lesson examines the different expansion slot types you will find on your PC's motherboard. By the time you finish this lesson, you will understand the following concepts:

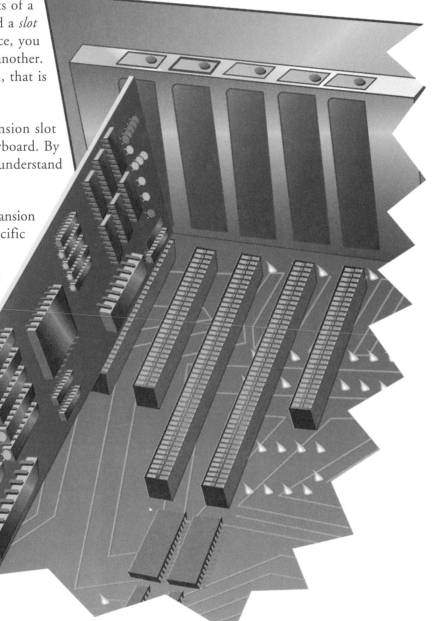

- Your PC may support different expansion slot types, each designed for a specific card type.

- A bus is a set of wires that let the CPU and a card communicate. When you insert a card into an expansion slot, you attach the card to the PC's bus.

- Different PCs support different bus types such as the ISA, EISA, VESA, Microchannel, PCI, and USB buses.

As you will learn in this lesson, telling one card type from another is quite easy. When you shop for hardware cards, your salesperson may ask you your PC bus type. By the time you finish this lesson, you will be able to answer such questions with confidence.

WHAT YOU WILL NEED

Before you get started on this lesson, make sure that you have the following readily available:

1. A PC tool kit with a screwdriver

2. A container within which you can place the chassis screws

3. A well-lit workspace with room for you to place the chassis

---

VIEWING YOUR SYSTEM'S EXPANSION SLOTS

Expansion slots reside within your PC system unit. To view your expansion slots, power off and unplug your PC. Remove your system unit cover, as discussed in Lesson 2, "Opening Your PC's System Unit." Several of your PC's expansion slots may be in use, while others are available for use.

If you examine the unused expansion slot openings, you will find that each has a small metal cover that is held in place by a small screw. This slot cover helps reduce the amount of dust that enters your system unit when the slot is not in use. When you install a card into an expansion slot, you first remove this cover. Hold on to the screw that held the cover in place. You will later use this screw to hold the card in the slot. Also, place the slot cover in a safe location. Should you ever remove the card, you will want to replace the cover.

When you insert a card into an expansion slot, never force the card into the socket. Instead, gently rock the card until it slides into place. After the card is in the slot, secure the card by replacing the screw that previously held the cover.

RECOGNIZING BUS TYPES

When the IBM PC was first released in 1981, the PC communicated with expansion slot cards using eight bits of data at a time. The original *bus* (collection of wires) was called the ISA bus. ISA is an acronym for *Industry Standard Architecture*. In short, the ISA defines a set of rules (standards) the bus, CPU, and cards you plug into the bus follow to communicate. In this way, when you buy and install a third-party card, such as an internal modem, the card will work in your PC.

When IBM released the 286-based PC AT in 1984, the AT supported a 16-bit bus, also called an ISA bus. By allowing the bus to transmit 16 bits of data at a time, this larger bus improved the PC's performance. Unfortunately, with the advent of faster 32-bit 386- and 486-based PCs, the 16-bit ISA bus became a performance bottleneck. As a result, many PCs started providing

32-bit EISA buses. EISA is simply an acronym for *Extended Industry Standard Architecture*. Because the 32-bit bus doubles the amount of data the bus can send, the EISA bus greatly improves system performance. Unfortunately, as video cards increased their resolution and began to support a larger number of colors (up to 16 million), the PC bus could not keep up. As a result, hardware designers created a new "local bus," which lets devices (such as a video card) talk directly to the CPU. Initially, the local-bus design and standards were controlled by VESA, the Video Electronics Standards Association.

Cards that support the VESA local bus are called VL-Bus cards. Eventually, Intel designed and released a more powerful local bus, called the *PCI local bus* (for Peripheral Component Interconnect) which has become the standard bus. Although the PCI bus began as a 32-bit bus, there are now 64-bit PCI cards and buses. Before you purchase a PCI-based card, make sure the card is compatible with your current bus.

One of the most important hardware developments to occur in the past few years is plug-and-play (PNP) support. As you will learn, the most difficult aspect of installing a card into your PC is assigning the card's settings so that the settings do not conflict with your existing cards. When such conflicts occur, one or more cards in your system will not work, or worse, your system itself may not work. Lesson 8, "Understanding Common Conflicts," discusses hardware conflicts in detail, as well as steps you can perform to resolve the conflicts.

The goal of the plug-and-play technology is to simplify hardware installations by letting the cards determine their own settings. In other words, you simply install the card and it will work. In general, when you install a plug-and-play card into a plug-and-play bus, the card asks the other cards that are connected to the bus which settings it can use. After the card learns which settings are unused, the card configures itself to use the settings and is then ready to use. In the future, all cards and PCs will support plug-and-play, thus making hardware upgrades much easier.

Recently, hardware developers have introduced the universal serial bus (USB) which lets you connect devices, such as joysticks, modems, scanners, and ZIP drives (up to 127 devices) to your PC. Lesson 28, "Using a Universal Serial Bus (USB)," discusses the universal serial bus in detail.

THE PC BUS SCORECARD

Keeping track of different bus types can be difficult. The following definitions may help you keep track:

Acronym	Name	Meaning
ISA	Industry Standard Architecture	A 16-bit expansion slot bus
EISA	Extended Industry Standard Architecture	A 32-bit expansion slot bus
VESA	Video Electronics Standards Association	A local bus that communicates directly with the CPU—sometimes called a VL-Bus
PCI	Peripheral Component Interconnect	Advanced local bus designed by Intel
PNP	Plug and Play	A bus that helps cards determine their hardware settings
USB	Universal Serial Bus	A high-speed bus for serial devices

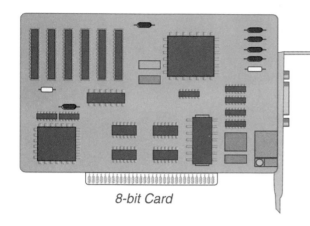

8-bit Card

DETERMINING A CARD'S TYPE

Just as there are different bus types, you will encounter different card types that were designed for use with a specific bus. To determine a card's type by inspection, you need to examine the card's connectors. To begin, simple devices, such as an internal modem or mouse, use an 8-bit card. Many older PCs support 8-bit expansion slots. Newer PCs, however, use 16-bit and 32-bit slots instead. However, you can plug an 8-bit card into a 16- or 32-bit expansion slot.

A 16-bit ISA card adds a notch to the 8-bit card (just shown) and increases the number of pins on the card. In short, the 16-bit slot adds a second socket into which the card is placed.

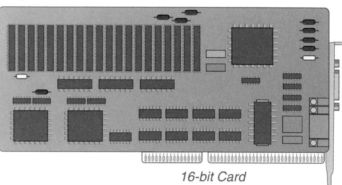

16-bit Card

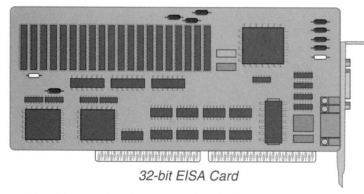

32-bit EISA Card

A 32-bit EISA card is very similar in size and shape to the 16-bit card. However, if you examine the card closely, you will find that the card doubles the number of pins.

As a general rule, you can place an 8-bit card into any expansion slot (8-bit, ISA, or EISA). Likewise, a 16-bit card can be placed into an ISA or EISA slot. A 32-bit EISA card, on the other hand, can only be used in an EISA slot.

A local-bus card contains pins that slide into an expansion slot socket and pins that slide into the local bus. The most common local bus cards are high-speed video cards, discussed in Lesson 20, "Upgrading Your Video Card." Finally, most desktop PCs sold today, make extensive use of PCI slots. Which look similar to an 8-bit card in appearance, but that contain many more pins. As you shop for hardware boards, you need to be aware of your PC bus types.

WHAT ABOUT IBM'S MICROCHANNEL?

If you use an IBM PS/2 computer, you will be concerned with another bus type called the Microchannel. In short, the Microchannel is a proprietary IBM bus. You cannot plug boards designed for the other buses discussed in this lesson into the Microchannel. Likewise, you cannot use Microchannel cards in a standard PC bus. The disadvantage of the Microchannel is that it and its cards are not compatible with standard PC devices. The Microchannel's advantage is that it eliminates the IRQ conflicts that challenge PC users, as discussed in Lesson 8.

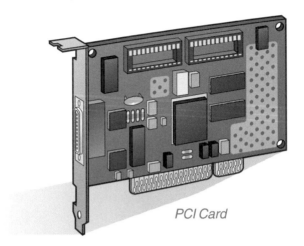

PCI Card

EXPANDING YOUR NOTEBOOK PC

In Lesson 27, "Upgrading Your Notebook PC," you will learn how to expand your notebook PC using PCMCIA cards. As you will learn, you can purchase one PCMCIA card that provides modem capabilities, another that provides RAM, and a third that may contain a network or SCSI interface. In addition, as discussed in Lesson 28, most new notebooks support the universal serial bus, that lets you connect up to 127 devices to the PC.

WHAT YOU MUST KNOW

In this lesson you learned about expansion slots into which you plug various hardware boards, or cards, such as an internal modem or mouse card. Throughout this book, you will perform different hardware upgrades by working with cards and chips. In Lesson 5, "Working with Boards and Chips," you will examine the steps you should perform to work with chips and boards. Before you continue with Lesson 5, however, make sure you have learned the following key concepts:

✓ When you add a hardware card, you install the card into one of the PC's expansion slots. Each consists of a slot opening in the back of the system-unit chassis and a slot socket on the motherboard.

✓ PC expansion slots are not created equal. As the PC has evolved, so too has the bus (collection of wires) used to connect expansion slot devices to the PC.

✓ PC buses are classified as ISA, EISA, VESA, PCI, and the Microchannel. When you purchase a hardware card, you need to know your PC bus type.

✓ To improve video performance, many newer PCs support a local bus, which the CPU uses to access directly the video card memory, bypassing the expansion slots.

Lesson 5

Working with Boards and Chips

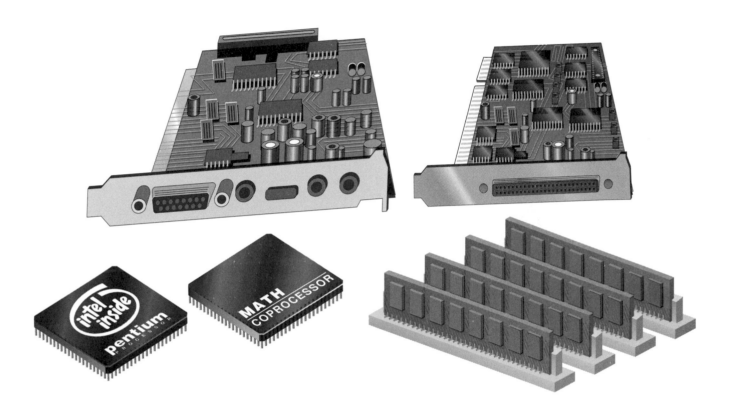

Throughout this book, you will install different hardware boards and chips. If you have never installed a board or chip before, relax. Installing boards and chips is very easy. However, you do need to work with care. Electronics are fragile. As long as you do not apply "brute force," however, you should not have any problems. This lesson examines the steps you should perform to work with boards and chips. By the time you finish this lesson, you will understand the following key concepts:

- Why you need to have a chip extractor in your PC tool kit
- How to install a hardware board in an expansion slot
- How to remove a hardware board from an expansion slot
- How to install and remove chips
- How to create your own board and chip extractors

WHAT YOU WILL NEED

Before you get started with this lesson, make sure that you have the following readily available:

1. A PC tool kit with a screwdriver

2. A container within which you can place the chassis screws

3. A well-lit workspace with room for you to place the chassis

4. A chip extractor

5. A screwdriver you can sacrifice (You will bend one to create a chip extractor.)

BEWARE OF STATIC ELECTRICITY!

When you work with cards and chips, be very careful to avoid damage from static electricity. Many computer boards are very sensitive to static discharge. To reduce the chance of static electricity damaging your hardware, some manufacturers recommend that you use a static mat that you connect to the PC chassis and to your wrist using a wristband. At the very least, it is important that you work in a static-free area. Also, always touch the PC chassis to ground yourself before working on senstive electornic equipment.

WORKING WITH HARDWARE BOARDS

When you perform hardware upgrades, such as installing an internal modem, sound card, or a new video card, you must work with electronic boards, called *cards*. A card has a tab with electrical connectors on it that slides into a socket on the motherboard. After you insert the card into a slot on the motherboard, one or more ports will protrude from the slot opening at the back of your PC's chassis. In Lesson 3, "Understanding Your Computer's Ports," you examined the PC's expansion slots, into which you install cards.

No matter which type of card you are installing, the steps you must perform are the same. To begin, turn off and unplug your PC. Next, remove your system unit cover, as discussed in Lesson 2, "Opening Your PC's System Unit." After you choose the slot into which you will insert the card, remove the small metal slot cover by unscrewing the screw that holds the cover in place. Store the screw in a safe place, because you will later use it to secure the card in place.

Place the slot cover in a safe location. Should you later remove the card, you will want to replace the slot cover to reduce the dust that enters the system unit.

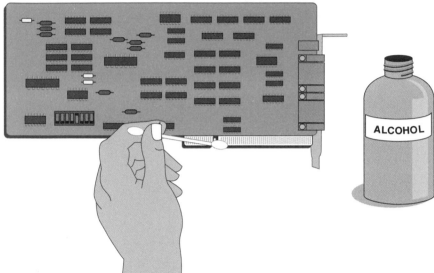

Examine the card you are going to install to ensure that the card's connectors are clean. Dirty connectors can prevent the board from working. To clean the connectors, use a Q-tip and rubbing alcohol.

Gently rock the card into place

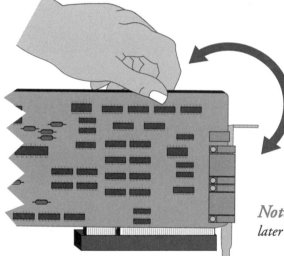

To install the card, gently slide the card's connectors into the expansion slot. You might need to rock the card slightly before the connector slides into place.

After the card is in place, secure the card by replacing the screw that previously held the slot cover in place. Next, replace and secure the system unit cover.

Note: *If your card is shipped in a static-proof bag, save the bag so you can later use it should you ever remove the card from your PC.*

INSTALLING A HARDWARE CARD

Regardless of the type of card you are installing, the steps you must perform are the same:

1. Turn off and unplug your system unit.

2. Remove your system unit cover.

3. Select the desired expansion slot.

4. Remove and store the small metal slot cover, placing the screw in a safe location. Save the small metal slot cover in case you must replace it later.

5. Gently insert the card's connector into the slot socket, securing the card in place with the screw that held the slot cover.

6. Replace and secure the system unit cover.

REMOVING A HARDWARE CARD

The steps for removing a hardware card are almost identical to those just discussed, with a few exceptions. First, after you remove the card, protect the card by placing it back into its static-proof bag. Next, store the card in a safe location, ideally protected by a cardboard box.

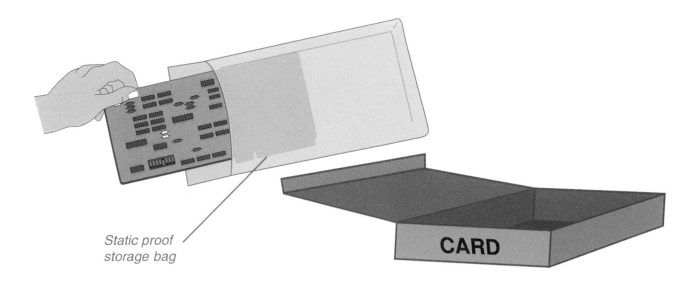

Static proof
storage bag

CARD

In some cases, you might have trouble removing a card from the expansion slot socket (don't forget to remove the slot cover screw, which now holds the board tight in the slot opening). If you have trouble, you might be able to remove the board from the slot gently using a bent flathead screwdriver as a sort of hook to gently pull each end of the board.

REMOVING A HARDWARE CARD

No matter which type of card you are removing, the steps you must perform are the same:

1. Turn off and unplug your system unit.

2. Remove your system unit cover.

3. Remove the slot cover screw, which now holds the board tight in the slot opening.

4. Gently remove card from the expansion slot.

5. Place the card into a static-proof bag and then into a cardboard box.

6. Replace the expansion slot cover to prevent dust from entering the system unit.

7. Replace and secure the system unit cover.

WORKING WITH CHIPS

Depending on the upgrade you are performing, you may need to install or remove one or more chips. Before you begin, make sure that you are working in a static-free environment. Next, ground yourself by touching the system unit chassis.

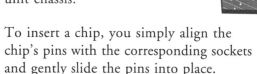

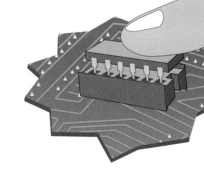

To insert a chip, you simply align the chip's pins with the corresponding sockets and gently slide the pins into place.

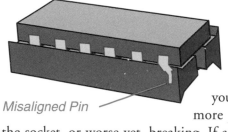

Misaligned Pin

As you insert the chip, make sure each pin is inserted successfully. If you are not careful, one or more pins will bend, missing the socket, or worse yet, breaking. If a pin is out of place, the chip will not work.

Notch

When you install a hardware card, correctly aligning the card is very easy. When you install chips, however, the correct alignment is not always obvious. If you examine a chip and its socket closely, you will normally notice small numbers.

To align the chip, align pin 1 with socket 1 and so on. If the chip is not numbered, many chips have a small notch next to pin 1.

The easiest way to remove a chip from a socket is to use a chip extractor, which lets you gently pull the chip from the socket.

If you do not have a chip extractor, you may be able to create a similar device by bending a small flathead screwdriver. Using the screwdriver, you can gently remove the chip, one end at a time.

After you remove a chip, you might want to store the chip by gently pressing the chip's pins into a small piece of styrofoam. In this way, you reduce the chance of any pins getting bent.

WHAT YOU MUST KNOW

In this lesson, you have learned how to install an expansion card into an expansion slot in your computer and a chip into its socket. You also learned how to remove them. In addition, you learned that a static electricity charge can destroy a chip or circuit board—make certain you discharge any static you have accumulated before you touch any components and work in a static-free environment.

In Lesson 6, "Understanding Your Computer's CMOS Memory," you will examine your PC's CMOS memory contents. Your PC uses a special memory called the CMOS memory within which it stores key system settings, such as the number and type of your disk drives, the amount of memory, your video type, and even the current system date and time. The CMOS memory is battery powered, which lets your PC remember these settings even when it is powered off. Before you continue with Lesson 6, however, make sure you have learned the following key concepts:

✓ If you are shopping for a PC tool kit, look for one that includes a chip extractor.

✓ As you perform various hardware upgrades discussed throughout this book, you will remove and install hardware cards. When you insert or remove a card, you should gently rock the card in the slot on the motherboard.

✓ As you install a chip, make sure that you do not inadvertently bend one of the chip's pins.

✓ If you do not have a chip extractor, you may be able to create a make-shift extractor by bending a small flathead screw driver.

✓ Static electricity can quickly destroy a chip or card. Never work with cards or chips without first grounding yourself by touching the system unit chassis. Also, you might want to consider buying and using a static mat.

Lesson 6

Understanding Your Computer's CMOS Memory

If you examine a hundred different PCs, you might find as many different hardware configurations. Computers may differ by the number or type of disks they contain, the type of video display, the amount of memory, and even their hard disk size. To help each computer keep track of its configuration, PCs use a special battery-powered memory called the *CMOS memory*. As you will learn, when you install new hardware, there will be times when you must update your system's CMOS memory. This lesson examines the CMOS memory contents and how you can update the memory settings. By the time you finish this lesson, you will understand the following concepts:

- The CMOS memory is battery powered so your PC will "remember" its settings when you power your PC off.

- How you can display your PC's CMOS memory contents

- How and when to update the CMOS memory settings

- You must be careful as you update your PC's CMOS settings because an incorrect setting can prevent your system from starting

It is important that you understand the CMOS memory. When you add a disk or increase your computer's RAM, you may need to update your computer's CMOS settings. Until you update the CMOS, your PC will not be aware of hardware updates.

UNDERSTANDING THE CMOS MEMORY

CMOS is simply an acronym for *complementary metal oxide semiconductor*. CMOS simply describes the type of material from which this special memory is made. To start successfully, your PC must know specifics about its disk types, available memory, video type, and so on. As you will learn in Lesson 12, "Adding Memory to Your PC," when you power off your PC, the information in your PC's random-access memory is lost. For the PC to remember its key hardware settings, the PC uses a small battery-powered CMOS memory. Because the CMOS memory is battery powered, the memory maintains its contents, even when the PC is unplugged.

HOW YOUR PC REMEMBERS KEY SYSTEM SETTINGS

PCs differ by the number and type of disks they contain, the amount of available memory, video type and more. When your PC starts, it must know these key settings. To remember its settings, the PC uses a small battery-powered memory called the CMOS. As you perform different hardware upgrades, you might have to update your system's CMOS settings. In addition to storing your PC's hardware settings, the CMOS memory keeps track of your system's date and time.

Your PC normally uses its CMOS memory settings only when it starts. Depending on your PC type, the way you access the CMOS settings will vary. When you first turn on your PC's power, the PC performs a self-test of its hardware components. During the self-test, the PC displays a count of its working memory.

Normally, you will access your system's CMOS settings by pressing one of the following keyboard combinations when your system completes its memory count:

- DEL
- ESC
- CTRL-ALT-ENTER
- CTRL-ALT-INS
- CTRL-ALT-ESC

Note: Very old PCs do not have a built-in setup program. Instead, you must boot (start) your computer using a special setup diskette to access the CMOS setup.

Depending on your system, your screen might display a menu of options, or it might immediately display the CMOS settings. If a menu appears, select the setup option. Next, your system will display a screen similar to that shown in Figure 6.1, which contains your current CMOS settings.

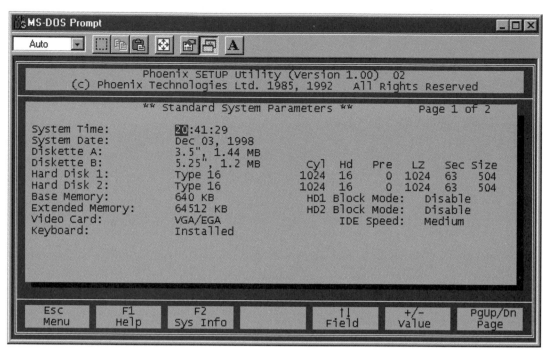

Figure 6.1 *Standard CMOS settings.*

As you can see, CMOS settings range from disk types to available memory. Also, the CMOS keeps track of the current date and time, which lets the PC know the current date and time, even after you turn off its power. Depending on your system, the steps you must perform to change a CMOS setting will differ. Read the instructions that appear on your screen display. In most cases, after you select a CMOS entry, you can change the entry's value using your keyboard PGUP and PGDN keys. After you change the entries you require, you can exit the setup program saving the new settings within the CMOS memory.

Note: Be careful as you change CMOS settings, an errant setting may prevent your system from starting.

RECORD YOUR SYSTEM'S CURRENT SETTINGS

Eventually, your system's CMOS battery will fail. After you replace the battery, you must restore your CMOS settings. To simplify this task, you should write down your current system settings, placing the settings in a safe location. Should you later need to restore your CMOS settings, you will be glad you took time to record the original values.

Note: If you have trouble invoking or using your PC's built-in setup program, you can purchase third-party software that lets you access the CMOS settings.

WHEN YOU MUST ACCESS CMOS ENTRIES

As long as your PC starts successfully, you can normally ignore the PC's CMOS settings. However, if you add memory to your system or install a new or different disk drive, you may need to update a CMOS setting. As you examine the lessons presented in this book, the lessons will tell you when you need to update one or more CMOS settings.

YOUR CMOS BATTERY CAN FAIL

Like all batteries, your CMOS battery will eventually die. When your PC's CMOS battery fails, your system will display an error message similar to the following when you first turn on the PC's power:

```
Invalid System Settings Run Setup
```

Should an error message similar to this appear, you must replace the CMOS battery by following the steps discussed in Lesson 7, "Replacing Your PC's CMOS Battery." After you replace the CMOS battery, you must restore the previous CMOS settings. At that time, you will be glad you recorded the CMOS settings, as previously discussed.

CHANGING THE CMOS SETTINGS

When you install different hardware devices, you may need to update your PC's CMOS memory settings to inform the PC of the new hardware. Depending on your system, the steps you must perform to access the CMOS settings will differ. In most cases, you will press a specific keyboard combination immediately after your PC displays its available memory count when you first power on your PC.

Like all batteries, the PC's CMOS battery will eventually fail. In such cases, follow the steps discussed in Lesson 7 to replace the battery. Next, you must restore the CMOS settings by following the steps discussed in this lesson.

ADVANCED CMOS SETTINGS

Depending on your system type, your CMOS may support several advanced settings that control low-level operations, such as your CPU's use of an instruction cache, your system's support for plug-and-play hardware, and so on. Figure 6.2, for example, illustrates advanced settings within a CMOS screen. Again, before you change a setting's value, make sure you write the down the setting's original value.

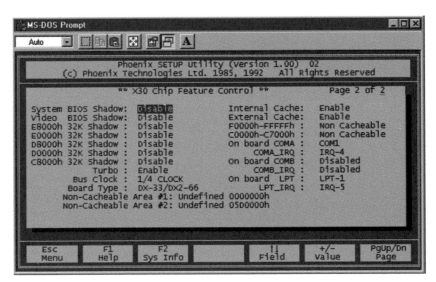

Figure 6.2 Advanced CMOS settings.

> ### PASSWORD PROTECTING YOUR SYSTEM
>
> Depending on your system type, you may be able to use a CMOS setting to password protect your system. When you assign a password to your system in this way, you system will require you to type in a password each time it starts. If you fail to type in the correct password, the system will not start.
>
> Should you forget your password, or should you need to access a system for which another user has assigned password protection, remove the CMOS battery, as discussed in Lesson 7. The PC, in turn, will forget its current system settings, including the password. You can then install the CMOS battery and restart the system. However, as discussed in this lesson, you must then reset each of the previous CMOS settings.
>
> *Note:* Some systems have a jumper on the motherboard that you can use to discard the current CMOS settings.

WHAT YOU MUST KNOW

In this lesson, you learned about your computer's CMOS memory—what it is, what it is made of, and when as well as how you must change its settings. Eventually, your PC's CMOS battery will fail. At that time, you must replace the battery. Lesson 7, "Replacing Your PC's CMOS Battery," examines the steps you must perform to replace your PC's CMOS battery. Before you continue with Lesson 7, however, make sure you understand the following key concepts:

- ✓ CMOS is an acronym for complementary metal oxide semiconductor. In short, CMOS defines the type of material from which the chip is made.

- ✓ Your PC uses a special memory called the CMOS memory to store specifics about your system, such as the number and type of disks, the amount of memory, the video type, and the current system date and time. If you change your hardware configuration, you may have to run the CMOS setup program to inform your computer of the changes.

- ✓ To access your PC's CMOS settings, you normally press a keyboard combination after your computer completes its power-on self-test. The documentation that accompanied your PC will specify the keyboard combination you must press.

- ✓ When you display your CMOS settings, write down the current values. Place your notes in a safe place. Should you ever need to restore the settings, you will be glad you took notes.

- ✓ Like all batteries, your CMOS battery will eventually fail. At that time, you will need to replace the battery and then restore the previous settings.

Lesson 7

Replacing Your PC's CMOS Battery

In Lesson 6, "Understanding Your Computer's CMOS Memory," you learned that your PC uses a small battery-powered memory, called the CMOS, to remember different system settings when the PC's power is off. Like all batteries, the PC's CMOS battery will eventually fail and you must replace it—fortunately, most CMOS batteries last several years. In this lesson, you will learn how to replace a CMOS battery. By the time you finish this lesson, you will understand the following key concepts:

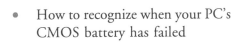

- How to recognize when your PC's CMOS battery has failed

- How to replace a CMOS battery

- How to restore your computer's previous CMOS settings

If you have not already read Lesson 6, which discusses the CMOS memory contents and how you access this special memory, do so now. As discussed in Lesson 6, you should take time now to write down your system's current CMOS settings, in case you have to restore them at a later time.

Before you get started with this lesson, make sure that you have the following readily available:

1. A PC tool kit with a screwdriver.

2. A container within which you can place the chassis screws.

3. A well-lit workspace with room for you to place the chassis.

4. A new CMOS battery—if you have a well-known brand of PC, you should be able to buy the correct battery without first looking inside your computer. If not, you might have to break up this lesson with a quick trip to your local computer-parts store.

RECOGNIZING A DEAD CMOS BATTERY

The PC's CMOS memory stores such information as the hard disk type, the number and size of floppy disk drives, the amount of random access memory (RAM), and the current system date and time. When the CMOS battery fails, your PC will forget these key settings. When you next turn on your PC's power, your system will display an error message similar to the following:

```
Invalid System Settings Run Setup
```

When this error message occurs, you must replace the CMOS battery.

REPLACING THE CMOS BATTERY

PCs use one of two types of CMOS batteries. The first CMOS battery type is a small, flat, nickel-shaped battery. The second battery type looks more like a battery pack.

The CMOS battery resides within the PC's system unit. Follow these steps, discussed in Lesson 2, "Opening Your PC's System Unit," to remove your system chassis:

1. Turn off and unplug your PC.

2. Remove the screws that connect the system-unit cover to the chassis and place the screws in a safe location.

3. Gently remove the system-unit cover.

Depending on your PC manufacturer, the location of the CMOS battery will differ. After you locate your CMOS battery, remove the battery and take it with you to your PC retailer. Purchase a similar battery type. If your system uses a battery-pack-like CMOS battery, note the orientation of the wires that connect the battery to your PC's motherboard. In other words, if the battery pack uses colored wires, write down the wire-color orientaion (such as red wire on the left).

To replace the small nickel-shaped CMOS battery, simply slide the new battery back into its holder. If you are replacing a battery-pack-like CMOS battery, make sure that you connect the battery cables to the motherboard in their original orientation.

RESTORING YOUR CMOS SETTINGS

When the CMOS battery dies, your PC will forget its key settings. After you replace the CMOS battery, you must restore the previous CMOS settings. To assign the CMOS settings, follow the steps discussed in Lesson 6.

REPLACING YOUR PC'S CMOS BATTERY

Over time, your PC's CMOS battery will eventually fail. At that time, perform these steps to replace the battery:

1. Turn off and unplug the PC system unit.

2. Remove the system unit cover.

3. Locate the CMOS battery, noting the battery's cabling, if applicable.

4. Replace the battery and, if necessary, connect the new battery's cable using the previous wire-color orientation.

5. Replace the system unit cover.

6. Plug in and start your PC, restoring the previous CMOS settings.

Replacing the CMOS Battery for a Notebook PC

If you use a notebook PC, you will eventually need to replace its CMOS battery. Depending on your notebook PC type, the steps you must perform to replace the battery may differ. In addition, because of the notebook PC's small size, you may need to order a special battery from your PC's manufacturer. The documentation that came with your notebook PC will tell you the battery type and the steps you must perform to replace the battery.

If you travel with your notebook PC, you may be used to shutting down and later starting your PC as you move from one office to the next or as your airplane gets ready to taxi for takeoff. To reduce the amount of time you must spending shutting down and later starting your PC, many notebook PC's provide a standby mode, which lets you leave your programs in their current state. When you select standby mode, the PC essentially remembers everything it has going on. Then, the next time you turn on your PC's power, you can resume your work right where you left off, without having to wait for your PC to shutdown and later restart. If you are running Windows 95 or 98, you can normally select the standby mode from the Start menu. When you place a PC in standby mode, the PC uses its battery-powered memory to store your system's current state.

What You Must Know

In this lesson, you learned how to recognize when your CMOS battery has failed and how to replace it. As hardware devices in your PC operate, they may periodically interrupt the CPU to request it to perform specific processing for them. To signal (interrupt) the CPU in this way, key devices in your PC have their own interrupt-request (IRQ) wire. When a device needs the CPU's attention, the device simply sends a signal down this wire. When you install a new hardware card, you might need to specify the board's IRQ setting. Each card you insert must have a unique IRQ number. If two boards have the same IRQ setting, the boards will not work. Lesson 8, "Understanding Common Conflicts," examines steps you can perform to avoid such conflicts. Before you continue with Lesson 8, however, make sure that you understand the following key concepts:

- ✓ When the PC's power is off, the PC uses a special battery-powered CMOS memory to remember key system settings.

- ✓ Over time, the CMOS battery will fail and you must replace it.

- ✓ If your CMOS battery has failed, your system will display a related error message the next time you start your computer.

- ✓ There are two types of CMOS batteries: one that looks like a nickel and one that looks like a battery pack.

- ✓ After you replace the CMOS battery, you must restore the previous CMOS settings.

Section Two

COMMON MOTHERBOARD UPGRADES

The PC's motherboard houses the majority of your computer's chips and circuits. In particular, you will find your computer's processor (the CPU or central processing unit) and random-access memory (RAM) on the motherboard. The lessons in this section examine several upgrades you can make to items found on the motherboard and include the following:

Lesson 8

Understanding Common Conflicts

When you install a hardware card, such as a modem, mouse, or network adapter, you may have to assign settings to the card, such as the interrupt-request (IRQ) line, a memory buffer, and possibly a direct memory access (DMA) address. To avoid hardware conflicts which prevent your system from working, each card within your computer must have unique settings. Within your PC, the CPU uses these settings to communicate with the device.

Depending on the settings of your existing cards, there will be times when a new card you install within your system conflicts with the settings of one of your existing cards. When such conflicts occur, either one or both of the cards will not work, or your system itself may not start.

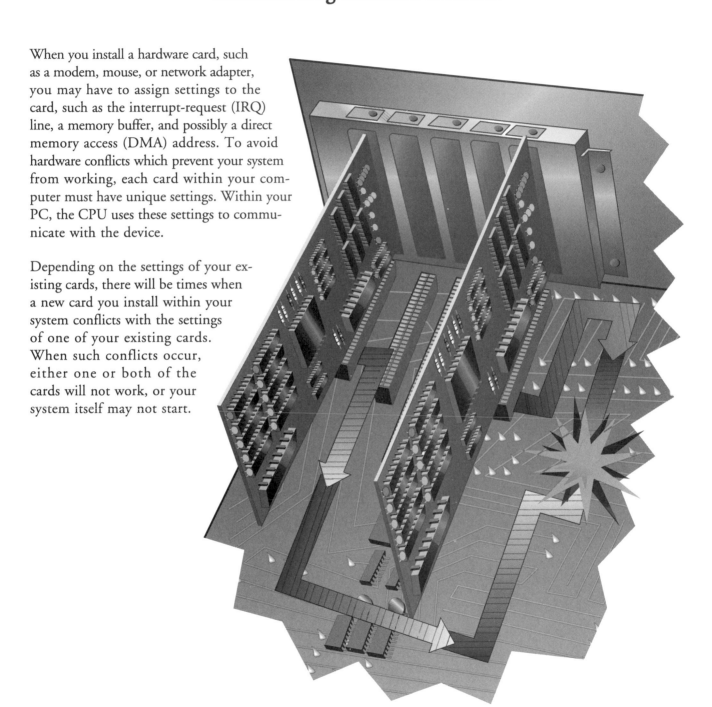

This lesson examines the steps you must perform to determine settings that will avoid conflicts and then the steps you must peform to assign the settings. By the time you finish this lesson, you will understand the following key concepts:

- The purpose of an interrupt request (IRQ)
- How to assign a card's IRQ setting
- The purpose of a card's I/O address
- How to assign a card's I/O address
- The purpose of a card's memory address
- How to assign a card's memory address
- The purpose of direct memory access (DMA)
- How to assign a card's DMA settings

Selecting the correct settings for a card is one of the most difficult steps to installing a new card. If the settings you select are already in use by a different card, your computer may behave erratically, or it might not work at all.

UNDERSTANDING INTERRUPT REQUESTS

Within your computer, the central processing unit (CPU) oversees all operations. As your CPU runs a program, there will be times when a device, such as a modem or mouse, needs the CPU's attention. In such cases, the device *interrupts* the CPU so the CPU can perform special processing for the device. For example, each time you move your mouse across your desk, the mouse notifies the CPU to move the mouse cursor across your screen display and update the screen. When the CPU completes the special processing, the CPU resumes the task it was performing prior to the interrupt.

Note: Every time you move the mouse, you interrupt the CPU from the task it was performing while it figures out where you are moving the mouse and adjusts the screen display of the cursor appropriately. This processing can consume significant amounts of CPU time. If you are waiting for a process to complete, try to refrain from wiggling the mouse to amuse yourself (a common temptation), and the process will go faster.

UNDERSTANDING INTERRUPTS

When a device interrupts the CPU, the device submits an *interrupt request* or *IRQ* to the CPU, whereupon the CPU stops working on its current task and performs special processing for the device. When the CPU completes the special processing, the CPU resumes its previous operation. Assume, for example, you are watching a video on TV and the phone rings. So you do not miss any part of the movie, you can pause the movie before you answer the phone (your interruption). When you have finished with the phone call, you can start the movie right where you left off. Wiggling the mouse while you wait for a process to complete is like receiving extra phone calls—the process takes longer. Each device within your system has its own IRQ setting which controls the wire the PC uses to signal the CPU. By knowing which device corresponds to each wire, the CPU can identify the device that is interrupting it and can then respond accordingly.

Because many different devices can interrupt the CPU, the CPU needs a way to determine which device is causing the interrupt. Thus, each device has its own *interrupt request line*.

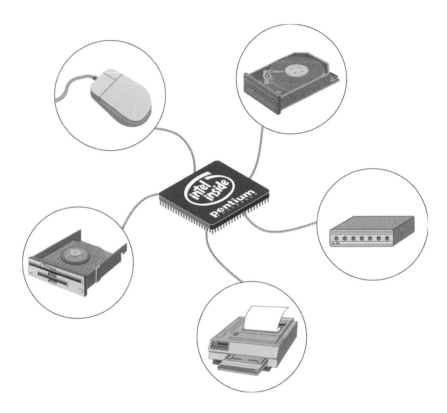

If you are using an older PC based on an 8-bit bus (see Lesson 4), your system will support eight IRQ lines, numbered 0 through 7. Table 8.1 lists the devices that normally correspond to these IRQ lines.

IRQ Number	Device
0	Timer
1	Keyboard
2	Available for use
3	COM2 (serial port)
4	COM1 (serial port)
5	Hard disk controller
6	Floppy disk controller
7	LPT1 (parallel port)

Table 8.1 *Devices that normally correspond to IRQ 0 through 7 on an 8-bit bus.*

If you are using a 286-based PC or higher, your system will use 16 IRQ lines, numbered 0 through 15. Table 8.2 lists the devices normally assigned to these IRQ lines.

IRQ Number	Device	IRQ Number	Device
0	Timer	8	Real time clock
1	Keyboard	9	Redirected as IRQ2
2	Cascaded	10	Available for use
3	COM2	11	Available for use
4	COM1	12	Available for use
5	LPT2	13	Math coprocessor
6	Floppy disk controller	14	Hard disk controller
7	LPT1	15	Available for use

Table 8.2 *Devices normally associated with IRQ 0 though 15.*

To support the 15 IRQ levels, PCs use two special chips called *interrupt controllers*. The first controller chip corresponds to interrupts 0 through 7 and the second to interrupts 8 through 15. To access this second set of interrupts, PCs actually steal the line for IRQ 2 and use it for a special purpose. To activate one of the interrupts on the second controller, the PC sends a signal on IRQ 2. In this way, IRQ 2 is said to be *cascaded*. When a device sends a signal on IRQ 2, the second interrupt controller jumps into action. Thus, your (286-based or higher) PC really only supports 15 interrupt request lines. If you examine different hardware cards, such as a modem or a mouse, you may find that a card's default setting is IRQ 2. As you just learned, however, IRQ 2 is not really used. When you set a card to IRQ 2, the PC routes the signal transparently to IRQ 9.

USING THE WINDOWS DEVICE MANAGER TO DETERMINE IRQ SETTINGS

If you are using Windows 95 or 98, you can use the Device Manager to display your system's current IRQ settings, as shown in Figure 8.1.

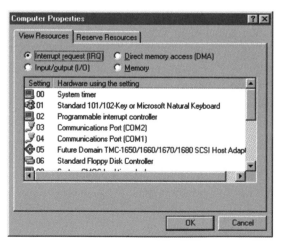

Figure 8.1 *The Windows 95 Device Manager IRQ settings display.*

Lesson 40, "Using the Windows Device Manager," discusses the Device Manager in detail. For now, however, to display available IRQ settings using the Device Manager, perform these steps:

1. Click your mouse on the Windows Start button. Windows will display the Start menu.

2. Within the Start menu, choose the Settings menu Control Panel option. Windows, in turn, will display the Control Panel window.

3. Within the Control Panel window, double-click your mouse on the System icon. Windows will display the System Properties dialog box.

4. Within the System Properties dialog box, select the Device Manager tab. Windows will display the Device Manager sheet.

5. Within the Device Manager sheet, select Computer and then click your mouse on the Properties button. Windows will display the Computer Properties dialog box.

6. Within the Computer Properties dialog box, click your mouse on the Interrupt request (IRQ) button. The Device Manager will display a list of IRQ settings that are currently in use. To determine an unused IRQ setting, simply select an IRQ number that is not in use.

USING THE MSD COMMAND TO DETERMINE IRQ SETTINGS

In Lesson 39, "Troubleshooting with MSD," you will learn how to use the MSD command to determine available IRQ settings. If you examine the MSD IRQ Status dialog box, you may find that IRQ 2 is set to something called *Second 8259A*—that's the second interrupt controller.

If you examine IRQ 9, you will see that it corresponds to the *Redirected IRQ 2*. Figure 8.2, for example, illustrates a sample MSD IRQ Status screen. When you need to assign an IRQ to a new device, search the MSD screen for a *(Reserved)* entry. These entries correspond to available IRQs.

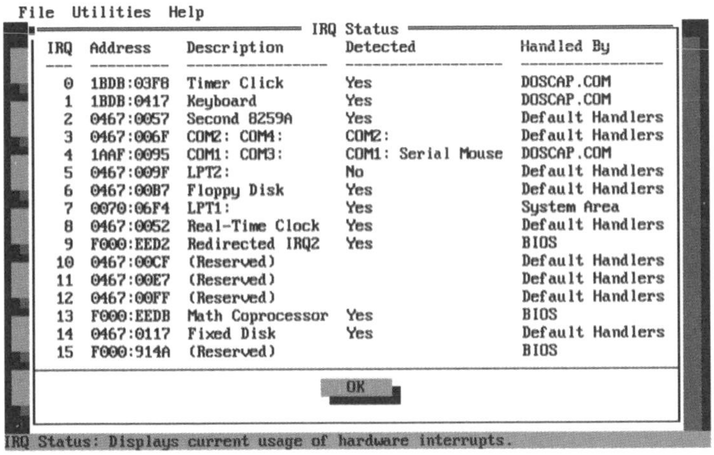

```
File  Utilities  Help
┌────────────────────── IRQ Status ──────────────────────┐
│ IRQ  Address   Description      Detected      Handled By │
│ ───  ───────   ───────────      ────────      ────────── │
│  0   1BDB:03F8  Timer Click      Yes           DOSCAP.COM │
│  1   1BDB:0417  Keyboard         Yes           DOSCAP.COM │
│  2   0467:0057  Second 8259A     Yes           Default Handlers │
│  3   0467:006F  COM2: COM4:      COM2:         Default Handlers │
│  4   1AAF:0095  COM1: COM3:      COM1: Serial Mouse  DOSCAP.COM │
│  5   0467:009F  LPT2:            No            Default Handlers │
│  6   0467:00B7  Floppy Disk      Yes           Default Handlers │
│  7   0070:06F4  LPT1:            Yes           System Area │
│  8   0467:0052  Real-Time Clock  Yes           Default Handlers │
│  9   F000:EED2  Redirected IRQ2  Yes           BIOS │
│ 10   0467:00CF  (Reserved)                     Default Handlers │
│ 11   0467:00E7  (Reserved)                     Default Handlers │
│ 12   0467:00FF  (Reserved)                     Default Handlers │
│ 13   F000:EEDB  Math Coprocessor Yes           BIOS │
│ 14   0467:0117  Fixed Disk       Yes           Default Handlers │
│ 15   F000:914A  (Reserved)                     BIOS │
│                      ┌──────┐                           │
│                      │  OK  │                           │
│                      └──────┘                           │
└────────────────────────────────────────────────────────┘
IRQ Status: Displays current usage of hardware interrupts.
```

Figure 8.2 *The MSD IRQ Status screen display.*

SETTING A CARD'S INTERRUPT REQUEST MANUALLY

When you purchase a hardware card, the card will normally come with a preselected IRQ. If the card supports the plug-and-play technology (discussed next), the card should automatically configure itself to avoid conflicts with your existing cards. Should your new card still conflict with your existing cards, you must change your card's settings.

Depending on your card's type, you may use jumpers, DIP switches, or software to change the card's settings. If you must change your card's settings via hardware switches or jumpers, examine the card closely. You will normally find a jumper or DIP switch that lets you select the IRQ setting. If your card supports software-based configuration, you can use the Windows Device Manager to assign the new settings.

Before you install the card, determine your PC's current IRQ use. If the your card's IRQ setting is not currently in use, install your card. If the IRQ setting is in use, change the jumper or DIP switches to change the IRQ setting to one that is not in use. Remember, if two cards have the same IRQ setting, the cards, and possibly your computer, will not work.

UNDERSTANDING PLUG-AND-PLAY DEVICES

To simplify hardware installations, newer cards support the plug-and-play technology which lets you install the cards without regard for your PC's existing card settings. In short, when you install a plug-and-play card and power on your PC, the card asks your

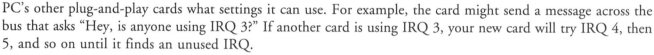

PC's other plug-and-play cards what settings it can use. For example, the card might send a message across the bus that asks "Hey, is anyone using IRQ 3?" If another card is using IRQ 3, your new card will try IRQ 4, then 5, and so on until it finds an unused IRQ.

Unfortunately, because most users have a mix of plug-and-play and older non-plug-and-play devices, there are times when the settings a plug-and-play card selects conflict with an older card. In such cases, you must determine the available IRQ settings and assign the correct settings to your card, normally using software as discussed next.

SETTING A CARD'S SETTINGS USING SOFTWARE

To simplify hardware installations, many newer cards let you assign their hardware settings using software as opposed to using jumpers or switches. In most cases, a newer card will come with software you can use to assign the card's settings. In addition, if you are using Windows 95 or 98, you may be able to use the Device Manager to assign the card's settings. To use the Device Manager to assign device settings to a card, perform these steps:

1. Click your mouse on the Start button. Windows, in turn, will display the Start menu.

2. Within the Start menu, choose the Settings menu Control Panel option. Windows will open the Control Panel window.

3. Within the Control Panel window, double-click your mouse on the System icon. Windows will open the System Properties dialog box.

4. Within the System Properties dialog box, select the Device Manager tab. Windows, in turn, will display the Device Manager sheet.

5. Within the Device Manager sheet, select the device you want to configure and then click your mouse on the Properties button. The Device Manager, in turn, will display a dialog box that contains the device properties.

6. Within the dialog box, click your mouse on the Resources tab. The Device Manager will display a page that contains the current device settings.

7. Within the device's settings page, click your mouse on the Use automatic settings checkbox to remove the checkmark from the box. Next, click your mouse on the settings you want to modify and then click your mouse on the Change button. The Device Manager will display a dialog box within which you can enter the setting you desire.

8. Within the dialog box, enter your setting and then choose OK.

UNDERSTANDING A CARD'S I/O ADDRESS

In addition to using an IRQ to signal the CPU, many cards also use a specific three-digit (hexadecimal) address users refer to as the card's *port address* or *I/O address*. These special address values correspond to memory locations on the card itself that the CPU uses to exchange data with the card. For example, when a program must send a character out of a serial port, such as COM1, the program places the character into a special port address on the serial card. Each card uses a unique port address.

Normally, you will not need to change a board's I/O address. However, if, after you install a card, the card or possibly another card quits working, you should examine both cards to check for an I/O address conflict. If you must change a card's port address, you will change a jumper, DIP switch, or software, as previously discussed.

UNDERSTANDING A CARD'S MEMORY ADDRESS

As you just learned, many cards perform I/O operations using small memory locations (which reside on the card) called ports. Depending on your card type, the card may require a range of bytes in the PC's upper-memory region as well. The upper-memory region is the 384KB range of memory that resides between the PC's 640KB conventional memory and extended memory.

Most of the upper-memory region is used by your video card to hold the image your PC is currently displaying on the screen. However, part of the region is not used. Thus, devices that must transfer larger amounts of data may reserve a portion of this unused memory. In such cases, you might have to specify the base or starting address for the device's memory range.

To specify a base address, you must determine a range of memory that is not currently in use by another device and then you must select that range on the card using DIP switches, jumpers, or software.

Next, you might need to tell your MS-DOS-based memory-management software and Windows 3.1 not to use the memory region. Normally, you tell your memory-management software not to use a memory range by using an exclude switch. If you are using MS-DOS, the following CONFIG.SYS entry, for example, excludes a region of memory using the EMM386 device driver:

```
DEVICE=C:\DOS\EMM386.EXE      X=EF00-EFFF
```

As you can see, the memory addresses used are in hexadecimal. The documentation that accompanied your card should include instructions for excluding memory in this way. If you are using Windows 3.1 you may have to place an EMMExclude statement within your *SYSTEM.INI* file as follows:

```
EMMExclude=EF00-EFFF
```

If you are using Windows 95 or 98, you can use the Device Manager to reserve the memory address. Admittedly, excluding a memory region for a card's use can be a challenging task. If you have difficulties, contact the card's technical support staff or a local PC user group and ask for help.

UNDERSTANDING DIRECT MEMORY ACCESS

As information flows through your computer, the information normally moves under the watchful eye of your computer's CPU. For example, if a program wants to display an image on the screen, the CPU moves the image into the computer's video memory. Although the CPU is well equipped to move information in this way, there are times when using the CPU as a "data mover" is a waste of the CPU's time. For example, when a program reads information from disk, the disk will normally transfer a sector of data (usually 512 bytes) to the computer's memory. Rather than having the CPU transfer the data, a special chip, called a *direct memory access* chip, oversees the operation, letting the CPU work on other tasks.

The term direct memory access (DMA) describes the process of moving data to or from memory without the use of the CPU. During a DMA operation, data flows down wires called a *DMA channel*. If you are using a 286-based PC or higher, the PC uses two DMA controllers with seven DMA channels, as listed in Table 8.3.

DMA Channel Number	Channel Use
0	8-bit data transfers
1	8-bit data transfers
2	Floppy disk transfers
3	8-bit data transfers
4	Cascade for DMA channels 0 through 3
5	16-bit data transfers
6	16-bit data transfers

Table 8.3 DMA channel use within the PC.

When you install a DMA device into your PC, you might need to select a DMA channel using DIP switches, jumpers, and software. Normally, two devices that use DMA will not conflict unless, for some reason, both devices try to perform a DMA operation at the same time. If you install a device that uses DMA and you begin to encounter intermittent errors, you might need to check your device's DMA channel settings. If you are using Windows 95 or 98, you can control most DMA settings using the Device Manager.

WHAT YOU MUST KNOW

In this lesson, you have learned about IRQ settings, port addresses, memory regions, and DMA channels, each of which must be set properly for the devices that use them to work properly. When you install a new hardware board, there will be times when you must change one or more board settings. To change a board setting, you will normally use jumpers and DIP switches. In Lesson 9, "Understanding DIP Switches and Jumpers," you will learn how to use a card's hardware switches to assign the card's settings. Before you continue with Lesson 9, however, make sure that you understand the following key concepts:

- ✓ When you install a card and the card or your PC fails to work, you might have a hardware conflict. Common hardware conflicts occur with IRQ settings, I/O addresses, memory regions, and DMA channels.

- ✓ Each card you install in your system uses a unique interrupt-request (IRQ) line to ask the CPU to perform special processing on its behalf. To set a card's IRQ, you use jumpers or DIP switches that reside on the card or software such as the Device Manager.

- ✓ To determine available IRQ settings under MS-DOS, use the MSD command.

- ✓ To determine available IRQ settings under Windows 95 or 98, use the Device Manager.

- ✓ An I/O address, or port address, is a special memory location built into the card itself that the CPU uses for small input and output operations or to set various card settings. Most cards use a three-digit (hexadecimal) port address.

- ✓ If a card must work with larger amounts of data, the card may request a range of memory from the PC's upper-memory region. If a card uses such memory, you must exclude the memory region from being used by Windows or your MS-DOS-based memory manager.

- ✓ Direct memory access is a technique that lets a special controller chip transfer large amounts of data from a device into the computer's memory without the use of the CPU as a "data mover." Devices that use DMA may require that you assign them to a specific DMA channel.

Lesson 9

Understanding DIP Switches and Jumpers

Within your computer, boards communicate with the processor by exchanging electronic signals. To let the processor know which board is signaling it, each board is assigned unique addresses and interrupt-request lines (IRQs). Lesson 8, "Understanding Common Conflicts," discussed several of these settings in detail. When you install a hardware board, such as an internal modem or sound card, there may be times when you need to change the board's hardware settings to avoid conflicts with an existing board within your computer. To change a board's settings, you may have to change one or more DIP switches or one or more jumpers, both of which are found on the board. If you are using a new card, you may need to change the card's settings using software.

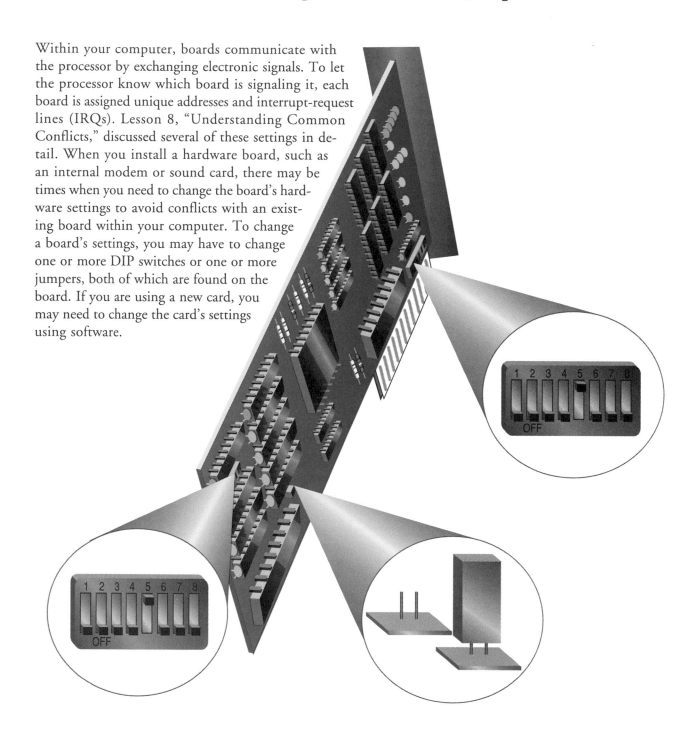

This lesson examines DIP switches, jumpers, and software settings. By the time you finish this lesson, you will understand the following key concepts:

- How to locate jumpers and DIP switches on a card
- How to change DIP switch settings
- How to change jumper settings
- How to change a card's settings using software

Hardware boards use jumpers and DIP switches for many different purposes. The documentation that accompanies the board will describe their use in detail. Do not let jumpers and DIP switches intimidate you. As you will learn in this lesson, they are very easy to use. As the number of hardware boards you install in your system increases, you may eventually need to change a jumper or DIP switch setting.

WORKING WITH DIP SWITCHES

The term DIP is an acronym for *dual inline package*, which describes how the switch components were designed. *DIP switches* look like a miniature collection of light switches.

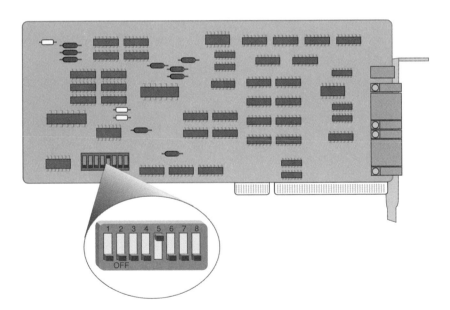

If you examine a DIP switch closely, you will find that the switches are labeled On/Off, Open/Closed, or 1/0.

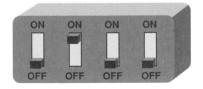
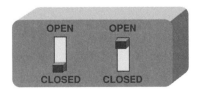

Hardware boards use DIP switches for many different purposes. In fact, a board may have several DIP switches. If you examine your hardware board closely, you will find that each switch has a unique number, such as switch 1 or switch 2.

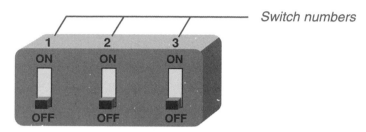

As you read the documentation that accompanies your board, you may be instructed to change a specific switch setting. Never change a DIP switch setting without first writing down the original settings. By keeping such records, if you ever must restore the board's original settings, you can refer to your notes. If you consistently keep such notes with the documentation that accompanied the card, when you must retrieve your notes, locating them should be easy.

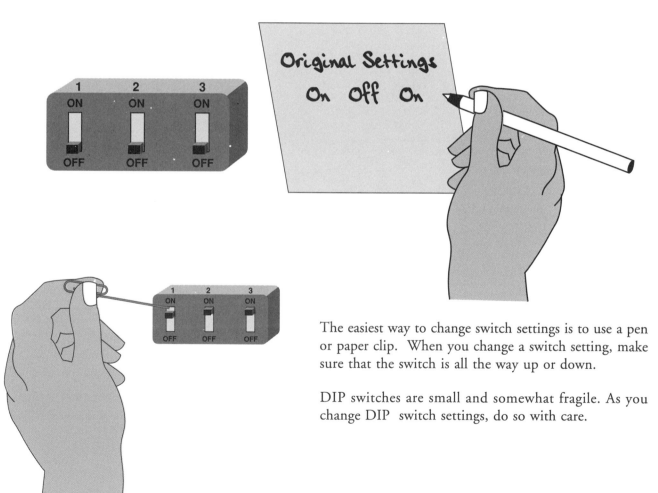

The easiest way to change switch settings is to use a pen or paper clip. When you change a switch setting, make sure that the switch is all the way up or down.

DIP switches are small and somewhat fragile. As you change DIP switch settings, do so with care.

UNDERSTANDING DIP SWITCHES

DIP switches provide one way for you to change (or configure) a hardware board. Depending on the board, two or more switches may be present. Most hardware boards clearly label each switch. The documentation that accompanies your hardware board will explain the purpose of each switch. The easiest way to change a switch is to use a pen or paper clip.

Note: *Never change DIP settings without first writing down the original switch settings.*

WORKING WITH JUMPERS

Jumpers provide a second way for you to configure a hardware card's settings. Jumpers let you physically connect two electrical pins, completing an electrical path. When you remove a jumper, you open (turn off) the path.

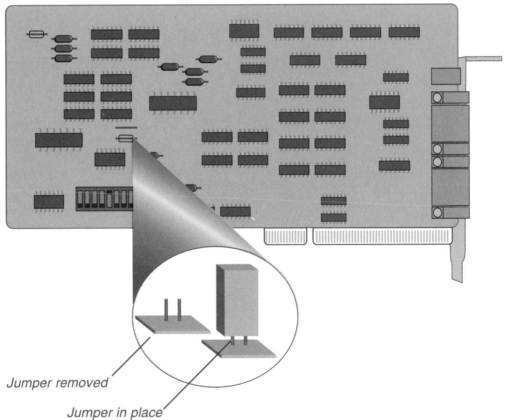

Jumper removed

Jumper in place

Like DIP switches, a hardware board can have two or more jumpers. If you examine the board closely, you will find that each jumper has a unique number, such as jumper 1 or jumper 2. The documentation that accompanies your board will define each jumper's purpose.

As was the case with DIP switches, never change jumper settings without first recording the jumper's original settings. Also, should you remove a jumper, place the connector in a safe location.

Rather than removing a jumper from within the PC, users often leave the jumper connected to one pin. In this way, the jumper connector does not complete a connection and it also does not get lost.

Note: *You should never change a jumper setting without writing down the original settings.*

In some cases, you can easily remove or add jumpers using only your fingers. In other cases, you will need to use needlenose pliers.

When using pliers, gently grip the jumper's center, sliding the jumper on or off.

CHANGING CARD SETTINGS USING SOFTWARE

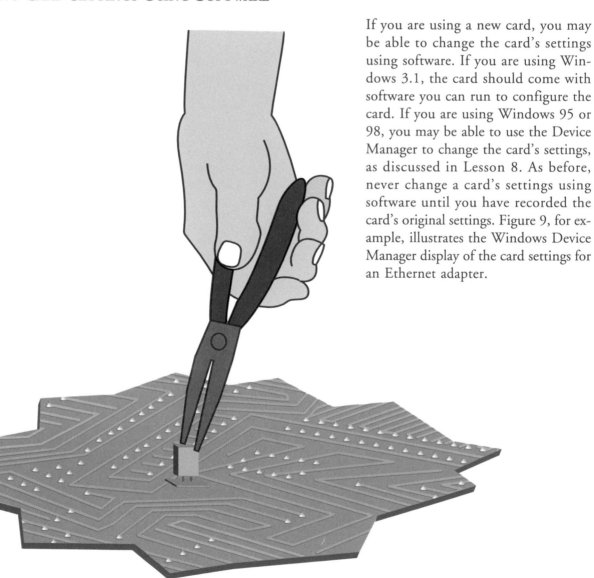

If you are using a new card, you may be able to change the card's settings using software. If you are using Windows 3.1, the card should come with software you can run to configure the card. If you are using Windows 95 or 98, you may be able to use the Device Manager to change the card's settings, as discussed in Lesson 8. As before, never change a card's settings using software until you have recorded the card's original settings. Figure 9, for example, illustrates the Windows Device Manager display of the card settings for an Ethernet adapter.

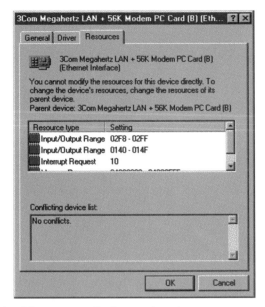

Figure 9 *Using the Windows Device Manager to display card settings.*

WHAT YOU MUST KNOW

In this lesson, you learned that, as you install more hardware cards, the likelihood that two or more devices will try to use the same address or interrupt line increases. PC cards use DIP switches, jumpers, or software to let you change the settings to an available memory location or request line. In anticipation of Intel's Pentium processor, many 486-based computers were designed to have their 486 processor upgraded to a Pentium. In Lesson 10, "Upgrading Your Processor," you will learn how to upgrade such "Pentium-ready" systems. Also, if you are using an older Pentium, you may want to upgrade it to a faster one. Before you continue with Lesson 10, however, make sure that you understand the following key concepts:

✓ You can configure most boards (change the board's settings) using DIP switches, jumpers, or software.

✓ A DIP switch is a small, normally plastic, group of switches. Using a paper clip, you can turn individual switches on or off to change the board's configuration.

✓ A jumper is a small connector that you slide over two pins to complete a circuit connection or that you remove to break a circuit. By changing the board's circuitry using jumpers, you change the board's configuration.

✓ Never change a DIP switch, jumper, or software setting without first writing down the original settings.

Lesson 10

Upgrading Your Processor

Historically, when a new PC processor ships, such as the Pentium, the processor's first-year prices are quite high. As a rule, if you can delay your upgrade 12 to 18 months, you will save considerable money. With the knowledge that many users often delay their processor upgrades, many PC manufacturers now sell PCs that are processor upgradeable. In the case of the Pentium processor, for example, these upgradeable PCs are often classified as "Pentium ready." This lesson examines the steps you must perform to upgrade your processor. By the time you finish this lesson, you will understand the following key concepts:

- The difference between the Pentium processor and a 486

- The steps you must perform to install a Pentium

- How you can upgrade your 386 or 486

- Why you might upgrade an older Pentium to a faster Pentium

- How a processor's speed influences its performance

If you are using a 486, you may be able to upgrade your system to use an older Pentium processor. Unfortunately, you cannot plug a Pentium processor into just any PC. Instead, your PC's motherboard must be designed to accept the Pentium. In other words, your motherboard must be *Pentium ready*. If your 486 is not Pentium ready, you may be able to increase your system performance by replacing your processor with an Intel OverDrive processor. Using the OverDrive processor, your system should run as much as 1-1/2 times faster.

WHAT YOU WILL NEED

Before you get started with this lesson, make sure that you have the following readily available:

1. A PC tool kit with a screwdriver

2. A container within which you can place the chassis screws

3. A well-lit workspace with room for you to place the chassis

4. A new processor

Note: Before you begin, make sure that you are working in a static-free environment. Also, ground yourself by touching your system unit chassis before you touch a processor chip.

HOW THE PENTIUM DIFFERS FROM A 486

When processor designers try to improve a processor's performance, they focus their efforts on the three following techniques:

- Increase the number of transistors on the processor chip

- Increase the processor chip's clock speed

- Increase the number of instructions per clock cycle

Computers execute programs by sending electronic signals from one component to another. By increasing the number of transistors in the processor chip, the Pentium allows more components to be placed within the processor itself. As a result, signals do not have as far to travel which reduces their transfer times. By reducing signal transfer times, the Pentium improves its performance. The 486 supports 1,250,000 transistors. The Pentium II, on the other hand, supports over seven million. Table 10.1 lists the number of transistors in PC processors over the years.

Processor Type	Number of Transistors
8088	30,000
80286	130,000
80386	250,000
80486	1,250,000
Original Pentium	3,000,000
Pentium II	7,500,000

Table 10.1 The number of transistors in different PC processor types.

Within the CPU, operations are controlled using a single *clock*, which keeps the computer's electronic components in sync. Each tick of the clock is called a *clock cycle*. In the original IBM PC, eleased in 1981, the clock ticked 4.7 million times per second. In older Pentiums, like many 486s, the clock ticks 66 million times per second. Newer Pentium processors, however, tick over 450 million times per second!

Note: As you shop for PCs, you will encounter different processor speeds, some faster or slower than 266MHz. Keep in mind that the faster the processor, the faster the PC.

A program is a list of instructions that the CPU executes. In the past, processors normally executed a single instruction with one or more clock ticks. The Pentium, however, can sometimes execute two instructions per clock tick. By combining these three techniques, newer Pentium processors are able to execute over 455-million instructions per second!

A Transistor Is a Chip's Workhorse

As electronic signals flow through the computer, devices need a way to store or hold signals. When computers were first built in the 1940s, the computers used vacuum tubes. Because the vacuum tubes were very large, hot, and subject to failure, the transistor was designed. Transistors are so named because they transmit signals across a resistor. Computer chips (sometimes called integrated circuits) are collections of many transistors. As Table 10.2 shows, chips are categorized by the number of transistors they contain.

Transistor Count	Chip Classification	Category
1 to 500	Small- to medium-scale integration	SSI or MSI
501 to 10,000	Large-scale integration	LSI
10,001 to 100,000	Very-large-scale integration	VLSI
Over 100,000	Ultra-large-scale integration	ULSI

Table 10.2 Chip classification by transistor count.

INSTALLING A PENTIUM PROCESSOR

If you are using a "Pentium ready" 486, you can upgrade your system to a Pentium processor. The Pentium processor you install, however, must fit into the 486 processor's socket, which means you can only insert an older (slower) Pentium. You could not, for example, insert a Pentium II processor within a 486 processor's socket (each uses different pins).

To install a Pentium processor, power off and unplug your PC. Next, remove the PC's system unit cover, as discussed in Lesson 2, "Opening Your PC's System Unit." Locate your current processor on the motherboard. Your processor chip will likely be labeled with the number 486.

Note: *Do not forget to discharge any static charge that your body may have accumulated before touching any chips. You can discharge such static by simply touching your system chassis.*

To simplify the removal and insertion of processor chips, many motherboards use a ZIF or *zero-insertion-force* processor socket. To remove the processor from a ZIF socket, simply raise up the socket lever. The processor chip should rise to the top of the socket.

To insert the Pentium processor into the ZIF socket, gently align the processor's pins into the socket and close the socket lever. The processor will slide gently and securely into place. The ZIF socket is so named because you apply no (zero) force to insert the chip into the socket.

Note: *When you are replacing any chip, make certain that the replacement is pointing the same way as the original.*

Replace and secure your PC's system unit cover. Next, plug in and power on your PC. When your PC starts, it will be using the Pentium processor.

UPGRADING A 386 TO A 486

If you are using a 386-based PC, you can now upgrade your PC by replacing the processor chip. If you examine PC magazine archives, you may find processors, such as the Cyrix 486, that you can plug directly into a 386 processor slot. In this way, you can upgrade your 386 to a 486 in a matter of minutes! Depending on the processor you buy, the steps you must perform to replace the processor may differ slightly. In general, however, you can follow the guidelines just discussed for the Pentium upgrade.

UNDERSTANDING HERTZ AND MEGAHERTZ (MHz)

If you've shopped for a new computer, you have probably been overwhelmed by the wide variety of systems on the market. You can buy PCs with 266MHz (266 megahertz) Pentium chips, 366MHz chips, and even 450MHz chips. Most salespeople will tell you that more megahertz means more speed. They are right, and here is why.

Inside your computer's processor, the CPU, is a small clock that coordinates the computer's processing. A processor's speed tells you how many times per second the clock ticks. A processor whose clock ticks 1 million times per second has a speed of 1MHz. A 450MHz Pentium, therefore, is a processor whose clock ticks 450 million times per second! Each time the processor's clock ticks, the processor can perform one and sometimes two instructions! As you might guess, one of the easiest ways to improve your system's speed is to upgrade to a faster processor. As the price of computers continues to drop, those users who insist on top performance should plan to purchase a new PC every 18 months.

THINK ABOUT UPGRADING YOUR PENTIUM

If you are using an older Pentium processor, such as a 60MHz Pentium, you should consider upgrading to a newer, faster Pentium. To upgrade your Pentium, you must select a new Pentium whose pins match your existing Pentium's socket. You could not, for example, insert a Pentium II processor into the socket for a 60MHz Pentium. As you plan to upgrade your processor, you should also consider adding memory as discussed in Lesson 12, "Adding Memory to Your PC." With the faster processor and additional memory, you will improve your performance under Windows 98 significantly.

UNDERSTANDING THE PROCESSOR'S INSTRUCTION CACHE

As you shop for processors, you may encounter the term *processor cache*. In short, a processor cache is a small very fast memory the processor uses to hold its current instructions or instructions it expects to execute in the near future. As a general rule, the larger the processor cache, the faster the system's performance. Unfortunately, the fast high-speed memory is also quite expensive. As the size of the processor cache increases, so too does the cost of the system. Newer processors provide two levels of cache, which users refer to L1 and L2 cache. The L1 cache resides within the chip itself. the L2 cache is an external cache that resides on the motherboard.

UNDERSTANDING MATH COPROCESSORS

To run programs, your computer relies on its central processing unit, or CPU. The CPU is the computer's electronic brain, which oversees most operations. A computer program is simply a list of instructions the computer performs, much like a recipe is a set of instructions a cook performs. When you run a program, the CPU executes the program instructions. An instruction might tell the CPU to add two numbers, to move a value in memory, and so on. In general, the CPU only executes simple instructions, such as adding two numbers. If a program needs to determine a value's square root or an angle's cosine, the program must break the operation into a series of more general instructions the CPU understands. Depending on the operation, the number of instructions can become long and time consuming for the CPU to execute. To improve the PC's performance, many users add a special math coprocessor, which can execute arithmetic operations quickly. Like the CPU, a math coprocessor is a chip.

A *math coprocessor* is a computer chip specifically designed to perform arithmetic operations quickly. If you use your computer to perform number-crunching applications, such as a spreadsheet, CAD, or scientific program, a math coprocessor should improve your system performance. On the other hand, if you normally just run word processor or database programs, the math coprocessor will not improve your system performance. Such programs normally do not perform complex arithmetic operations. Thus, the math coprocessor is not used.

DETERMINING WHETHER YOUR PC NEEDS A MATH COPROCESSOR

In the past, if you were using a 386-based PC or older, you had to buy and install a math coprocessor. Newer CPUs, such as the Pentium and *some* 486s, however, have a built-in math coprocessor. If you are using Windows 95 or 98, you can use the Device Manager to determine if your system has a math coprocessor. To display math-coprocessor information using the Device Manager, perform these steps:

1. Select the Start menu Settings option and choose Control Panel. Windows, in turn, will display the Control Panel window.

2. Within the Control Panel window, double-click your mouse on the System icon. Windows will display the System Properties dialog box.

3. Click your mouse on the Device Manager tab.

4. Within the Device Manager's list of devices, double-click your mouse on the System devices entry.

5. If your system has a math coprocessor, the list of system devices will contain a Numeric data processor entry. Double-click your mouse on the entry. The Device Manager, in turn, will display the math coprocessor's properties as shown in Figure 10.

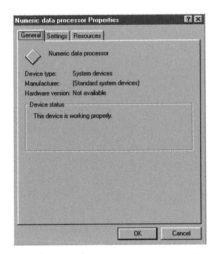

Figure 10 *Using the Device Manager to display math-coprocessor properties.*

If you are using MS-DOS, the way you can determine if your PC has a math coprocessor is to use the MSD (Microsoft Diagnostic) command provided with DOS 6 and Windows. Lesson 38, "Troubleshooting with MSD," examines the MSD command in detail. For now, run MSD from the DOS prompt. MSD will display its main menu. Press **P** to select MSD's Computer option. MSD will display the Computer dialog box, which states whether or not a math coprocessor is present. Press Enter to remove the dialog box. Next, press Alt-F to select MSD's File menu and choose the Exit option.

SHOPPING FOR A MATH COPROCESSOR

As you know, the computer's CPU type is identified by a unique number, such as a 286 or 386. When you purchase a math coprocessor, you must match the CPU type. Math coprocessors are identified by similar numbers, such as a 287 or 387, to facilitate proper matching. If you are using a 486, however, things get a little more difficult. If you examine advertisements for 486 computers, you will find 486DX and 486SX processors. As it turns out, 486DX processors have a built-in math coprocessor and 486SX processors do not. As a result, 486DX computers tend to be more expensive. When you price a 487 math coprocessor, you may find it is more expensive than its 287 and 387 counterparts. As it turns out, the 487 math coprocessor is actually a 486 with a built-in math coprocessor. In other words, it is almost identical to the 486DX processor. The difference between the 486DX and the 487 is simply an extra pin that prevents the chips from being plug compatible. When you install the 487, it takes over all processing, and the original 486SX becomes idle.

INSTALLING A MATH COPROCESSOR

To install a math coprocessor, turn off and unplug your PC. Next, open your system unit, as discussed in Lesson 2, and free yourself of all static charge. If you examine your motherboard, you will find a coprocessor socket very close to your processor socket. You might need to refer to the documentation that accompanied your PC to locate the coprocessor socket. Align the coprocessor pins to the socket and gently slide the coprocessor into place. Replace and secure your system unit cover and power on your PC. After your system starts, run the MSD command, as before. If your PC does not see the math coprocessor, access your PC's setup program and change your PC's CMOS settings, as discussed in Lesson 6, "Understanding Your Computer's CMOS Memory."

THE FAMOUS PENTIUM MATH-COPROCESSOR ERROR

When Intel released their 90MHz Pentium processor, they were soon informed by users that the math coprocessor contained a bug which produced errant results. However, in addition to telling Intel about the error, the users also posted specifics about the error on the Internet. Within days, reports of the Pentium bug appeared on the front page of major newspapers. If you examine Figure 10, you may be able to read the screen text that states the math coprocessor is working correctly. If you are using a Pentium chip that contains the math bug, the Device Manager's math-coprocessor status message will so inform you. In such a case, contact Intel and ask them to provide you with a replacement Processor.

WHAT YOU MUST KNOW

In this lesson, you learned that you may be able to upgrade your 486 to a Pentium or your 386 to a 486 with one simple operation. Likewise, you may be able to upgrade a Pentium processor to a faster Pentium, provided new processor's pins match the existing processor's socket. Upgrading the processor is the biggest single operation most users can do to speed up their computers. When your computer performs keyboard input, writes to the screen display, or reads or writes files on disk, your computer normally uses a special chip called the BIOS (Basic Input Output System). Depending on the age of your PC, there may be times when you must replace the BIOS. In Lesson 11, "Upgrading the PC BIOS," you will examine the steps required to replace the BIOS. Before you continue with Lesson 11, however, make sure that you have learned the following key concepts:

- ✓ The Pentium is a processor chip capable of executing over 200 million instructions per second.

- ✓ The Pentium improves its performance by integrating more transistors, over three million, and by increasing the number of instructions it can execute in a single clock tick.

- ✓ You may be able to upgrade your 386 to a 486 simply by replacing the processor chip.

- ✓ You cannot install a Pentium processor into every 486-based PC, only a PC which is "Pentium ready."

- ✓ When you upgrade your processor, you must choose a processor whose pins match your existing processor's socket.

Lesson 11

Upgrading the PC BIOS

The PC BIOS is a chip (or pair of chips, depending on the age of your PC) that oversees all of the input and output operations your PC performs. When programs read keystrokes from the keyboard or display text or pictures to the screen display, the programs rely on the BIOS.

In addition, the BIOS oversees disk I/O and other key operations. BIOS is an acronym for Basic Input Output System.

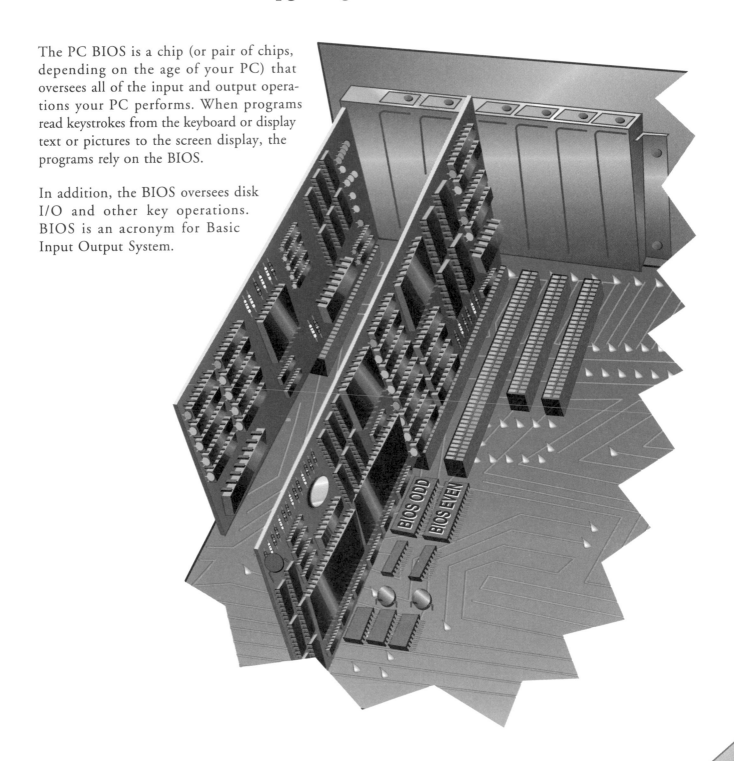

If you have an older PC, there may come a time when you need to upgrade your PC BIOS before you can use a new device. If you are using a newer PC, you may upgrade your BIOS using software, as opposed to replacing the BIOS chips. This lesson examines the steps you must perform to upgrade your PC BIOS. By the time you finish this lesson, you will understand the following key concepts:

- How you know when you must upgrade the BIOS
- How replacing the BIOS can lead to compatibility problems
- How to replace the BIOS chips or how to update a flash-BIOS chip using software

---

WHAT YOU WILL NEED

Before you get started with this lesson, make sure that you have the following readily available:

1. A PC tool kit with a screwdriver and chip extractor
2. A container within which you can place the chassis screws
3. A well-lit workspace with room for you to place the chassis
4. New, compatible BIOS chips or BIOS software

Note: Before you begin, make sure that you are working in a static-free environment. Also, ground yourself by touching your system unit chassis before you touch a BIOS chip.

HOW YOU KNOW WHEN YOU NEED TO REPLACE YOUR BIOS

Most users will never upgrade their PC BIOS because, quite frankly, they will have no reason to do so. Normally, the need to update your BIOS occurs when you install a new floppy disk or other BIOS-based device into an older system. When the device does not work, an often overlooked cause is incompatibility between the device and BIOS. Users normally do not intentionally set out to upgrade their BIOS. Instead, an incompatibility forces the upgrade. Some users might suggest that replacing an older BIOS is a good way to improve your system performance. Although newer BIOS chips may indeed be faster, they might not be compatible with your system. In such cases, the net result is a fast system that does not work. Before you upgrade your BIOS, always check with your PC manufacturer first to ensure that the BIOS upgrade is compatible with your system.

UNDERSTANDING THE PC BIOS CHIPS

The PC BIOS is a pair of computer chips that oversees input and output operations. To upgrade the BIOS, you simply replace the chips with new ones. Most users never have a need to upgrade the BIOS. Before you upgrade your BIOS, check with your PC manufacturer to ensure that the BIOS upgrade is compatible with your system.

Keep in mind that most users normally do not upgrade their BIOS chips to improve their system performance. Instead, users upgrade the BIOS to gain support for a new device.

DETERMINING YOUR BIOS TYPE

If you experience problems using a new hardware device or software program, the product's technical-support staff may ask you about your BIOS type or date. There are three easy ways for you to get information about your BIOS. First, each time your system starts, your screen will normally display the BIOS information briefly on your monitor. If you are using MS-DOS, you can use the MSD command discussed in Lesson 38, "Troubleshooting with MSD" to display BIOS specifics, as shown in Figure 11.1.

Figure 11.1 *Using MSD to display BIOS specifics.*

If you are using Windows 95 or 98, you can run Registry Editor, *RegEdit.EXE*, and search the Registry database for the words BIOSDATE or BIOSNAME as shown in Figure 11.2.

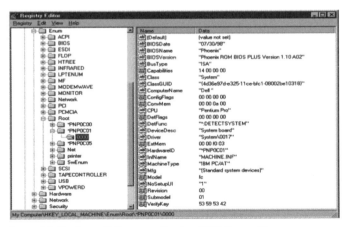

Figure 11.2 *Using the Windows 95 Registry Editor to display BIOS specifics.*

To use the Registry Editor to display BIOS information, perform these steps:

1. Select the Start menu Run option. Windows, in turn, will display the Run dialog box.

2. Within the Open field, type **RegEdit** and press ENTER. Windows will display the Registry Editor window.

3. Within the Registry Editor, Use the Edit menu Find option to search for the word BIOSDATE or BIOSNAME.

UNDERSTANDING FLASH BIOS CHIPS

If you are using a newer PC, it is quite likely that your PC may use a flash-BIOS, that (unlike a chip-based BIOS) uses settings you can change using software. If your system uses a flash-BIOS (the documentation that accompanied your system should tell you), you will perform your BIOS upgrades by running a program. Normally, you can download BIOS upgrades from the Web site of your PC manufacturer. For specifics on upgrading your system, contact your PC manufacturer's technical support staff or search the manufacturer's Web site for flash-BIOS information.

UPGRADING YOUR SYSTEM BIOS CHIPS

If your PC uses BIOS chips that you must replace, that is, your system does not use a flash BIOS, and after you ensure that the new BIOS chips are fully compatible with your system, power off and unplug the PC's system unit. Next, remove the system-unit cover as discussed in Lesson 2, "Opening Your PC's System Unit." Locate the BIOS chips on the motherboard. Before you touch the BIOS chips, make sure you discharge static electricity by grounding yourself to your system chassis.

The BIOS uses a pair of chips—one called *odd* and one *even*. When you replace the chips, you must place the odd and even chips in the correct sockets. Stop now and make a note of the chip orientation.

Using a chip extractor, gently remove each BIOS chip from its socket, replacing the chip with the corresponding odd or even new chip. After you replace both chips, replace your system-unit cover. Plug in and power on your PC. If you have installed the new BIOS chips correctly, your system will perform its power-on self-test. After your system starts, make sure you can access your disk drives and can perform screen and keyboard I/O.

Upgrading Your BIOS Chips

Before you purchase new BIOS chips, make sure the chips are fully compatible with your system. One way to increase the likelihood that your chips are compatible is to purchase the chips from the same manufacturer who built your PC. To change your BIOS chips, perform these steps:

1. Power off and unplug your PC system unit.

2. Remove the system-unit cover, as discussed in Lesson 2, and discharge static from your body.

3. Locate the pair of BIOS chips on the motherboard. Remove the chips from their sockets using a chip extractor.

4. Insert the new odd and even BIOS chips into the correct sockets.

5. Replace the system-unit cover.

6. Plug in and power on your PC system unit.

Note: If your system does not start, verify that you have placed the odd and even BIOS chips into the correct sockets.

What You Must Know

Throughout this book, you will learn how to install various hardware devices into your PC. If you are upgrading an older PC, there may be times when your PC BIOS does not recognize the device. In this lesson, you learned how to upgrade your BIOS. If you use your computer to run math-intensive programs, such as a computer-aided design (CAD) program, or to create complex spreadsheets, you might improve your system performance by adding a math coprocessor. Lesson 12, "Adding Memory to Your PC," discusses ways you can improve your system performance by adding more random-access memory (RAM). Before you continue with Lesson 12, however, make sure that you understand the following key concepts:

✓ BIOS is an acronym for Basic Input Output System. Your computer's BIOS is a pair of chips that oversee most input and output (I/O) operations.

✓ Most users do not upgrade their BIOS to improve their system performance. Instead, users upgrade the BIOS to obtain support for a new device.

✓ Before you upgrade your BIOS, you need to ensure that the new BIOS will be fully compatible with your system. One of the best sources to ask is your original PC manufacturer.

✓ Older systems use BIOS chips that come in pairs, one called the odd BIOS chip and one called the even. When you upgrade your BIOS chips, you need to ensure that you install the odd chip into the odd socket and the even chip into the even socket.

✓ Many newer systems use flash-BIOS chips you can update using software. Normally, most PC manufacturers offer such BIOS upgrades that you can download from their Web site.

Lesson 12

Adding Memory to Your PC

As you have learned, a program (software) is simply a list of instructions the computer performs. Before your computer can run a program, the program must reside in your computer's random-access memory (RAM). As programs become more powerful, they also become larger, requiring more RAM. Further, within Windows, you may have several different programs running at the same time, each of which requires its own memory space. When Windows runs out of memory, it temporarily moves programs in and out of memory to the much slower disk to make room in RAM for the current application. Although swapping programs in and out of memory in this way lets Windows run multiple programs at the same time, the disk operations required during the swaps significantly slow your system performance.

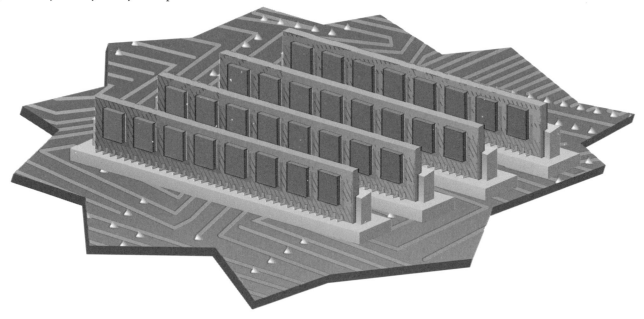

One of the best ways Windows users can improve system performance is to add memory. In the future, as programs become more complex or take advantage of multimedia video, 8MB of RAM will become the standard, and fast systems will have more. This lesson examines the steps you must perform to add memory to your PC. By the time you finish this lesson, you will understand the following key concepts:

- How to determine how much memory your PC currently contains and if adding memory will improve your system performance

- How to install SIMM and DIMM chips

- How to upgrade a notebook computer's memory

- The differences between memory types, such as DRAM, VRAM, and SRAM

Normally, when you add memory to your system, you will see immediate performance improvement. As such, everyone should consider adding more memory.

HOW MUCH MEMORY DO YOU HAVE?

Before you make the decision to add more memory to your PC, you should determine how much memory your PC already has. If you are using Windows 95 or 98, you can use the System Properties dialog box to determine how much memory your PC contains, by performing these steps:

1. Select the Start menu Settings option and choose Control Panel. Windows 95, in turn, will display the Control Panel window.

2. Within the Control Panel window, double-click your mouse on the System icon. Windows 95 will display the System Properties dialog box.

3. Click your mouse on the Performance tab. Windows 95, in turn, will display the Performance tab, shown in Figure 12, that lists how much RAM your PC contains.

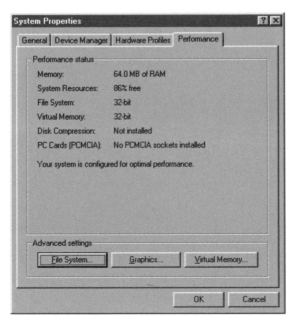

Figure 12 The System Properties Performance tab.

If you are using MS-DOS, you can find out how much memory your system contains by issuing the MEM command, which you run from the DOS prompt, as shown here:

```
C:\> MEM     <ENTER>

Memory Type          Total  =   Used  +   Free
Conventional          640K       48K       592K
Upper                 155K       155K      0K
Reserved              128K       128K      0K
Extended (XMS)      7,269K     6,245K    1,024K
Total memory        8,192K     6,576K    1,616K


Total under 1 MB     795K        203K      592K


Largest executable program size      592K (605,696 bytes)
Largest free upper memory block        0K      (0 bytes)
MS-DOS is resident in the high memory area.
```

Next, before you add memory, evaluate how you use your PC. If you normally run multiple programs from within Windows, you will improve your system performance by adding memory. However, if you run only one program at a time from MS-DOS, you probably won't see a tremendous performance improvement by adding more memory.

WILL ADDING MEMORY IMPROVE YOUR SYSTEM PERFORMANCE?

If you make extensive use of Windows and you normally have multiple programs running at the same time, adding memory to your system will improve your performance. If, however, you work from the MS-DOS environment, you might not see a great change in performance by adding memory.

LOCATING YOUR SYSTEM MEMORY

PC memory resides on your system's motherboard. To locate your system's memory, first power off and unplug your PC. Next, remove your system unit cover, as discussed in Lesson 2, "Opening Your PC's System Unit," and discharge any static that has accumulated on your body.

Your computer's random-access memory uses upright chips, called *SIMMs* or *DIMMs*. SIMM is an acronym for *single inline memory module*. In short, the term refers to the fact that several memory chips are stored in the same module, in line, as shown. DIMM, in turn, is an acronym for dual inline memory module. In general, a DIMM doubles the chip's storage capacity by placing chips on both sides of the card. When you purchase memory, you must purchase either SIMMs or DIMMs based on your PC's motherboard slots. You cannot use a SIMM chip in a DIMM slot and vice versa. The documentation that accompanied your PC will tell you whether your PC uses SIMM or DIMM chips.

Within your system unit, locate the SIMM or DIMM chips on your motherboard. Also, note the number of unused sockets.

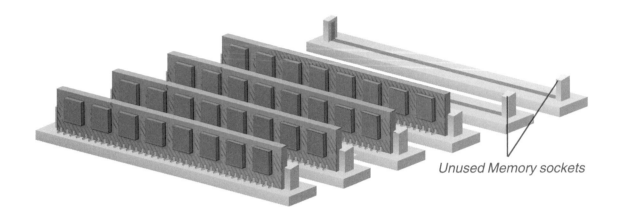

Unused Memory sockets

Note: Before you begin, make sure that you are working in a static-free environment. Also ground yourself by touching your system unit chassis before you touch a processor chip.

WHAT TYPE OF MEMORY CHIPS DO YOU NEED?

SIMM and DIMM chips are sold as 1MB, 2MB, 4MB, 8MB, and so on—even up to 128MB chips! However, your PC may only support 4MB or 8MB chips. Turn to the documentation that accompanied your PC or call your manufacturer's technical support to determine the size of memory your system can use. In most cases, the memory size you add to your system must match the memory size your PC is currently using. In other words, if your PC contains 2MB SIMMs, you probably cannot add 4MB chips. Instead, you must keep using 2MB chips.

With the cost of SIMM chips constantly decreasing, you may find that if your PC supports larger SIMMs, you will want to remove the smaller chips. For example, if the price of 32MB chips becomes affordable and your system supports 32MB chips, you may want to simply remove any 8MB chips from your system.

Manufacturers classify memory chips by speed and size. Memory speed is expressed in terms of nanoseconds (ns), that is, billionths of seconds that a given task (such as a memory read) takes—the lower the number, the faster the chip. For example, you might buy 16MB, 70ns SIMMs. Your system documentation will specify the minimum memory speed your system can use. As a rule, if you buy memory that is at least as fast as your system's current memory chips, you will be fine.

INSTALLING MEMORY CHIPS

To add memory to your system, you simply insert a SIMM or DIMM chip into the next available socket. Sounds easy, right? Unforunately, it is not. In addition to the socket, PCs hold SIMMs or DIMMs in place using small notches that appear at the end of the socket.

You need to be very careful when you insert the SIMM chip into these notches. If you break a notch off, the PC may not be able to hold the chip in place. As a result, the socket cannot be used and you cannot use other sockets! Worse yet—in many cases, the socket cannot be fixed!

Because an errant snap can have devastating results, I strongly recommend that you let your computer retailer add memory to your system for you. Should your retailer break a SIMM socket, your retailer is responsible. The money you spend having the chips installed will be much less than having to replace a motherboard because you have broken a socket.

Socket notch

Note: If you choose to have your retailer install your SIMM or DIMMchips for you, examine the chips before you leave the store to ensure that the retailer has not inadvertently broken a socket.

If you choose to install a memory chip, you normally insert the chip into the slot at an angle, and then stand the chip upright, inserting the chip into notches that hold the chip in place.

INSTALL SIMM OR DIMM CHIPS WITH GREAT CARE

If you choose to install your own SIMM or DIMM chips, do so with great care. When you install a memory chip, you slide the chip into the slot and then you snap the chip into notches that hold the chip in place. If you accidentally break one of these notches, you might not be able to use the socket or sockets that follow. New users might want their computer retailer to perform their memory-chip upgrade for them. To install memory chips, perform these steps:

1. Power off and unplug your PC system unit.

2. Open your system unit, as discussed in Lesson 2, and remove any static charge from your body by touching your system-unit chassis.

3. Locate the unused memory slots.

4. Gently insert the memory chip into the next unused slot.

5. Replace and secure your system-unit cover.

6. Plug in and power on your PC system unit.

MANY OLDER PCS USE MEMORY CARDS

Many older 286- and 386-based PCs do not use SIMM or DIMM chips. Instead, the systems use a memory card. If you open your PC system unit and you do not see SIMM chips or SIMM slots, your PC may use card-based memory. In such cases, contact your PC retailer to determine the correct memory card type. To install card-based memory, perform these steps:

1. Power off and unplug your PC system unit. Open your system unit, as discussed in Lesson 2, and free yourself of static.

2. Use the card's jumpers or DIP switches to configure the card's starting address, as discussed in the documentation that accompanies your card.

3. Locate an unused expansion slot and gently insert the card into the unused slot. Replace and secure your system-unit cover.

4. Plug in and power on your PC system unit.

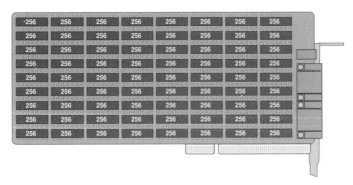

ADDING MEMORY TO A NOTEBOOK PC

If you are using a notebook PC, you may have two ways to add memory to your system. First, most notebook PCs support SIMM or DIMM chips. Although the documentation that accompanies your notebook PC may show you the steps you must perform to install the chips, you should strongly consider letting your PC retailer install the chips for you. Most notebook PCs are difficult, at best, to open so you can access the motherboard. To reduce your risk of damaging the notebook, let a service technician who works on notebooks every day perform the installation for you. Second, you may be able to add memory using a PCMCIA card.

TELLING YOUR SYSTEM ABOUT THE NEW MEMORY

After you install additional memory, you can normally simply power on your PC and your system will find its new memory. As your system starts, your PC will display its memory count on your screen display. If, for some reason, your system does not recognize the new memory, you may have to tell your computer's CMOS about the new memory before you can put it to use. To inform the CMOS about the memory, access your CMOS setup program, as discussed in Lesson 6, "Understanding Your Computer's CMOS Memory."

UNDERSTANDING MEMORY TYPES

As you shop for PC memory, you may encounter several different memory types. The following list defines several of the acronyms you may encounter.

RAM is an acronym for random-access memory. It is a generic term that describes memory that can be both written to by programs and read (as opposed to read-only memory, ROM, which can only be read and not written).

DRAM is an acronym for dynamic RAM. It is the least expensive and most commonly used memory. The word dynamic appears in the name to indicate that the microprocessor must periodically refresh the chip's contents or the contents will be lost.

SRAM is an acronym for static RAM. It is much faster and much more expensive than DRAM. Because of its speed, systems often use SRAM for their fast (and small) processor cache. Unlike DRAM chips, whose contents the processor must refresh continually, SRAM chips are static and do not need refreshing, which is one reason why SRAM chips are faster than DRAM. In addition, SRAM chips take advantage of newer, faster technology to increase their speed.

VRAM is an acronym for video RAM. It is very similar to DRAM in that its contents must be refreshed continually. Unlike DRAM and SRAM chips, VRAM chips can be written to and read at the same time (they are dual ported). The ability to be read and written simultaneously makes the VRAM chips ideal for video operations for which the video card can update the current image in memory while the card displays the image to the monitor.

What You Must Know

If you are using Windows, it seems that you can never have too much RAM. As you learned in this lesson, one of the fastest ways to improve your system performance is to add more RAM. In this lesson, you learned how to install more random-access memory into your computer. In Lesson 13, you will learn how to install a floppy disk within your PC. Before you continue with Lesson 13, however, make sure that you have learned the following key concepts:

✓ A program is a list of instructions the computer executes. Before the computer can run a program, the program must reside within the computer's random-access memory (RAM). Likewise, before a program can access data, such as a word processing document or a spreadsheet, the data must reside in memory.

✓ As programs become larger and more complex, their memory needs increase. In the future, as programs begin to make more use of multimedia video, sound, and pictures, your PC memory requirements will increase greatly.

✓ To determine how much memory your PC currently contains, you can use the Windows Device Manager or the MS-DOS MEM command.

✓ You add memory to your PC (in most cases) by installing SIMM or DIMM chips. When you shop for memory chips, you must know the size and speed you require. The documentation that accompanied your PC will specify the chip sizes your system supports, as well as the chip speed. In most cases, you cannot use two different sizes of memory chips. In other words, you cannot use 8MB and 32MB chips at the same time.

✓ The speed of a RAM chip is considered as a measure of access time, in nanoseconds (ns). The lower the number, the faster the chip. Choose replacements that are at least as fast as the originals.

✓ Not all PCs use SIMM or DIMM chips. Instead, some older PCs use card-based memory. In such cases, you install the memory cards much like you would any expansion slot card.

Section Three

COMMON HARDWARE UPGRADES

When you think of upgrades, the first thing that comes to mind is hardware. The most spectacular upgrades, generally, are made by upgrading physical hardware, for example, getting a new hard disk, CD-ROM, multimedia sound board, video card, monitor, floppy drive, modem, fax/modem, or printer. When you upgrade hardware, the results are immediate and visible. The lessons in this section show you when, why, and how to perform these upgrades. Once again, you can do this! The lessons presented in this section include the following:

Lesson 13

Installing a Floppy Disk

A few years ago, when 3 1/2 inch disks first became widely available, users often installed a second floppy-disk drive, giving them a 3 1/2 and a 5 1/4 inch drive. Today, very few users, anywhere, use the the old 5 1/4 inch disks. As a result, the only time users normally install a floppy drive is when their existing drive fails.

This lesson examines the steps you must perform to install a floppy disk drive. By the time you finish this lesson, you will understand the following key concepts:

- How to install and mount a floppy disk drive
- How to cable and power a floppy disk drive
- The advantages of using a dual-floppy drive

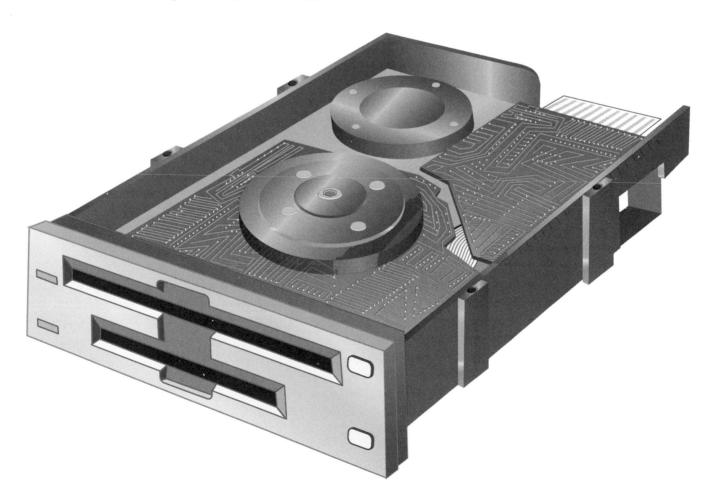

WHAT YOU WILL NEED

Before you get started on this lesson, make sure that you have the following readily available:

1. A PC tool kit with a screwdriver

2. A container within which you can place the chassis screws

3. A well-lit workspace with room for you to place the chassis

4. A new floppy drive and possibly a floppy drive ribbon cable

---

INSTALLING A FLOPPY DISK DRIVE

In most cases, installing a floppy disk drive is very straightforward. You will begin by looking at a standard installation and then you will examine some exceptions. To begin the installation, turn off and unplug your PC's system unit. Next, remove the system-unit cover, as discussed in Lesson 2, "Opening Your PC's System Unit."

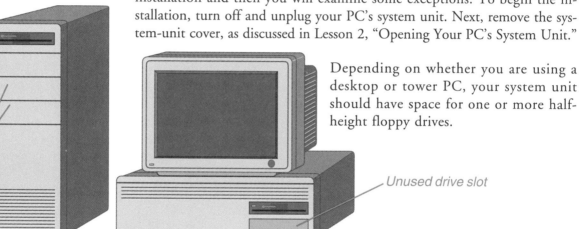

Depending on whether you are using a desktop or tower PC, your system unit should have space for one or more half-height floppy drives.

Unused drive slots

Unused drive slot

On the front of each unused *drive bay* (the space the drive goes into) is a slot that is covered by a small piece of plastic. Remove the screws that attach the cover to the system unit.

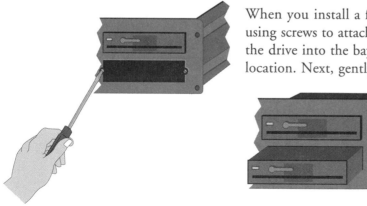

When you install a floppy drive, you will secure the drive in place using screws to attach the drive to the system unit. Before you insert the drive into the bay, remove these screws and place them in a safe location. Next, gently slide the floppy disk drive into the drive bay.

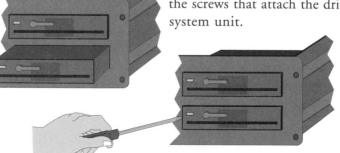

Secure the drive in place by inserting the screws that attach the drive to the system unit.

For the computer to access the floppy drive, you must connect the drive to the disk controller, an expansion slot card which contains the electronics that control the drive. Within your system unit you should find an unattached ribbon cable coming from the controller.

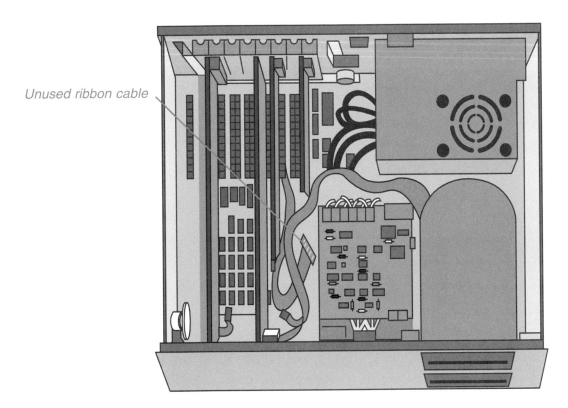

Unused ribbon cable

Pin connector

Edge connector

Align the ribbon cable to the drive connector and gently slide the cable into place. If you are connecting a 5 1/4-inch floppy, the drive will normally use edge connectors. Align the cable so that the split in the cable aligns with the connector's notch. If you are installing a 3 1/2-inch drive, the drive might use a pin connector. In this case, align the connector so that the cable's pin 1 matches the socket's pin 1. Remember, most cables indicate pin 1 by using a distinctive wire color. Next, you must provide power to the floppy drive by connecting a power-supply cable (see Lesson 22, "Replacing the PC's Power Supply,") to the drive.

Replace your system unit cover and plug in and power on your PC. As your system starts, access your system's setup program, as discussed in Lesson 6, "Understanding Your Computer's CMOS Memory." You must tell your PC's CMOS memory about the floppy-drive type before you can use the drive. After you specify the drive type, exit the setup program. When your system has started, the drive should be fully accessible.

INSTALLING A FLOPPY DISK DRIVE

To install a floppy disk drive, perform these steps:

1. Power off and unplug your PC system unit.

2. Remove your system unit cover, as discussed in Lesson 2.

3. Remove the small plastic cover that protects the drive slot. Remove the screws that will connect the drive to the system unit. Place the screws in a safe place.

4. Gently slide the drive into the drive bay. Secure the drive in place using the screws you just removed from the system unit.

5. Attach the drive controller ribbon cable to the drive.

6. Plug the drive into the power supply.

7. Replace and secure the system unit cover.

8. Plug in and power on your PC system unit. As your system starts, access the setup program and notify the CMOS about the new drive.

POSSIBLE INSTALLATION CHALLENGES

In most cases, installing a floppy disk drive is relatively simple. Sometimes, however, things can get more challenging. If you encounter one of the following scenarios, you might find it simpler to have a computer service person perform the installation for you.

NO DRIVE RAILS

Normally, you insert the floppy disk drive into the drive bay by sliding the disk along drive rails. If your PC does not have rails for the floppy, you will need to buy and install the rails. Your challenge may become finding rails that fit both your PC and the floppy you plan to install.

Drive rails

WRONG RIBBON CABLE CONNECTORS

As you have learned, 5 1/4- and 3 1/2-inch floppy drives sometimes use different ribbon cables. If your ribbon cable does not have the connection type you need, you will have to purchase a new cable. Before you buy a new cable, however, you will need to ensure that the cable you need is compatible with your disk controller—the electronics that operate the drive.

WRONG BIOS TYPE

In Lesson 11, "Upgrading the PC BIOS," you learned that the PC BIOS is a pair of chips that oversee input and output operations. Depending on the type of floppy drive you are installing, there may be times when you first must upgrade your BIOS. When you shop for drives, determine the drive's BIOS requirements.

REVERSING DRIVES A AND B

If your system has two floppy drives, there may be times when you will want to change which drive is A and which is B. The easiest way to make this switch is simply to flip-flop the ribbon cable connectors on the floppy drives within your system unit. If your drives use different connector types, preventing the cable swap, you can buy a new cable that contains the correct connectors. After you complete the switch, you will need to notify your PC's CMOS using the setup program previously discussed.

USING A DUAL-FLOPPY DRIVE

If you install a CD-ROM or tape drive, you may find that drive bays are prime real estate. To free up a drive bay, many users are installing dual-floppy drives that combine a 5 1/4- and a 3 1/2-inch floppy into the same drive.

The steps you must perform to install the dual-floppy drive are identical to those just discussed. In most cases, the dual-floppy drive uses only one ribbon cable connector. Attach the drive A cable connector to the floppy. After you configure the CMOS setup, the drive itself will correctly determine when you want to access drive A or B.

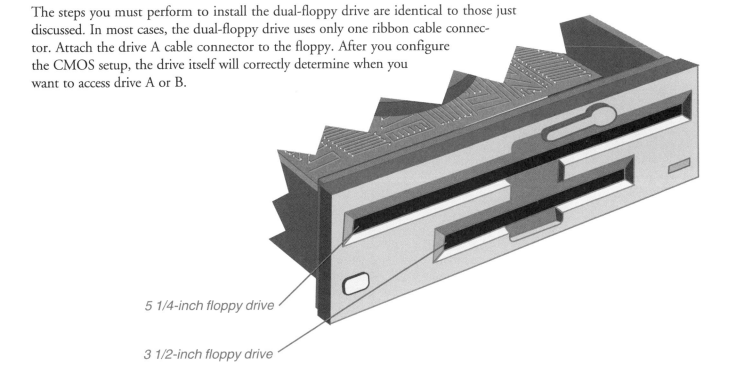

5 1/4-inch floppy drive

3 1/2-inch floppy drive

What You Must Know

A few years ago, users often installed a second floppy drive into their PCs. Today, the only time most users install a floppy disk is when their existing disk fails. In this lesson, you learned how to replace a floppy-disk drive.

In Lesson 14, "Installing a SCSI Adapter," you will examine the steps you need to perform to install a SCSI adapter and then how you later connect devices to create a SCSI device chain. As you will learn, many hard disks, CD-ROM drives, and tape drives now connect to a special adapter card called a SCSI (pronounced "scuzzy") adapter or SCSI controller. Before you continue with Lesson 14, however, make sure that you have learned the following key concepts:

- ✓ If your system only has a 5 1/4- or 3 1/2-inch floppy drive, you can easily install a new floppy.

- ✓ When you shop for floppy drives, make sure the drive is compatible with your system BIOS.

- ✓ If your system does not have available drive bays, you might want to consider a dual floppy, which combines a 5 1/4- and 3 1/2-inch drive into the same unit.

- ✓ To exchange drives A and B, exchange the ribbon-cable connectors that attach the floppy drive to a disk controller. When you restart, you will need to inform your CMOS memory of the new setup.

Lesson 14

Installing a SCSI Adapter

SCSI (pronounced "scuzzy") is an acronym for *Small Computer Systems Interface*. A SCSI adapter is a hardware board that lets you connect up to seven high-speed devices, such as disks, CD-ROM drives, or tape drives, to your computer. With the growing need for PCs to use such devices, the SCSI adapter is becoming a key PC component. This lesson examines the steps you must perform to work with SCSI devices. By the time you finish this lesson, you will understand the following key concepts:

- How to attach devices to a SCSI adapter card

- How to install a SCSI adapter

- Why you must terminate the SCSI device chain

- Why each device requires a unique SCSI address and how to assign a SCSI adress to a device

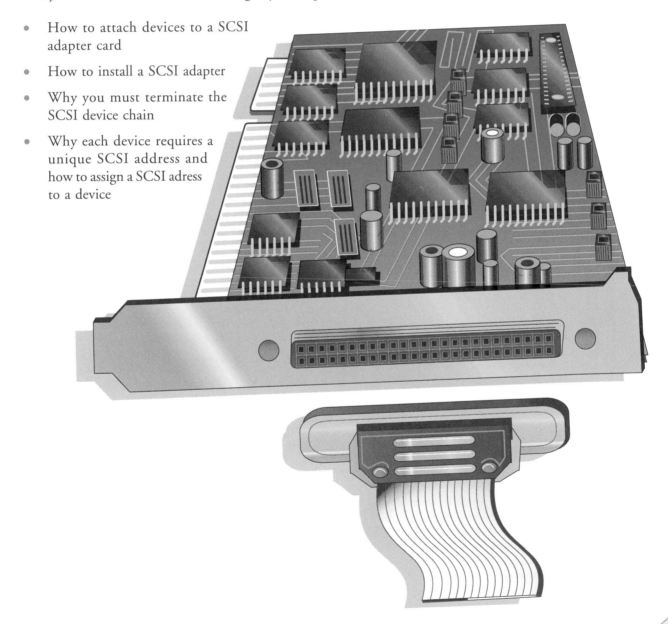

UNDERSTANDING THE SMALL COMPUTER SYSTEMS INTERFACE (SCSI)

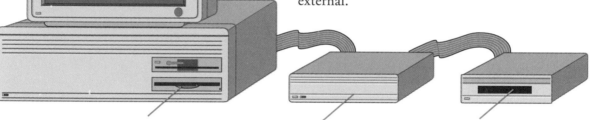

For your computer to communicate with a hardware device, the device must be connected to the PC. In Lesson 3, "Understanding Your Computer's Ports," you examined your PC's expansion slots, into which you can install hardware cards. A *SCSI adapter* provides a second way for you to connect devices to the PC. In short, the SCSI adapter creates a second bus to which you can attach devices. The devices you attach can be internal, residing within the system unit, or external.

Internal CD-ROM   External hard disk   External tape drive

You can connect up to seven devices to a SCSI adapter. The devices you connect must be SCSI devices, which contain their own controller electronics. SCSI devices normally use 50-pin cables, terminated with a 50-pin connector.

Each SCSI device has two ports, one for an incoming cable and one for an outgoing cable that connects to a subsequent device. When you connect SCSI devices, you create a device chain, expanding the bus length with each device you attach.

For example, assume you connect an external hard disk to the SCSI adapter. To connect the hard disk, you would use a 50-pin cable, as just discussed.

50-pin SCSI cable

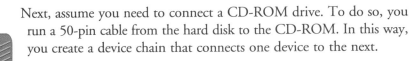

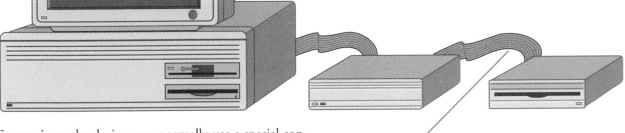

Next, assume you need to connect a CD-ROM drive. To do so, you run a 50-pin cable from the hard disk to the CD-ROM. In this way, you create a device chain that connects one device to the next.

As you build your device chain, you must *terminate* the last device in the chain to tell the SCSI adapter where the chain ends.

To terminate the device, you normally use a special connector called a *terminator*. You place the terminator where you would normally connect a cable to the next device.

50-pin SCSI cable

Note: Some devices let you terminate devices with jumpers or even DIP switches. Refer to the documentation that accompanied your device for more specifics.

SCSI terminator

SCSI DEVICES REQUIRE POWER

The 50-pin SCSI cable transmits the signals used to control or communicate with a SCSI device. In addition to connecting the SCSI cable to the device, you must also provide power to the device. In the case of an internal device, you will use one of the power-supply cables, as discussed in Lesson 22, "Replacing the PC's Power Supply." For external devices, you must plug the device into a power outlet.

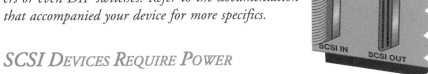

UNDERSTANDING SCSI

SCSI is an acronym for *Small Computer Systems Interface*. You pronounce SCSI as "scuzzy." A SCSI adapter is a hardware card that lets you connect up to seven SCSI devices. When you connect SCSI devices, you run separate SCSI cables from one device to the next, creating a device chain. To end the chain, you terminate the last device by placing a special terminator in the cable port.

UNDERSTANDING SCSI DEVICE NUMBERS

When you connect devices to the SCSI adapter, the adapter must have a way to distinguish one device from the next. Thus, you must assign each device a number (called a *SCSI address*) that ranges from 0 through 7. Normally, the SCSI adapter uses device number 7. When you connect multiple devices to the SCSI adapter, there may be times when two or more devices require the adapter's attention at the same time. In most cases, you will have one or more devices, such as a disk drive, for which a fast response is critical (if a scanner has to wait an instant, for example, the system performance will not suffer, but delaying a disk drive's response would slow down the entire system). The SCSI adapter number lets you specify device priorities. The higher the SCSI address (such as 6 or 7), the higher the device priority. Normally, you set a device's SCSI address using DIP switches or jumpers.

INSTALLING A SCSI ADAPTER

Normally, when you install a non-plug-and-play SCSI-adapter card, you must specify a DMA channel, IRQ, and port address for the adapter (a plug-and-play SCSCI adapter will configure itself), as discussed in Lesson 8, "Understanding Common Conflicts." The documentation that accompanies your adapter should specify the board's default settings. If you must specify device settings for your adapter, use the Windows Device Manager or the MS-DOS MSD command to determine your system's current settings. If a conflict exists, you will, depending on your SCSI adapter type, change the card's settings using jumpers, DIP switches, or software.

To install the SCSI-adapter card within your system, first power off and unplug your system unit. Then, remove the system unit cover and discharge all static from your body, by touching your system chassis. Select the expansion slot into which you will install the adapter. Remove the small metal slot cover and gently insert the adapter card. Replace the screw to hold the adapter securely in place.

If you are using one or more internal SCSI devices, cable and terminate the devices. Replace and secure the system unit cover. If you are using external SCSI devices, cable and terminate the last device in the chain. Plug in and power on your PC.

Depending on your adapter or the devices you are attaching, you might need to install device-driver software. In such cases, follow the instructions specified in the manual that accompanied your device. Lesson 30, "Understanding Device Drivers," discusses device drivers in detail.

INSTALLING A SCSI ADAPTER

To install a SCSI adapter card, perform these steps:

1. Use the Windows Device Manager or the MS-DOS MSD command to determine if the card's default settings are OK. If necessary, use the card's jumpers, DIP switches, or software to change the board's settings so there are no conflicts.

2. Power off and unplug your PC system unit.

3. Remove your system unit cover, as discussed in Lesson 2, and discharge any static from your body.

4. Remove the expansion slot cover and gently insert the SCSI adapter card.

5. Use DIP switches or jumpers to assign the desired SCSI address to each device.

6. If you are installing internal devices, cable the devices and terminate the last one. If you are installing external devices, replace the system unit cover and then cable and terminate the devices.

WATCH YOUR SYSTEM STARTUP

After you install a SCSI adapter, watch your monitor closely when your system starts. In most cases, your system's SCSI software will display, on your screen, the names of each drive it encounters in the SCSI device chain. If, for some reason, the software does not see a device, examine the following items:

1. Is the device plugged in and powered on?

2. Is the device cabled correctly to the SCSI chain?

3. Does the device's unit number conflict with another device in the chain? (Remember, your system may have one or more internal devices in the SCSI chain that you do not see, such as an internal CD-ROM drive.)

4. If you move the device to a different location in the chain (by changing the chain's cabling), does the device appear? If so, one of your cables may be damaged.

UNDERSTANDING SCSI-1 AND SCSI-2

As you read magazines, books, and product documentation, you may encounter the terms SCSI-1 and SCSI-2. SCSI defines a standard interface. Many users refer to the original SCSI standard as SCSI-1 and the new SCSI specification as SCSI-2. In general, you can include SCSI-1 and SCSI-2 devices within the same device chain. Likewise, you can attach SCSI-1 devices to a SCSI-2 adapter and vice versa.

WHAT YOU MUST KNOW

Regardless of how users work with their computers, users have one thing in common—no matter how much hard disk space they have, they find a way to consume it. In Lesson 15, "Installing a New Hard Drive," you will learn how to install a hard disk. Before you continue with Lesson 15, however, make sure that you understand the following key concepts:

✓ A SCSI (pronounced "scuzzy") adapter provides a way for you to connect internal and external SCSI devices. You connect one device to the adapter and subsequent devices to one another to create a SCSI device chain.

✓ You can connect up to seven devices to a SCSI adapter. You must terminate the last device in the chain, normally using a special SCSI terminator.

✓ SCSI devices normally use a 50-pin cable.

✓ Each device in the SCSI chain must have a unique SCSI address from 0 through 7. The higher the SCSI address, the higher the device priority.

Lesson 15

Installing a New Hard Drive

No matter how users use their computers, they normally have a similar problem—too little disk space. As programs become more complex, their storage requirements also increase. As you will read in Lesson 38, "Cleaning Up Your Existing Disk Space," a first step you should take to combat insufficient disk space is to use the Windows 98 Disk Cleanup Wizard to remove unnecessary files from your disk. Next, as discussed in Lesson 34, "Doubling Your Disk's Storage Capacity," you can compress the files on your disk using a program such as DriveSpace. When your compressed disk runs out of space, your next resort is to add or upgrade a new hard drive. Hard drives are mechanical devices with moving parts. Not only do the moving parts slow down the drives, they can also fail. When a hard disk fails, you will need to replace the drive. This lesson examines the steps you must perform to install a new hard drive. By the time you finish this lesson, you will understand the following key concepts:

- How to estimate your disk storage requirements
- The differences between IDE, EIDE, ESDI, SCSI, and USB drives
- What to look for when shopping for a drive
- The steps you must perform to install an internal or external hard drive
- The software steps you must perform to access a drive

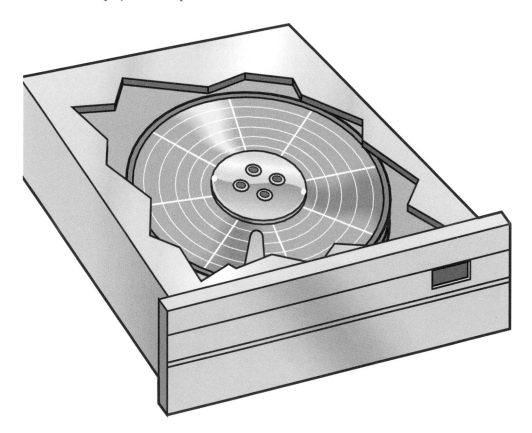

Your first hard disk installation can be challenging. Ideally, you should perform the upgrade with the assistance of an experienced user. Most cities have PC user's groups with members who would be very happy to assist you.

DETERMINING YOUR DISK STORAGE REQUIREMENTS

In the past, users adding a new hard disk multiplied their current disk capacity by a factor of 2 to 2.5 to determine their new storage requirements. At that time, hard disk drives were much more expensive than they are today (more specifically, the price per megabyte was much higher). Today, users often work with large documents that contain illustrations and pictures. As a rule, most user's disk requirements grow by a factor of 5 annually. That means that if you currently use a 300MB drive, next year you will very likely need a 1.5GB drive.

One way to estimate your future disk requirements is to multiply your current disk storage requirements by a growth factor of 5 or higher. To estimate your current requirements, add your current disk usage to disk requirements of programs you plan to purchase over the next six months:

New disk space = factor × (current disk space + new programs)

To start, make a list of the programs you plan to add to your disk. If you do not know a program's disk requirements, you can get a fairly close estimate from members of a local user's group.

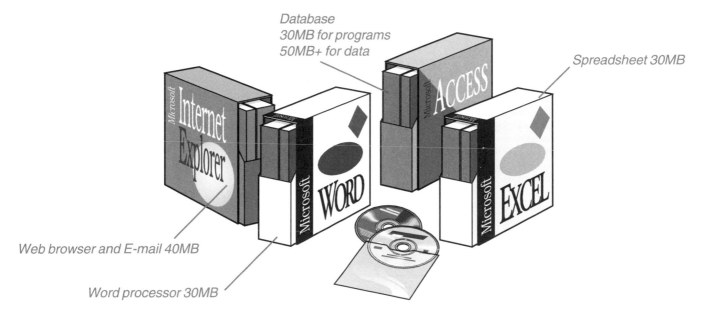

Database
30MB for programs
50MB+ for data

Spreadsheet 30MB

Web browser and E-mail 40MB

Word processor 30MB

In this case, assuming you plan to add these software programs and you currently use 100Mb of disk space, your future storage requirements would become the following:

New disk space= 5 × (100 + 30 + 30 + 30 + 50 + 40)
= 5 X (280)
= 1.4GB

Do not try to save a few dollars by buying a smaller drive. Most users have the ability to fill any hard drive, regardless of the disk's size.

UNDERSTANDING DISK DRIVE TYPES

As you shop for hard disks, you will encounter drives labeled as ESDI, IDE, SCSI, or USB. In short, these drive labels describe how the disk drive attaches to your computer. ESDI is an abbreviation for *Enhanced Small Device Interface*. An ESDI drive (which is an older drive) normally connects to a drive controller card that you install into an expansion slot. IDE is an abbreviation for *Integrated Drive Electronics*. Normally, an IDE drive does not require an expansion slot card. Instead, the drive controller is built into the drive itself. In many cases, you connect an IDE drive directly to your system's motherboard. An EIDE drive is simply an *Enhanced IDE* drive that provides support for disks 1GB and larger. A SCSI (*Small Computer Systems Interface*) drive connects to a SCSI adapter card, as discussed in Lesson 14, "Using a SCSI Adapter." Finally, a USB-based disk drive is one that you can connect to the universal serial bus, as discussed in Lesson 28, "Using a Universal Serial Bus (USB)."

Before you purchase a hard drive, ensure that your system will support the drive. For example, if you purchase an ESDI drive, you need to ensure that the drive will be compatible with your existing drive controller. Likewise, if you purchase an IDE drive, your computer's motherboard must support an IDE drive connection or you will need an IDE card. Finally, if you purchase a SCSI- or USB-based drive, you will need to have a SCSI or USB adapter.

WHAT TO LOOK FOR IN A NEW DRIVE

As you shop for hard drives, you should first determine the size of the disk you need and then you should consider the drive's *access time*. In short, the drive's access time specifies the average time it takes for the information a program requests from the disk to arrive within the computer's memory. The smaller a disk's access time, the faster your disk, and hence the better your system performance. Disk manufacturers measure access time in milliseconds (ms), such as an 8ms drive. Because a disk drive is a mechanical device (one with moving parts), the drive will eventually fail. In addition to the disk's access time, you might want to examine the disk's mean time between failure (MTBF), a measurement supplied by the manufacturer that can give you a guideline about how long your disk should continue to work before a failure occurs.

INSTALLING A NEW HARD DRIVE

Hard drives can be internal (residing within a drive bay in the PC system unit) or external. Depending on your drive type, the steps you must perform to install the drive will differ.

INSTALLING AN INTERNAL HARD DRIVE

To install an internal hard drive, power off and unplug your PC. Next, remove your system unit cover as discussed in Lesson 2, "Opening Your PC's System Unit," and ground yourself to remove any residual static electricity from your body. If you are replacing a hard drive, first remove the ribbon cable that connects your drive to the controller. Next, remove the power plug that connects the drive to the power supply. Unscrew the drive from the drive bay, placing the screws in a safe location. Slide your drive out of the drive bay. Examine your new drive's case. Some drives have a small metal label that specifies a drive type number, such as type 30. If your drive contains such a label, write down the drive type number and any other information such as the number of heads, cylinders, sectors, and so on. You will use this information later when you update your computer's CMOS after your drive installation is complete. If you are installing a new drive, remove the plastic cover from the desired drive bay and then remove the drive bay screws. Place the screws in a safe location. If the drive bay contains drive rails, slide your new drive into place, securing the drive with the drive bay screws.

Note: *If your drive bay does not contain drive rails, you can purchase the rails from your computer retailer. However, you might find it easier to let your retailer complete the drive installation for you.*

After the drive is secure within the drive bay, connect a power supply cable to the drive.

Next, use the drive's ribbon cable to connect the drive to the controller, motherboard, or to a SCSI adapter, depending on your drive type.

If you are installing a SCSI drive, make sure you correctly terminate the SCSI device chain, as discussed in Lesson 14. Replace your system unit cover and plug in your PC.

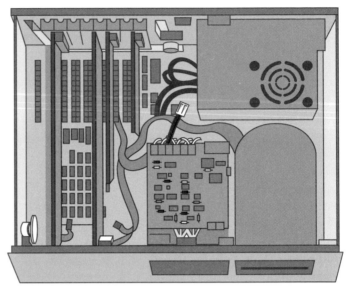

INSTALLING AN EXTERNAL HARD DRIVE

External hard drives connect to a SCSI adapter or to a proprietary card. If you need to install a special disk controller card, power off and unplug your PC. Install the card as discussed in Lesson 5, "Working with Boards and Chips." Likewise, if you need to install a SCSI adapter, follow the steps discussed in Lesson 14. Next, attach the drive's ribbon cable to the adapter card and plug in the drive's power connector. Depending on where, in the SCSI device chain, you place the drive, you may have to terminate the device as discussed in Lesson 14. If you are connecting your drive to a universal serial bus, you can simply connect and then plug in your drive.

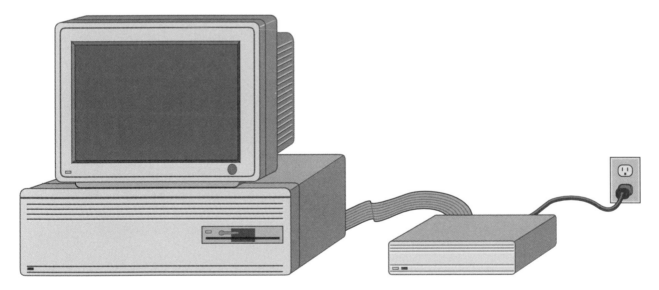

TELLING YOUR CMOS ABOUT THE DRIVE

Before your computer can access your new drive, you must assign your new drive's settings to the computer's CMOS memory. Follow the steps discussed in Lesson 6 to update the settings. Use the setting values you previously found on the drive's casing or within the documentation that accompanied your drive.

Note: Record your drive's CMOS settings and keep your notes in a safe location. If you ever must replace your CMOS battery, the drive's many settings are often impossible to remember. If, when you update your CMOS settings, you cannot locate your drive setting values, you should be able to get the setting values from the manufacturer's technical support or the service division at your computer retailer. Also, several books contain listings of the settings for virtually every drive known.

PREPARING YOUR NEW DISK FOR USE

Before Windows (or MS-DOS) can store information on your new disk, you must first partition and then format your disk. To partition your disk, you use the MS-DOS FDISK command. To format your disk, you use the MS-DOS FORMAT command. Preparing a disk for use is the one aspect of PC computing that has not yet migrated from the MS-DOS command set. If you are not familiar with running MS-DOS commands, you should ask an experienced user to help you.

If you are adding a second hard drive, your existing hard drive should contain the FDISK and FORMAT commands. If you do not have an existing hard drive (you are replacing your previous drive), you must work from a floppy disk that contains the commands. To work from a floppy, you must start your system using a bootable floppy disk. Next, you need to ensure that the floppy disk contains the FDISK and FORMAT commands. To create a bootable floppy disk from within Windows, peform these steps:

1. Click your mouse on the Windows Start button. Windows will display the Start menu.

2. Within the Start menu, select the Settings menu Control Panel option. Windows will open the Control Panel window.

3. Within the Control Panel window, double-click your mouse on the Add/Remove Programs icons. Windows, in turn, will display the Add/Remove Programs Properties dialog box.

4. Within the dialog box, click your mouse on the Startup Disk tab. Windows will display the Startup Disk sheet.

5. Within the Startup Disk sheet, click your mouse on the Create Disk button. Windows will create your bootable disk.

6. Using the Windows Explorer, copy the FDISK and FORMAT command files to the floppy disk from the *Windows\Command* folder.

PARTITIONING YOUR DISK

Before you can use a hard disk, you must format the disk. Likewise, before you can format a hard disk, you must partition the disk into one or more logical collections called *partitions*. In some cases, your manufacturer or retailer may have partitioned the drive for you. If not, you must partition the disk using the MS-DOS FDISK command. (Before you partition a drive, you must first inform the CMOS about the disk and its type.)

Using the FDISK command, you will divide your disk into one or more partitions, each having a minimum size of 1MB. The total size of all partitions cannot exceed the capacity of the disk. Windows (and MS-DOS) will view each partition as a logical disk drive and will assign each partition its own drive letter. For example, if you have a 3GB drive, you might prefer that Windows think of the drive as three 1GB drives named C, D, and E.

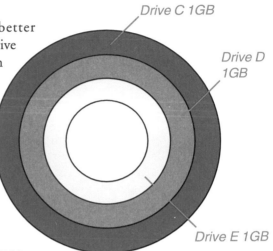

Users often divide a hard disk into multiple drives to better organize their files. For example, they might store programs on drive C, files for work on drive D, and files for school on drive E. When you use multiple drives to store your files, a command you execute for drive D, such as the delete command, will not affect files on a different drive. In this way, users have an additional level of file protection.

Users who have different operating systems (such as Windows NT or Unix) on the same drive, use one partition for each operating system. Then, when they start their PC, they can choose the operating system they desire.

To partition your disk, you invoke FDISK from the DOS prompt:

```
A:\> FDISK    <ENTER>
```

FDISK will display a menu of options similar to that shown in Figure 15.

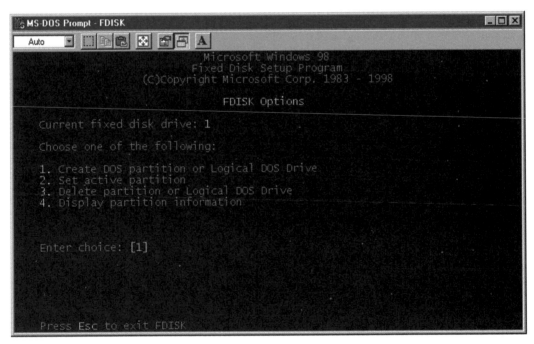

Figure 15 *The FDISK main menu.*

Using FDISK menu options, you will first create one or more partitions. When you create a partition, you must specify the partition's size in megabytes. Then, you must create a logical drive (assign a drive letter) to each partition. For the detailed steps you must perform from the FDISK menu, turn to the MS-DOS documentation that accompanied your disk drive.

Note: *If you are installing a second hard drive, choose the option that lets you select the new drive before you create a partition. Also, do not use FDISK to partition a disk that contains files whose contents you need. When you create a partition, you will lose any information you have previously stored on the disk.*

FORMATTING YOUR DISK PARTITIONS

After you use FDISK to partition your hard disk, you must format each disk partition. To format your disk, you will use the MS-DOS FORMAT command. If you have a working hard drive (which means you are adding a second drive), your existing drive should contain the FORMAT command. If you are replacing your hard drive, you must work with a floppy disk that contains FORMAT.

For your computer to start (boot) from your new hard disk, your disk must contain special operating system files. To place these system files on your disk, you invoke the FORMAT command using the /S switch.

Warning! *Use the FORMAT command with great care. If you inadvertently format the wrong drive, the information the drive contained will be lost! If you are not sure how to format the correct drive, have an experienced user assist you.*

FORMATTING A SECOND HARD DRIVE

If you are installing a second disk and you have partitioned the second hard drive, you can format that drive using the FORMAT command contained on your existing hard drive (drive C). Assuming that your new hard drive is drive D (the FDISK command will determine the drive letter), you would format the drive as follows:

If your new disk drive uses a different drive letter, simply substitute your disk drive letter for drive D in the command just shown.

FORMATTING A DRIVE FROM A FLOPPY

If you have replaced your computer's only hard drive, you must format your drive from a floppy disk. To begin, the floppy disk must be bootable. In other words, the floppy must contain the files that your system needs to start. Next, the floppy must also contain the FORMAT command.

Note: *If you intend to replace your only hard drive, make sure you have a* **dependable** *boot floppy disk that has the FORMAT command on it* **before** *you remove the old drive.*

To format your hard disk as a bootable disk, use the following FORMAT command:

FORMATTING EACH DRIVE PARTITION

As you have learned, using the FDISK command, you can divide a single hard disk into multiple drives called partitions. For example, you might divide a 2GB hard disk into two 1GB drives named C and D. After you partition the drives, you must format each drive.

INSTALLING A HARD DISK DRIVE

Depending on whether you are installing an internal hard drive or external drive, the steps you must perform will differ slightly.

Internal Drive

To install an internal drive, perform these steps:

1. Power off and unplug your system unit and remove the system unit cover.
2. Secure the drive into a drive bay slot.
3. Connect the drive's ribbon cable to the drive controller.
4. Plug the drive into the power supply.
5. Replace and secure the system unit cover.

External Drive

To install an external drive, perform these steps:

1. Power off and unplug your system unit.
2. If necessary, install a hard drive adapter card within the system unit.
3. Connect the drive's ribbon cable to the adapter card.
4. Plug in the drive's power cable.

Software Operations

After you have installed the drive, closed up the system unit, and powered up and started the computer, perform these steps:

1. Update your computer's CMOS settings.
2. Use the FDISK command to partition the drive.
3. Use the FORMAT command to format the disk drive.

USING *FAT32* UNDER *WINDOWS 98*

If you are using Windows 98, you can take advantage of a new file system (the software that manages how Windows stores files on your disk) to support larger disk partitions, increase your available disk space, and to improve your disk performance. Using FAT32, your system can support a 2TB (terabyte or trillion byte) disk. When you partition a large disk using the Windows 98 FDISK command, FDISK will ask you if you want to install the FAT32 file system on the disk. In most cases, you should say yes. In addition, if you are running Windows 98 and you have a hard disk that is using the FAT16 (the older) file system, you can increase your disk's available space by converting the disk to FAT32. To convert a disk to FAT32, perform these steps:

1. Click your mouse on the Windows Start button. Windows will display the Start menu.

2. Within the Start menu, select the Programs menu and choose Accessories. Windows will display the Accessories submenu.

3. Within the Accessories submenu, select the System Tools option and choose Drive Converter (FAT32). Windows, in turn, will start the Drive Convert Wizard, which will take you step by step through the file-system conversion process.

WHAT YOU MUST KNOW

In this lesson, you learned the steps you must perform to replace an existing hard disk or to add a new hard drive. In Lesson 16, "Installing a Zip Drive," you will learn how to connect a Zip drive to your system. As you will learn, Zip disks look much like a large floppy disk and are capable of holding over 100MB of data. Using Zip disks is a very convenient way to move large files or a number of files from one system to another. Before you continue with Lesson 16, however, make sure that you understand the following key concepts:

✓ Before you purchase a hard disk, estimate your disk storage requirements. To estimate your new requirements, multiply your current disk requirements by a factor of 5.

✓ As you shop for a disk, you will encounter the terms ESDI, IDE, SCSI, and USB. In short, these terms describe how you connect the drive to your computer.

✓ After you install your hard disk, you must update your computer's CMOS settings.

✓ Before you can use a newly installed drive, you must first use the MS-DOS FDISK command to partition the drive and then you must format each disk partition.

✓ If you have never used the FDISK or FORMAT commands in the past, have an experienced user assist you. An inadvertent error with either of these commands can quickly destroy all the information a second disk contains.

✓ If you are using Windows 98, you should update your disk's file system to the new FAT32 file system.

Lesson 16

Installing a Zip Disk

In Lesson 13, "Installing a Floppy Disk," you learned how to install a floppy-disk drive within your PC. Because of their limited storage capacity (a floppy disk can only store 1.44MB), many users have now turned to Zip drives, whose disks can store over 100MB! This lesson examines the steps you must perform to connect a Zip drive to your PC. By the time you finish this lesson, you will understand the following key concepts:

- A Zip disk is a high-capacity, removable disk that can store over 100MB.

- Although a Zip disk looks much like a floppy disk, you cannot use a Zip disk within a floppy-disk drive and vice versa.

- Depending on the type of Zip drive you buy, you will connect the Zip drive to a parallel port, a SCSI adapter, or to a universal serial bus. If you are using an internal Zip drive, your drive may connect to your PC's IDE controller.

- Within Windows, the Zip drive will appear like any other drive, meaning, you can use programs, such as the Windows Explorer, to copy, delete, rename, and move files on the Zip drive.

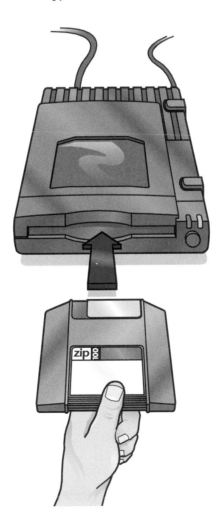

ZIP DISKS ARE CAPACITY DISKS

As briefly discussed, a Zip disk is a high-capacity removable disk that can store over 100MB of data. Although Zip disks look similar to a floppy disk, a Zip disk is actually quite a bit bigger than a standard floppy. You cannot, therefore, use a Zip disk within a floppy drive, or a floppy disk within a Zip drive. As you will learn, a Zip drive is very easy to connect to a PC. Assume, for example, that you must share a large file with the user in the office next to you, who does not have a Zip drive or access to a local-area network. If you have a Zip drive, you can simply copy the file from your system onto a Zip disk. Then, you can connect the Zip drive to the other user's system, run the Zip disk's software installation on the user's system, and then copy the file from the Zip drive onto the user's system.

CONNECTING YOUR ZIP DRIVE TO YOUR PC

Depending on your Zip drive's type, you will connect your Zip drive to your PC in one of four ways. First, if your Zip drive is a "Parallel Zip Drive," you will attach your drive to your PC's parallel port—the port to which you normally attach your printer. To attach your Zip drive to your parallel port, you must disconnect your printer from the port. On the back of your Zip drive, you will find a parallel port to which you will attach your printer. In this way, you will have access to both your Zip drive and your printer.

If your Zip drive is a "SCSI Zip Drive," you must connect the drive to a SCSI adapter or to a device within the SCSI chain. Lesson 14, "Installing a SCSI Adapter ," discusses SCSI ports in detail. Depending on the location within the device chain where you attach the Zip drive, you may have to terminate the drive as discussed in Lesson 14. If you are using a "USB Zip Drive," you must attach the drive to a universal serial bus, as discussed in Lesson 28, "Using a Universal Serial Bus (USB)." If you have an internal Zip drive, your drive probably connects to an IDE controller that may also control your hard disk. As you shop for a Zip drive, you must keep in mind, how you will attach the drive to your system (parallel, SCSI, or USB). Then, you must buy the appropriate Zip-drive type. Figure 16.1 shows one Zip drive within the SCSI device chain and a second Zip drive connected to a notebook PC's universal serial bus.

Figure 16.1 *Connecting a (SCSI-based) Zip drive within the SCSI device chain and a (USB-based) Zip drive to a notebook PC's universal serial bus.*

USING YOUR ZIP DRIVE

After you connect your Zip drive to your PC, you will run a Setup program that installs the software Windows will use to access your Zip drive. After the Setup program completes, you can use your Zip drive just as you would any drive on your system. In other words, Windows will list your Zip drive within the Explorer's drive list and within the File Open and Save As dialog boxes, as shown in Figure 16.2.

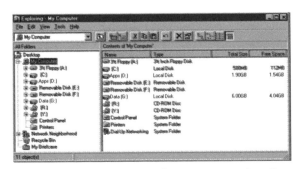

Figure 16.2 *Windows will display a drive letter for your Zip drive, just as it does for each of your drives.*

What You Must Know

With the average size of most documents continuing to grow, floppy disks simply cannot store enough information. To exchange large documents (or a large number of small documents), many users are turning to Zip disks. In this lesson, you learned how to connect a Zip drive to your PC. In Lesson 17, "Installing a Modem," you will learn ways you can improve your system performance by upgrading to a faster modem. Before you continue with Lesson 17, however, make sure you understand the following key concepts:

✓ A Zip disk, which looks similar to a large floppy disk, is a high-capacity removable disk that can store over 100MB.

✓ Although a Zip disks looks like a floppy disk, you cannot use a Zip disk within a floppy drive or a floppy disk within a Zip drive.

✓ Depending on your Zip-drive type, you will either connect your Zip drive to a parallel port, a SCSI adapter, or to a universal serial bus. If you are using an internal Zip drive, you may connect the drive to an IDE adapter.

✓ After you connect your Zip drive and install your Zip drive's device-driver software, Windows will display a drive letter for your Zip drive, just as it would any drive.

Lesson 17

Installing a Modem

With the tremendous success of the Internet and the World Wide Web, today's information highway, users are always looking for ways to improve the performance of their Internet connection. Today, users can connect to the Net using standard telephone lines, an ISDN connection, or a cable-modem link.

This lesson examines these various connection types and the steps you must perform to install a modem.

**Internet
E-Mail
Faxes**

By the time you finish this lesson, you will understand the following key concepts:

- How modems work
- The difference between modem speeds
- The various ways users can connect their PC to the Internet
- The benefits of a fax/modem
- The steps you must perform to install a modem
- The purpose of data communications settings and how you assign them
- The purpose of fax and modem software

HOW MODEMS WORK

A *modem* is a hardware device that lets you connect two computers using standard phone lines. First, the sending computer's modem **mo**dulates the computer's digital signals into analog signals that pass over the phone lines. Then, the receiving computer's modem **dem**odulates the analog signal back into the digital signal that the computers understand.

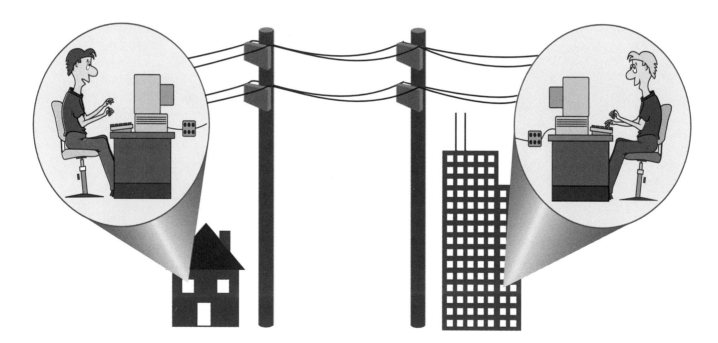

Using the modem, your computer essentially calls the second computer which, in turn, answers the incoming call. The two computers can reside across town, across the country, or even around the world. The cost to call a second computer outside of your city is identical to making a long distance phone call.

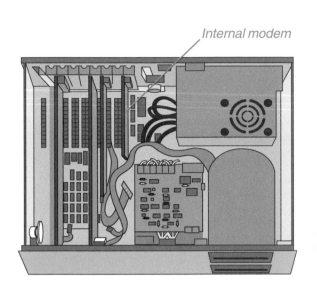

Internal modem

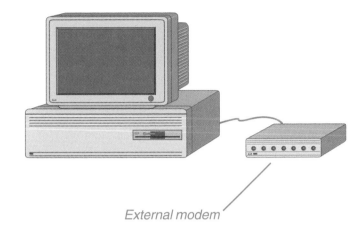

External modem

Modems can be internal (residing within your system unit) or external. In either case, the modem's purpose is identical.

UNDERSTANDING MODEMS

A modem is a hardware device that lets two computers communicate over standard phone lines. When you use a modem, one computer calls a second computer, much as you would make a long distance phone call. Using modems, you can exchange files, or chat with other users, or send electronic mail. A fax/modem is a modem that has the ability to send or receive information to or from a remote fax machine. When you use the Internet, the notion of "long distance" does not really exist. Instead, after you connect to the Internet, you can access computers across the world or chat with other users worldwide for free! To access the Internet, you will normally dial into a local Internet provider, which means you do not incur any phone charges. Unfortunately, for those users who live in remote places, their call to the Internet provider may be a long-distance call.

UNDERSTANDING MODEM SPEEDS

When two modems communicate, they must first agree on a communication speed. As you shop for modems, you will encounter speeds such as 28.8 (for 28.8Kbs or 28800 bits per second) and 56Kbs (56,000 bits per second). A few years ago, users made extensive use of modems with speeds of 1200 to 2400 bits per second. Users express modem speed in terms of *baud rate*. In general, baud stands for *bits per second*.

14.4Kbs

56Kbs

As you know, computers work in terms of 1s and 0s—bits (binary digits). The same is true for modems. A 28.8Kbs modem, for example, can send or receive 28800 bits of information in a second. Likewise, a 56Kbs baud modem can send or receive 56000 bits per second. As you can see, the 56Kbs baud modem is three times faster than its 14.4Kbs baud counterpart, which can save you considerable time when you download information from a Web site.

MODEM UPGRADES ARE A SMART INVESTMENT

If you are using an older modem whose speed is less than 56Kbs and you spend an hour or more connected to the Internet each day, you should consider an immediate modem upgrade. Like all PC hardware, the price of modems has come down drastically over the last few years. You can now buy a fast 56Kbs modem for less than $50. With the rapid growth of the Internet and World Wide Web, your modem use is likely to increase. The faster your modem, the less time you will waste waiting for your modem to send or receive information.

When you download files from across the Internet (which you do each time you view a Web site), keep in mind that file sizes are expressed in terms of bytes (eight bits), not bits. To download a 64KB (65,536 bytes) file, for example, means you must receive over 524,288 bits (65,536 bytes × 8 bits/byte). Table 17 lists the approximate amount of time the file transfer would require at different modem speeds.

Modem Speed	File Size	Transfer Times
300 baud	64KB	Over 29 minutes
1200 baud	64KB	Over 7 minutes
2400 baud	64KB	Over 3 minutes
9600 baud	64KB	About 1 minute
14.4K baud	64KB	About 30 seconds
28.8K baud	64KB	About 15 seconds
56K baud	64KB	About 7 seconds

Table 17 *Transfer times for a 64KB file at different baud rates.*

Note: *When you view a Web page, it is not uncommon for your browser to download several hundred kilobytes for each Web page. As you can see, by using a 56Kbs modem, you will spend much less time waiting for information to make its way across the phone lines to your PC.*

BENEFITS OF A FAX/MODEM

A fax/modem is simply a modem that can send and receive faxes. Most newer modems are fax/modems. Using a fax/modem, you can connect to both fax machines and other computers. Fax/modems are ideal for travelers who carry a laptop PC with them. When you receive a fax using a fax/modem, you can view the fax on your screen or you can print it on your printer.

To send a fax, however, the document must be in an electronic format; in other words, it must be stored on your disk. The disadvantage of a fax/modem compared to a fax machine is that you cannot send a paper fax, such as a contract you just signed, using a fax/modem. Unless, that it is, you have a scanner you can use

Modem

Phone Lines

Fax/Modem

Fax

to scan the paper image into your computer as an electronic image. Many fax programs let you "print" to the fax/modem directly from the current application (such as a word processor, draw program, or spreadsheet). In this way, to send a fax from within your word processor, for example, you would use the File menu Print option to select the Fax

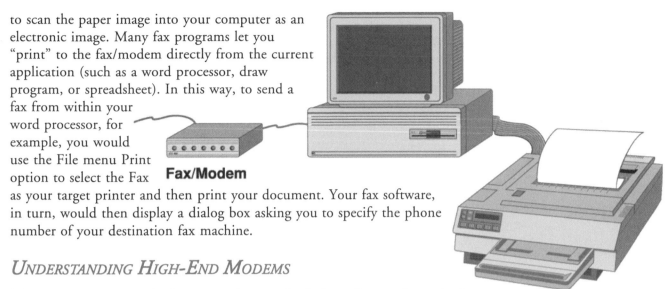

Fax/Modem

as your target printer and then print your document. Your fax software, in turn, would then display a dialog box asking you to specify the phone number of your destination fax machine.

UNDERSTANDING HIGH-END MODEMS

Most users connect to the Internet using standard phone lines and standard modem (such as a 28.8Kbs or 56Kbs modem). Users who want faster performance and who are willing to pay considerably more for their connection have several different options. First, the user might ask the phone company to install an ISDN connection, which requires a special phone lines, an ISDN modem, and an Internet Service Provider who supports ISDN. In addition to the extra phone charges for the ISDN line, your provider will also charge you a higher monthly fee for an ISDN connection. Recently, cable-TV companies have started to offer high-speed (and relatively inexpenisve) cable connections. When you subscribe to a cable-modem service, your cable company will provide your modem and the software you need.

INSTALLING YOUR MODEM

As you have learned, a modem can be internal, residing within your system unit. This section examines the steps you must perform to install both modem types.

INSTALLING AN INTERNAL MODEM

When you install a modem, you normally must identify which interrupt-request line (IRQ) the modem will use to signal the CPU. In addition, you must normally specify the serial port (such as COM1 or COM2) the modem will use (there are new high-speed modems that connect to parallel ports).

As discussed in Lesson 8, "Understanding Common Conflicts," the modem must use a unique IRQ number. Likewise, when you select a serial port, you must select a port that is not in use by another device (such as a mouse or printer). To determine the available IRQ settings, use the Windows Device Manager, discussed in Lesson 40, "Using the Windows Device Manager," or the MS-DOS-based MSD command discussed in Lesson 36, "Troubleshooting with MSD." To select the modem's serial port setting, you must determine which serial ports are currently in use. If you are not using a serial printer, then you normally only have to worry about a serial mouse. If your mouse uses COM1,

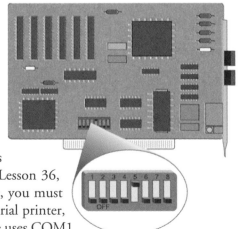

for example, you would assign your modem to COM2. The PC can support up to four serial ports, COM1 through COM4. Unfortunately, in most cases, you can only use two serial devices at any given time. As it turns out, COM1 and COM3 share a key address, as do COM2 and COM4. If you attach your mouse to COM1 and your modem to COM3, a conflict will occur due to this shared address. After you determine the correct IRQ and COM-port settings, you can normally use a jumper or DIP switch that you find on the modem card to specify the settings.

After you determine the correct IRQ and serial port, power off and unplug your system unit. Next, remove your system unit cover, as discussed in Lesson 2, "Opening Your PC's System Unit," and rid yourself of any static charge. Locate an unused expansion slot and gently insert the modem card. Secure the card in place and replace the system unit cover.

If you examine the back of the PC system unit, you will find modem ports for phone lines. Connect a phone cable from your phone wall outlet to the modem port labeled **Line**.

Next, if you like, connect your phone to the port that is labeled **Phone**. By connecting your phone to the modem port in this way, your phone and modem can share the same line, meaning, when you are not using your modem, you can use your phone, and vice versa.

Connecting your phone to the modem is optional; the modem will work perfectly well without a phone attached to it. Plug in and power on your PC system unit.

INSTALLING AN INTERNAL MODEM

To install an internal modem, perform the following steps:

1. Determine the IRQ and serial port the modem will use.

2. Power off and unplug your PC system unit.

3. Remove your system unit cover, as discussed in Lesson 2, and rid yourself of static charge.

4. Gently insert the modem card into an expansion slot.

5. Replace and secure your system unit cover.

6. Connect your phone wall outlet to the modem port labeled **Line**. If you wish, connect your phone to the modem port labeled **Phone**.

7. Plug in and power on your PC system unit.

INSTALLING AN EXTERNAL MODEM

Installing an external modem is much easier than installing an internal modem because you do not have to worry about IRQ settings. Instead, you simply connect the modem to a serial port, such as COM1 (if your modem connects to a parallel port, connect your modem to the port your printer is not currently using). Next, you must plug your modem into a power source.

TELLING WINDOWS ABOUT YOUR MODEM

After you install your modem, you must install device-driver software that lets Windows use the modem. If you are using Windows 3.1, follow the steps specified in the documentation that accompanied your modem. If you are using Windows 95 or 98, you can take advantage of special software, called a Wizard, that will help you install and configure your modem software. To use the Windows Install New Modem Wizard, perform these steps:

1. Select the Start menu Settings option and choose Control Panel. Windows, in turn, will open the Control Panel window.

2. Within the Control Panel window, double-click your mouse on the Modem icon. Windows will display the Install New Modem Wizard, as shown in Figure 17.1. (If your PC already contains a modem, Windows will display the Modem Properties dialog box. Within the Modem Properties dialog box, click your mouse on the Add button to start the Install New Modem Wizard.)

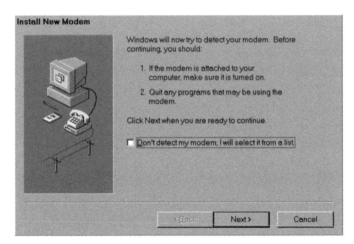

Figure 17.1 *The Install New Modem Wizard.*

The Install New Modem Wizard will walk you through the steps you must perform to install and configure your modem software. To use the Wizard, simply complete the steps the Wizard presents on the current screen and then click your mouse on the Next button to move to the next step. If you must go back a step, simply click your mouse on the Back button. By working the Wizard's steps in this way, you can install your modem software quickly.

USING YOUR NEW MODEM TO CONNECT TO THE NET

After you install your modem device driver, you must tell your Internet software to use your new modem. If you are using America Online (AOL) or the Microsoft Network (MSN) to connect to the Net, the steps you must perform to configure your software to use your new modem will differ.

If you are using an Internet Service Provider to connect to the Net, you can use the Windows Dial-Up Networking folder, shown in Figure 17.2 to create a new connection or to change your existing configuration's modem settings. For more information on Windows 98 Dial-Up Networking, refer to the book *1001 Windows 98 Tips*, Jamsa Press, 1998.

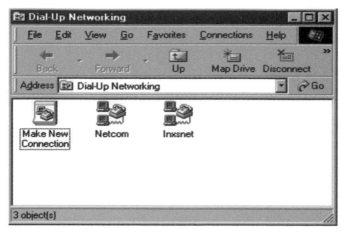

Figure 17.2 *The Dial-Up Networking folder.*

UNDERSTANDING MULTILINK CONNECTIONS

If you are using Windows 98, you can use two or more modems to create a multilink connection to your Internet Service Provider. To use a multilink connection, your must have a phone line for each modem. Next, your Internet Service Provider must support multilink connections for your account (which may cost you slightly more a month for your connection). When you connect to the Internet, Windows 98 will use each of the modems to send and receive data. If you do not live in an area that provides either ISDN or cable modem connections, you may find that multilink connections provide you with an alternative way to improve your connection speed.

WHAT YOU MUST KNOW

The modem (especially fax/modem) is becoming a very important piece of equipment for computer users. Using a modem, you can deliver a document across the country (or the world!) in seconds for the price of a long distance phone call. In this lesson, you have learned how to install a modem into your system. Over the next year, more than five million users will install multimedia sound cards within their systems. In Lesson 18, "Installing a Multimedia Sound Card," you will learn how to install a sound card. Before you continue with Lesson 18, however, make sure that you have learned the following key concepts:

- ✓ When you shop for modems, you will encounter different speeds, such as 28.8Kbs or 56Kbs. The faster a modem's speed, the faster your response time. When you connect to a remote computer, you can only send data as fast as the other modem can receive it and vice versa.

- ✓ A fax/modem is a modem that lets you connect to a remote fax to send or receive faxes. When you shop for a modem, make sure you purchase a fax/modem—as you work, you will find it quite convenient to send and receive your faxes using your PC.

- ✓ To use your modem to connect to a remote computer to send or receive faxes, you must use special modem or fax/modem software. In most cases, when you purchase a modem, you will receive a floppy disk that contains the necessary software.

- ✓ After you install or connect your modem, you must install software (a device driver) that Windows will use to communicate with your modem.

Lesson 18

Installing a Multimedia Sound Card

With the multimedia craze sweeping the nation, users are quickly adding sound boards to their PCs. In the past, very few programs could take advantage of a sound board. Today, however, that situation is changing quickly. Newer programs use sound effects, audio and video instruction, and can even play back audio CDs!

This lesson presents the steps you must perform to install a sound card. By the time you finish this lesson, you will understand the following concepts:

- The purpose of a sound card and the different sound-card capabilities you will encounter
- How you use the different sound-card ports
- The steps you must perform to install a sound card
- The common conflicts you may encounter when you install a sound card

If you have not yet purchased a sound card, you should visit your computer retailer and take one for a test drive. As the growth of multimedia programs continues to explode, a sound card has become a must-have device.

WHAT YOU WILL NEED

Before you get started on this lesson, make sure that you have the following readily available:

1. A PC tool kit with a screwdriver
2. A container within which you can place the chassis screws
3. A well-lit workspace with room for you to place the chassis
4. A new sound card and speakers

Although sound cards differ in price and quality, most sound cards provide the following capabilities:

- Recording via an external microphone
- Recording via a line-in source
- MIDI interface
- WAV file playback
- Audio CD-ROM playback

There are several ways sound cards differ from one another. Some points to consider when you look for a sound card include:

- If possible, listen to play back on computers with each card.
- There are 8-bit sound cards and 16-bit sound cards. The 16-bit cards, which are slightly more expensive, use more data to describe the notes and, thus, the sound is better. If you can, buy a 16-bit card.
- Some sound cards come bundled with powered speakers (with a small amplifier built into each speaker), which sometimes saves some money over a separately purchased card and speakers. With others, you must buy the speakers separately, which could be an advantage if you are plugging right into a stereo that has its own speakers.

- Some sound cards provide a SCSI-compatible interface you can use to attach a CD-ROM drive to the card.

- Sound cards purchased for general use should be "Sound Blaster compatible."

- Better sound quality comes from boards using "wave-table synthesis" than comes from those using "FM synthesis."

- Sound boards with a Digital Signal Processor (DSP) move processing from the CPU to the DSP on the sound board, freeing up your CPU to perform other tasks.

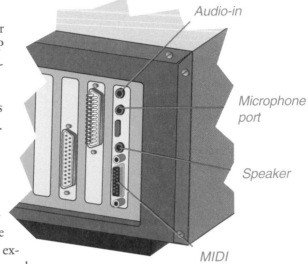

Audio-in

Microphone port

Speaker

MIDI

A sound board is simply a card you install into one of the PC's expansion slots. As you can see, a sound card has several ports.

The sections that follow discuss each port in detail.

USING THE SOUND CARD'S SPEAKER PORT

When you use a sound card, you can connect external speakers, headphones, or even (if you are a big sound fan) a line from your stereo to the card's speaker port. If you are using external speakers, you will plug one speaker into the sound card and the second speaker into the first.

Some speakers let you power the speaker's amplifier using a battery. In most cases, however, you will want to invest in a small power supply, which lets you plug the speakers into a standard wall outlet.

USING THE SOUND CARD'S MICROPHONE PORT

You can use the sound card to record voice, music, or other sounds using an external microphone. When you connect a microphone to the sound card's port, you do not have to provide the microphone with any additional power. The sound card will provide the necessary power to the microphone.

Many microphones provide an On/Off switch that you can use to control recording. In most cases, however, you will use a software program to tell the sound card when to record and when to stop.

USING THE SOUND CARD'S AUDIO LINE INPUT AND *CD-ROM* INPUT

In addition to using a microphone for recording, most sound cards provide a port for direct audio input. Using the audio-in port, you can record music from a stereo system or other sources, such as a television or VCR. By using the audio-input port, you can record from a device without picking up the background noise that you might experience if you record using a microphone.

Also, most sound cards provide a connector to which you can attach a cable to your CD-ROM drive. By directly connecting the CD-ROM drive to the sound card in this way, you can use the sound card to play the same audio CDs you would play using your stereo system.

USING THE SOUND CARD'S *MIDI* INPUT

MIDI is an acronym for *Musical Instrument Digital Interface*. In short, MIDI defines the standard that lets digital electronic instruments, such as an electronic piano keyboard, interface with a computer and its software. Most sound cards provide a MIDI interface that looks similar to a small parallel or serial port. When you connect a MIDI device to this port, you can use the device to play back songs that have been recorded digitally or to record your own MIDI music. MIDI devices have opened a whole new world of recording, sequencing, and tone control for musicians and recording engineers. In addition, most sound cards let you connect a joystick device to the MIDI port for use with computer games.

INSTALLING A SOUND CARD

The steps you must perform to install a sound card are very similar to those you perform for other cards. To begin, power off and unplug your PC system unit. Next, remove the system unit cover, as discussed in Lesson 2, "Opening Your PC's System Unit," and discharge any static from your body. Locate an unused expansion slot and remove the slot's metal cover. Gently insert the sound card into the slot, securing the card in place with the screw you just removed from the slot cover.

Replace and secure the system unit cover. Next, connect your external speakers to the sound card's speaker port. Then, if you are using an external microphone, connect the microphone to your sound card's microphone port. Plug in and power on your PC and the external speakers. When your system starts, you will need to install device-driver software and run other programs in order to use the card.

INSTALLING A SOUND CARD

To install a sound card, perform these steps:

1. Power off and unplug your PC system unit.

2. Remove the system unit cover, placing the screws in a safe location, and discharge any static from your body.

3. Locate an unused expansion slot and remove the slot's metal cover.

4. Gently insert the sound card into the expansion slot and secure the card in place.

5. Replace and secure the system unit cover.

6. Connect the external speakers to the sound card's speaker port and your microphone to the sound card's microphone port.

7. Plug in and power on the PC system unit and the external speakers.

INSTALLING SOUND CARD SOFTWARE

After you install the sound card, you must install device driver software before you can put the card to use. If you plan to use the card for Windows and MS-DOS, you must install device drivers for both. As you unpacked your sound card, you should have found one or more floppy disks that contain the device-driver files. The documentation that accompanied your sound card should specify the steps you must perform to install the device driver software. Also, Lessons 30, "Understanding Device Drivers," and 31, "Telling Windows about Your Hardware Upgrade," discuss MS-DOS and Windows device drivers.

The disks that accompany your sound card might also include sample Windows and MS-DOS programs that support sounds, and might even provide some sample sound files. Within Windows, the Accessories group provides the Sound Recorder program, with which you can record and play back sound files. For more information on using the Sound Recorder program, turn to the book *1001 Windows 98 Tips*, Jamsa Press, 1998. Figure 18 illustrates the Windows Sound Recorder program.

Figure 18 *Recording sounds using the Windows Sound Recorder.*

RESOLVING COMMON CONFLICTS

If your sound card does not work or another card stops working when you use your sound card, your PC has a hardware conflict, as discussed in Lesson 8. The most common conflict is selecting a sound-card interrupt-request (IRQ) that is already in use by a different card. In addition, most sound cards require an I/O address as well as a DMA channel. To change a sound card's settings, you may have to change jumpers or DIP switches that reside on the card or use software to change the card settings. If you experience problems with your sound card, follow the steps discussed in Lesson 8, "Understanding Common Conflicts," to resolve the conflict.

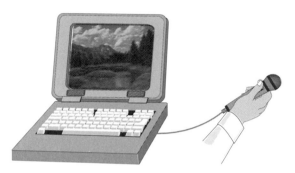

SOUND CARDS AND NOTEBOOK PCS

The popularity of sound cards has not bypassed notebook PCs. Today, many notebook PCs provide a built-in sound card and speakers. Using a standard microphone that you attach to your notebook PC, you can record your own sounds. If your notebook does not provide a built-in sound card, you may be able to purchase a PCMCIA card that provides sound-card support.

WHAT YOU MUST KNOW

As interest in multimedia explodes around the PC world, a sound card has become a must-have item for PC users. In this lesson, you examined sound cards and how to install them. As more and more users spend longer hours in front of their monitors, many users have realized how a quality monitor can reduce their eye strain. In Lesson 19, "Upgrading Your Monitor," you will examine the different ways two monitors can differ. You will also examine the steps you must perform to upgrade your monitor. Before you continue with Lesson 19, however, make sure that you have learned the following key concepts:

✓ A sound card is a hardware board that lets your PC record and play back sounds. The sound card can play back sounds using external speakers or headphones. In addition, you can connect the audio-out line to a stereo amplifier or other device with line-level inputs.

✓ With a sound card, you can record sounds using an external microphone or an audio-in source. Using the audio-in source, you can record music from a stereo or other device with line-level outputs, such as a VCR.

✓ Many sound cards include a MIDI interface, which lets musical instruments and recording and sequencing devices interface with your computer and special music software.

✓ When you install a sound card, you can experience three types of conflicts: an IRQ, I/O address, or DMA channel conflict. To resolve these conflicts, follow the steps listed in Lesson 8.

✓ After you install a sound card, you must install a device driver and software programs that let you use the card.

Lesson 19

Upgrading Your Monitor

As the number of hours you spend in front of your PC increases, so too does the importance of having a good monitor. In Lesson 20, "Upgrading Your Video Card," you will learn about video cards, which provide the first half of the picture, so to speak. In this lesson, you will learn about monitors, which provide the second half of the picture. If you think about it for a moment, installing a monitor is very easy. You simply connect the monitor to the video adapter card, and then plug in and power on the monitor. Thus, this lesson takes a look at several factors you should consider when you shop for a monitor. By the time you finish this lesson, you will understand the following key concepts:

- How monitor ergonomics make your monitor easier to use

- How a monitor displays an image

- How resolution and sharpness relate

- The difference between interlaced and non-interlaced monitors

- How dot pitch affects a monitor's resolution

- How you can use a glare-reduction screen to minimize the amount of light that reflects off your screen display

- The angle at which you should place your monitor on your desk

UNDERSTANDING MONITOR ERGONOMICS

Because of the long hours users spend in front of their monitors, designers have invested tremendous efforts to make monitors more people friendly. In the past, an ergonomic monitor was one that would adjust up and down or rotate from left to right.

Today, however, you can rotate some monitors 90 degrees, to better represent the shape of your current document.

Also, most monitors let you reduce glare by adjusting the monitor's brightness and contrast, much as you would adjust a TV.

In addition to using the controls to adjust your screen image, you can also use the controls to move the image left or right as well as up and down. Normally, most monitors will place their controls behind a small plastic cover that you will find on the front of the monitor.

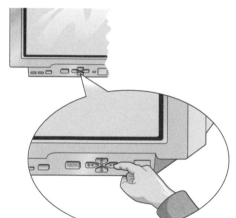

Today, many monitors support glare suppressing screens that you can insert or remove, as you require. In addition to these mechanical improvements, newer monitors support sharper images and truer colors. The sections that follow discuss the behind-the-scenes operations that control your monitor's capabilities.

HOW A MONITOR DISPLAYS AN IMAGE

Monitors display characters and images by illuminating small dots on the screen called picture elements or *pixels*.

As it turns out, each pixel is actually made up of red, green, and blue elements. By illuminating these three elements at different intensities, the monitor is able to change the pixel's color.

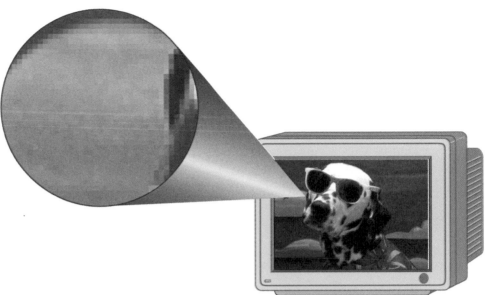

These three small elements are actually three different types of *phosphors*, which illuminate in a distinct color when heated.

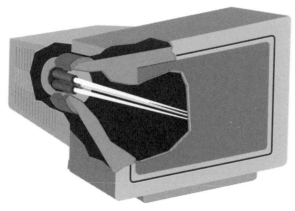

To illuminate the phosphors, the monitor contains three precise electron guns (one for each phosphor color) that it can aim and fire.

To display characters or images on your screen, the monitor quickly fires the electron guns across and then down your screen.

UNDERSTANDING MONITOR FREQUENCIES

As you just learned, the monitor displays images by illuminating phosphors using three electron guns. To display an entire screen image, the monitor repeatedly scans the guns across and down the screen. With each scan, the monitor illuminates a row of red, green, and blue phosphors. Unfortunately, to maintain an image, the phosphors must be continually refreshed (reheated). So, the monitor must move the electron guns very quickly. In fact, VGA monitors, for example, refresh a new line of pixels over 30,000 times per second!

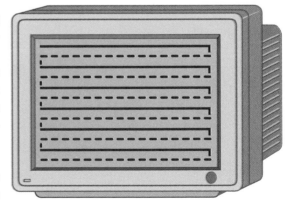

The speed at which a monitor starts refreshing a new line of pixels is called the *horizontal refresh rate*. Monitors refresh lines of pixels from left to right across the screen. When the guns reach the right edge of the screen, the monitor turns the electron guns off as it aims the guns at the start of the next line.

In a similar way, the speed at which the monitor refreshes the entire screen is called the *vertical refresh rate*. Common vertical refresh rates range from 50 to 72 times per second. Recently, however, new monitors support refresh up to 160 times per second. When the electron guns reach the bottom of the screen display, the monitor turns off the guns while it aims them back at the upper-left corner of the screen.

UNDERSTANDING HZ AND KHZ

When you express the number of times an operation is performed per second, you can use the term *hertz,* which is often abbreviated as Hz. A monitor that refreshes the screen 72 times per second is refreshing at 72Hz. If an operation is performed thousands of times per second, you can use the term *kilohertz,* which is abbreviated as KHz. A monitor that refreshes lines of pixels 15,000 times per second, for example, refreshes at 15KHz.

Monitor speeds are expressed in terms of their vertical refresh rate. Monitors support either a fixed refresh rate or multiple rates. For example, an EGA monitor supports a refresh rate of 60Hz. Likewise, a VGA monitor will support a rate of either 60 or 70Hz. *Multisynch* monitors have the ability to refresh the screen at different rates. Thus, you can typically plug a multisynch monitor into any video card. Although multisynch monitors are very flexible, they are also more expensive. If you are shopping for a fixed-rate video monitor, make sure the monitor will support your video card.

THE ADVANTAGE OF MULTISYNCH MONITORS

A multisynch monitor is a monitor that you can plug into a video card that refreshes the screen at 60, 70, or up to 160Hz. Thus, you can view a multisynch monitor as plug and play. If you are working with a monitor that is not multisynch, you will not have such a luxury.

UNDERSTANDING RESOLUTION AND SHARPNESS

As you have learned, the monitor displays images by illuminating pixels. *Resolution* is the measure of the number of pixels the monitor can display on your screen. Common resolutions include 640×480, 800×600, 1024×768, 1280x1024, and 1600x1200.

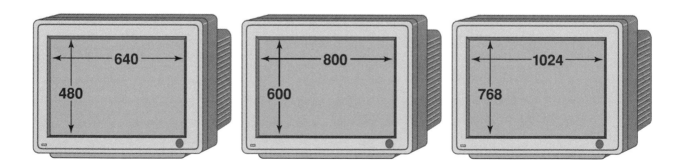

As a rule, the higher the image resolution, the sharper the image. The following images illustrate how the same image might appear at three different resolutions.

UNDERSTANDING DOT PITCH

When you shop for a monitor, it is important that you consider the monitor's resolution. Equally important, however, is the resolution your video card supports. Keeping in mind that the higher the resolution, the sharper the image, you then need to compare monitors, ideally side-by-side and definitely with both using the same video card and video mode (resolution and number of colors), to compare sharpness. Just because two monitors have the same resolution does not mean the monitors will have the same image *sharpness*. Other factors, such as hardware design and quality, influence monitor sharpness.

One feature often used to measure a monitor's sharpness is *dot pitch*, which describes the distance between successive phosphor colors, such as the difference between two successive red phosphors. In most cases (for monitors of the same size), the smaller the dot

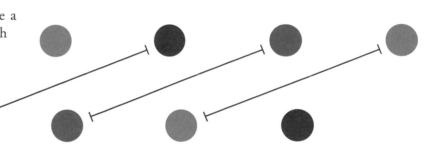

pitch, the sharper the image. As a rule, look for a dot pitch of 0.28mm or less. If you are considering a larger monitor, such as a 17- or 21-inch monitor, a slightly larger dot pitch will produce equivalent sharpness.

UNDERSTANDING RESOLUTION

As you have learned, monitors display images by illuminating small picture elements (pixels) on your screen display. Resolution describes the number of pixels on your screen display. As a general rule, the larger a monitor's resolution, the sharper its image display. Monitor resolution is expressed in terms of *x* by *y* (horizontal by vertical) pixel counts. Common resolutions include 640×480, 800x600, 1024×768, 1280x1024, and 1600x1200.

UNDERSTANDING INTERLACING

To display an image, the monitor constantly receives signals from the video card that tell it which colors to use for each pixel. Each time the monitor refreshes the screen (many over 70 times per second), the monitor must receive the corresponding pixel colors.

As the resolution increases, so too does the number of pixels the monitor must track. Unfortunately, some monitors simply cannot keep up. In such cases, the monitors use a technique called *interlacing* when they refresh the screen. Using interlacing, the monitor refreshes every other line of pixels as it refreshes the screen.

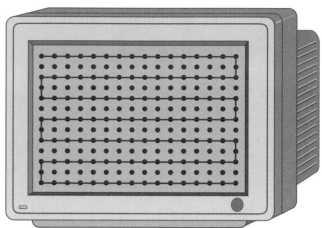

Although interlacing lets slower monitors support higher resolutions, it can produce a wave-like screen appearance that is distracting to work with all day. If you plan to spend long hours in front of your monitor, you'll want to invest extra money and buy a non-interlaced monitor.

INTERLACED VERSUS NON-INTERLACED MONITORS

When you shop for a monitor, be aware of interlaced monitors, which display higher resolutions by refreshing every other line with each screen refresh operation. Unfortunately, by refreshing pixels in this way, interlaced monitors often produce a wave-like display. Although the lower price of the interlaced monitor may seem appealing, you will not be happy with the end result.

UNDERSTANDING SCREEN SAVERS

As you have learned, monitors display images by illuminating red, green, and blue phosphors. As it turns out, if the image a monitor displays never changes (perhaps a screen constantly displays a menu of options), the phosphors can become damaged causing the image to appear "burned into" the screen. To prevent such damage to your monitor, you should use a screen-saver program. A screen saver is simply a program that becomes active when you are not currently using your PC, and displays changing images to the screen. The actual images the screen saver displays are not important. Rather, it is important only that the screen saver move or change the images constantly to prevent screen burn in. When you later press a key or move the mouse, the screen saver program will stop running and your previous screen contents will appear.

UNDERSTANDING ENERGY-STAR COMPLIANT MONITORS

As you have learned, to prevent image "burn in," many users run screen-saver programs that change screen images constantly. The problem with screen savers, however, is that while the program is running, the monitor remains fully powered and it consumes electricity. Although the amount of electricity a monitor consumes is not significant, there are currently millions of PCs active right now with their screen savers running. To reduce the amount of electricity inactive monitors consume, hardware designers have created Energy-Star compliant monitors that screen-saver programs can shut off when the monitors are not in use! Later, when the user presses a key or moves his or her mouse, the screen-saver program can turn the monitor back on. As you shop for a new monitor, look for a monitor that is Energy-Star compliant.

POSITIONING YOUR MONITOR TO REDUCE YOUR NECK AND SHOULDER STRAIN

As you fine-tune your monitor settings, take time to ensure that you position your monitor so that it reduces your neck and shoulder strain, and if possible, reduces reflection and glare from nearby windows. Ideally, the top of your monitor should be at, or slightly below your eyes.

TAKING ADVANTAGE OF A FLAT-SCREEN MONITOR

If you are thinking about upgrading your monitor, you should consider a flat-screen monitor, which may consume less space on your desk. In general, you can attach a flat-screen monitor your video card, just as you can any monitor. If space on your desk is at a premium, you will find a flat-screen monitor to be a great solution.

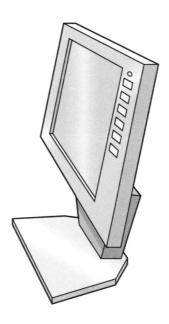

WHAT YOU MUST KNOW

As you learned in this lesson, the monitor provides the one half of your computer's video image display. The video card, which contains the electronics responsible for generating the screen image, is the other half. Lesson 20, "Upgrading Your Video Card," examines video cards in detail. Before you continue with Lesson 20, however, make sure that you understand the following key concepts:

✓ Upgrading your monitor is very easy. You simply power off and unplug your system unit and your monitor. Unplug your existing monitor's power and video card cables, replacing them with your new monitor's cables.

✓ A monitor displays images on your screen by illuminating small picture elements called pixels. To illuminate the pixels, the monitor uses three electron guns.

✓ Pixels are composed of small phosphors that, when heated, illuminate in different colors. To maintain their color, phosphors must be continually refreshed (reheated). Thus, the monitor must continually move the electron guns across and down your screen. The speed at which your monitor refreshes your screen is called the monitor's refresh rate.

✓ Resolution specifies the number of pixels on your screen display. The greater the number of pixels, the sharper the images a monitor displays.

✓ Sharpness refers to the amount of space between phosphors (dot pitch). The smaller the dot pitch, the sharper the image.

✓ As a monitor's resolution increases, so too does the amount of information the monitor must handle with each screen refresh operation. Because some monitors simply cannot keep up, some monitors employ a technique called interlacing. An interlaced monitor skips every other row of pixels during each screen refresh operation. Unfortunately, such interlacing can lead to a wave-like screen appearance. Be wary of interlacing when you shop for a monitor.

Lesson 20

Upgrading Your Video Card

In Lesson 19, "Upgrading Your Monitor," you examined various monitor characteristics and how monitors display images on your screen. If you have not yet read Lesson 19, do so now. This lesson examines video cards, which provide the first half of the video process. In short, your video card contains the electronics that tell the monitor what to display and how to display it.

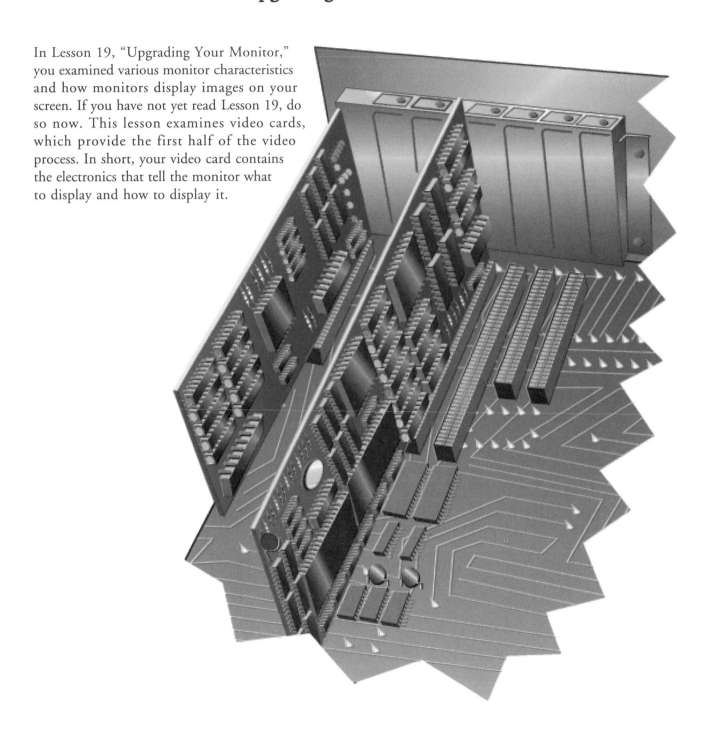

By the time you finish this lesson, you will understand the following key concepts:

- The purpose of a video accelerator
- How a video card's type controls the number of colors you can display
- The importance of video-card memory
- How you might be able to get much faster performance from your existing video card or a new one at little or no extra expense
- Why you need a video-card device driver

With the tremendous capabilities being included in multimedia programs, a fast, high-resolution video card that supports a large number of colors is becoming a must.

WHAT YOU WILL NEED

Before you get started on this lesson, make sure that you have the following readily available:

1. A PC tool kit with a screwdriver
2. A container within which you can place the chassis screws
3. A well-lit workspace with room for you to place the chassis
4. A new video card

UNDERSTANDING THE VIDEO CARD

A video card contains the electronics that let your computer display text and graphics on your screen. In most cases, the video card resides in one of the PC's expansion slots. However, some PCs place the video card electronics directly on the motherboard.

Before you can upgrade the video card for a motherboard-based video system, you must disable the motherboard video electronics. Normally, you will disable the motherboard video using a jumper or DIP switch, as discussed in Lesson 9, "Understanding DIP Switches and Jumpers."

As you know, your monitor attaches to the video card. To display an image, the CPU sends information to the video card which, in turn, sends the information to the monitor.

To improve your computer's video resolution or video speed, normally you must replace the video card in your computer.

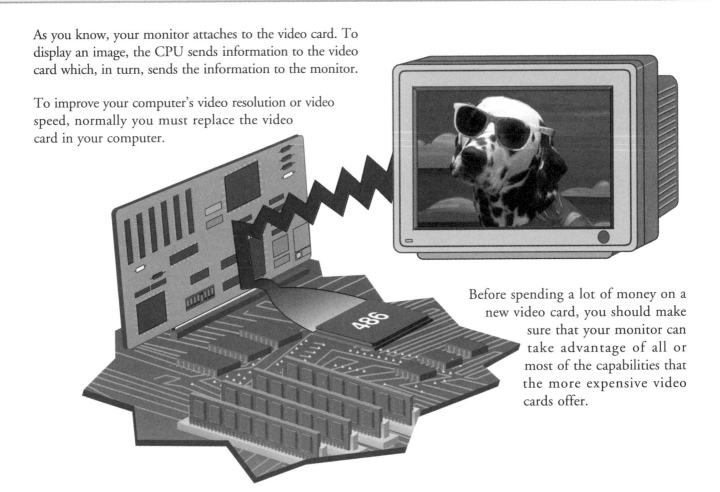

Before spending a lot of money on a new video card, you should make sure that your monitor can take advantage of all or most of the capabilities that the more expensive video cards offer.

UNDERSTANDING VIDEO ACCELERATORS

If you work with Windows, you are well aware that Windows succeeds by presenting commands and operations as pictures (graphics-based icons). To improve the performance of Windows, hardware developers have created enhanced video cards that accelerate common graphics-based operations. For example, a video accelerator card might have chips (processors) that Windows can take advantage of to move or size a window quickly. Likewise, the card can improve multimedia (video-based) operations by increasing the rate at which the screen can be updated. If you are shopping for a "fast" PC, make sure that you purchase a video accelerator. Recently, many video cards are providing support for fast 3D graphics which are required for high-end computer games.

HOW VIDEO CARDS DIFFER

As you shop for video cards, you will find that cards differ greatly in price. In addition, video cards can differ in four other ways:

- The card's speed (accelerated or not)
- The number of colors the card can display

- The card's resolution
- The card's on-board memory amount and type

If you make extensive use of Windows or other graphics-based programs, you will find that a video accelerator card significantly improves your system performance. In the near future, as more multimedia applications include video, an accelerator card will be a must. As you learned in Lesson 19, monitors display images by illuminating small phosphor dots called pixels. Resolution specifies the number of pixels that appear on the screen display. The higher a card's resolution, the greater the number of pixels and the sharper the screen image.

A video card also defines the number of colors your monitor can use to display an image. Video cards are often classified as 8-bit, 16-bit, or 24-bit cards, based on the number of bits the card uses to represent each pixel's color. Table 20 lists the number of colors these video card types can display.

Video Card	Number of Colors
8-bit	256
16-bit	65,536
24-bit	16,777,216

Table 20 *The number of colors different video cards can display.*

When you shop for video cards, you need to be careful. The ideal video card has high resolution and can display a large number of colors at that resolution. Be wary of advertisements that state a card can display over 16 million colors. Instead, look for cards that can display over 16 million colors with a high resolution, such as 800 × 600 or even 1280 × 1024. The key factor in determining how many colors a video card can display at different resolutions is the card's onboard memory (RAM).

As you shop, you will encounter video cards that have varying amounts of onboard memory (normally 1Mb or 2Mb). Within its onboard memory, the video card holds a color value for each pixel. If your monitor is running at 1280 x 1024 resolution, the card must hold values for 1,310,720 pixels. If the card can display 256 colors, each pixel color requires 8 bits or one byte. If the card can display 65,536 colors, each pixel color requires 16 bits or two bytes. In this case, the card's video memory must hold 2,621,440 bytes. Finally, to display over 16 million colors, each pixel color requires 24 bits (or three bytes) and the card's memory would have to hold 3,932,160 bytes! As you can see, the amount of onboard memory a video card contains defines the number of colors the card can display at different resolutions. As you shop for video cards, you will find cards with 1Mb, 2Mb, or 4Mb of RAM. As you just learned, the card's onboard memory controls the card's resolution and available colors.

INSTALLING A VIDEO CARD

To replace your existing video card, power off and unplug your PC system unit. Unplug your monitor from the video card. Remove your system unit cover, as discussed in Lesson 2, "Opening Your PC's System Unit," and discharge any static electricity from your body. Locate and remove your existing video card—it is the card into which your monitor was plugged. If your video electronics reside on the motherboard, you must disable the electronics, as you read earlier. To determine the actual steps you must perform to disable motherboard electronics, refer to the documentation that accompanied your PC.

Next, gently slide and secure the new video card into an expansion slot. Replace your system unit cover. Attach your monitor to the new video card. Plug in and power on your PC and monitor. As your system starts, you should see a count of your system's memory on the screen display.

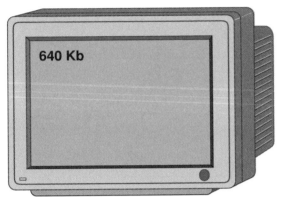

If the memory count appears, your video card installation was successful. If the memory count does not appear, first ensure that you have correctly cabled the card to your monitor and that your monitor is plugged in. Second, double-check that you have securely inserted the video card within the expansion slot. Next, your video card might conflict with another card. You might have to remove one or more cards until you identify the source of the conflict. If the error persists, you should contact your retailer or the card's technical support staff.

INSTALLING A VIDEO CARD

To install a video card, perform the following steps:

1. Power off and unplug your PC system unit and monitor.
2. Unplug your monitor from the current video card.
3. Remove your system unit cover and discharge any static from your body.
4. Remove your existing video card.
5. Insert and secure the new video card into an expansion slot.
6. Replace the system unit cover.
7. Plug in and power on your PC and monitor.

MATCH YOUR VIDEO CARD TO YOUR PC'S BUS TYPE

When you shop for a video card, you need to purchase a card that is compatible with your PC's expansion slots. Many video cards, for example, use a local bus to improve their performance. Unfortunately, if your PC does not have a local bus, you cannot take advantage of such boards. Lesson 4, "Understanding the PC's Expansion Slots," examines PC expansion slots in detail. Before you shop for a video card, read through Lesson 4. If your system has a PCI bus, purchase a video card that will take advantage of the local bus speed. Recently, many newer PCs are shipping with video cards that use a 64-bit or 128-bit bus to further speed graphics operations. Before you upgrade to such a video card, make sure your PC supports the video-card type.

UNDERSTANDING VIDEO RAM (VRAM)

As you have learned, your video card contains onboard memory within which it stores the image that appears on your screen display. To change the screen image, programs change the contents of this video memory. Likewise, to refresh the screen contents, the video card examines the video-memory contents to determine which signals it should send to the monitor. To speed up video operations, some video cards use a fast video-memory chip called VRAM. The advantage of a VRAM chip over standard DRAM is that your video card can read and write the chip's contents at the same time—which speeds up video operations significantly. If you are looking for the best performance, shop for a video card that provides VRAM. However, the card's faster performance is not without cost. As you shop, you will find that cards that use VRAM are more expensive than cards that use DRAM. Recently, hardware designers have released a new memory chip called WRAM which offers the speed of VRAM at less cost.

UNDERSTANDING VIDEO CARD DEVICE DRIVERS

In Lesson 30, "Understanding Device Drivers," you will examine device drivers, which are special software programs that let Windows or MS-DOS use a hardware device. By default, Windows, MS-DOS, and your PC BIOS provide support for basic devices, such as the keyboard, screen, and printer. As you add devices (perhaps a mouse, scanner, or CD-ROM), you may have to install device-driver software. If you purchase a video-accelerator card, you may need to install a device driver for MS-DOS, as well as Windows. If you do not install the device driver, your system might be able to use the card, however, your system will probably use the card in its most basic ways, failing to take advantage of an accelerator or increased resolution.

When you purchase a video card, you will normally receive a floppy disk that contains the card's Windows (and possibly an MS-DOS) device driver. The documentation that accompanies your video card will specify the steps you must perform to install the device driver. For more information on how to tell Windows about a new device, turn to Lesson 31, "Telling Windows about Your Hardware Upgrade."

USING WINDOWS TO CONTROL VIDEO SETTINGS

In the past, Windows 3.1 users often had difficulty changing their video resolution or the number of colors they wanted their video cards to display. Under Windows 3.1, users could change such settings for some video cards using the Windows 3.1 Setup program, while other cards required their own custom software. If you are using Windows 95 or 98, the process of changing screen colors and video resolution is much easier. To change your screen colors or video resolution under Windows 95 or 98, perform these steps:

1. Click your right-mouse button on an unused area on the Windows Desktop. Windows, in turn, will display a popup menu.

2. Within the popup menu, select the Properties menu option. Windows will display the Display Properties dialog box.

3. Within the Display Properties dialog box, select the Settings tab. Windows, in turn, will display the Settings tab page, as shown in Figure 20.

4. Within the Settings page, you can drag the Desktop area scroll bar to change your screen resolution and you can use the Color palette pull-down list to select the number of colors you desire.

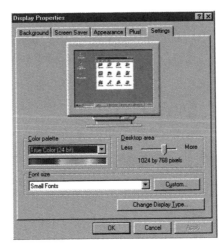

Figure 20 *The Windows Display Properties dialog box Settings tab.*

WHAT YOU MUST KNOW

Thanks to the visual nature of the World Wide Web, multimedia presentations, and animations, video card upgrades have become a must-have device for users wanting to take full advantage such programs as well as their new monitors. In this lesson, you learned how to upgrade your video card.

Today, all desktop and notebook PCs ship with a CD-ROM drive. Like most hardware devices, newer and faster CD-ROM drives reach the market on a regular basis. In Lesson 21, "Installing a CD-ROM Drive," you will learn how to install a CD-ROM drive. Before you continue with Lesson 21, however, make sure that you have learned the following key concepts:

✓ A video accelerator is an expansion slot card that contains special processing chips that can speed up different video operations. As the number of Windows-based multimedia programs and video games increase, video accelerators will become standard equipment.

✓ Different video card types support different capabilities (resolutions and colors). If you are concerned about system performance, you should begin your search with only those video cards that include an accelerator. However, such video cards are significantly more expensive than their slower counterparts.

✓ Video cards contain their own memory, which actually stores the image that is displayed on the screen. The more memory a video card contains, the more colors the card can display at one time.

✓ Depending on your video card type, you might have to install special device-driver software before Windows can take advantage of the card's capabilities.

Lesson 21

Installing a CD-ROM Drive

With the explosive growth of multimedia-based software, and with larger more complex programs (such as Windows 98 and Office 2000) requiring distribution on a CD-ROM, virually every PC sold today ships with a CD-ROM drive. Like most hardware devices, over time, newer CD-ROM drives become available that are faster and less expensive. Today, you can buy 36-speed CD-ROM drives that support the DVD storage format (which can store up to 4.7GB on a CD-ROM, which is ideal, for example, to store a movie). You can also purchase drives that are capable of recording their own CDs. This lesson examines the different CD-ROM drive types and the steps you must perform to install each. By the time you finish this lesson, you will understand the following key concepts:

- You can connect a CD-ROM drive to a sound card, a SCSI adapter, a parallel port, or a universal serial bus

- CD-ROM drives can be internal or external, and come in different speeds

- If your notebook PC does not have a built-in CD-ROM, you can connect an external CD-ROM drive to a PCMCIA card or to the PC's universal serial bus

- A CD-R drive is a drive that lets you read or record CDs

WHAT YOU WILL NEED

Before you get started on this lesson, make sure that you have the following readily available:

1. A PC tool kit with a screwdriver

2. A container within which you can place the chassis screws and a container for drive slot screws

3. A well-lit workspace with room for you to place the chassis and drive

4. A new CD-ROM drive and cables

SHOPPING FOR A CD-ROM DRIVE

If you have not yet purchased a CD-ROM, consider the following factors as your shopping guide:

Cost   As you shop, you will find that the cost of CD-ROM drives can differ considerably. Normally, the major factor affecting CD-ROM drive cost is drive speed. The faster the drive, the more expensive the drive's price. Today, for example, you can find readily afordable 36-speed CD-ROM drives (most books and magazines will represent a 36-speed drive as 36X speed). If you wait for the cost of 36X drives to come down, you will then have the same dilemma with even faster drives. The second factor affecting drive cost is whether the drive is an internal or external drive. You will normally pay more for an external drive because of the cost of the case and wiring and because you can quickly move the drive from one system to another, which eliminates your need to buy multiple drives.

Speed   CD-ROM drives differ in speed. The original drives transferred data at a rate of 150KBs (approximately 150,000 bytes per second). Next, double-speed (2X) drives transferred data at a rate of 300KBs. Soon after, quad-speed (4X) drives transferred data at 600KBs. Today, 36X speed drives transfer data at 5.4MBs. If you are using multimedia programs that display video, the faster your drive, the better your video quality. As a rule, if you plan to hold on to your drive for some time, spend extra money now and buy a faster drive.

Internal versus External   You can install a CD-ROM drive within one of your system-unit drive bay slots or you can use an external drive. The advantage of an external drive is that you can easily move the drive from one computer to another. If you have multiple computers, you might want to consider an external CD-ROM drive.

Connection Type   Depending on your hardware, you can connect a CD-ROM drive to a SCSI adapter, a sound card, a parallel port, or to a universal serial bus (USB). Each connection type has its advantages and disadvantages. A SCSI connection is fast, but requires that you set the CD-ROM drive's SCSI address and that you power off your system to install or remove the drive. A parallel port connection is simple, but slow. Connecting a drive to a universal serial bus is easy, but many users do not yet have USB-based hardware. Connecting the drive to a sound card may be the least expenisve route, but it ties your drive to the sound card. Should you decide to replace a sound card that provides the drive interface, you might be forced to replace the drive itself (a costly proposition).

Multimedia Upgrade Kit   Many CD-ROM drives sold today are packaged in a multimedia upgrade kit that also provides a sound card, speakers, and several sample CDs. Many stores offer aggressive pricing on multimedia upgrade kits. However, before you purchase an upgrade kit, make sure that the CD-ROM drive and sound card provided meet your needs. Otherwise, purchase both separately. If you want a SCSI-based CD-ROM drive, make sure the kit provides one.

CONNECTING A CD-ROM DRIVE

Depending on your CD-ROM drive type, you connect the drive to either a sound card, SCSI, or USB adapter. If you have purchased a multimedia upgrade kit, your drive will very likely connect to the sound card in the kit. CD-ROM drives can be internal (residing within a drive bay in the system unit) or external. The steps you must perform to install an internal or external drive will differ, as discussed next.

Internal CD-ROM drive

External CD-ROM drive

Note: The next two sections tell you how to install an internal or an external CD-ROM. If you do not already have a SCSI adapter card or the proper sound board installed, you will have to install one. Lesson 5, "Working with Boards and Chips," describes installation of hardware cards in general, Lesson 14, "Installing a SCSI Adapter," describes installation of a SCSI adapter, and Lesson 18, "Installing a Multimedia Sound Card," describes installation of a multimedia sound card.

INSTALLING AN INTERNAL CD-ROM DRIVE

To install an internal CD-ROM drive, power off and unplug your PC's system unit. Next, remove the system unit cover, as discussed in Lesson 2, and discharge any static from your body. Locate the drive bay into which you will insert the drive. Remove the drive bay screws and store them in a

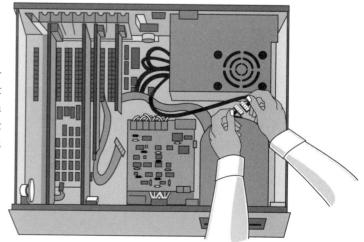

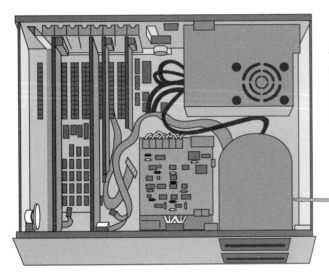

safe place so you can later use the screws to secure the drive in place. If you are replacing an existing drive with the CD-ROM, first remove the ribbon cable that connects the drive to the controller. Next, remove the power cable that connects the drive to the power supply.

Note: *If your PC's drive bay does not contain rails into which you will slide the drive, you can buy the rails at your computer retailer. If your PC needs drive rails, you might find it easier to let your computer retailer complete the installation for you.*

After you slide the drive into place, secure the drive to the drive bay using the screws you previously removed.

Next, use the ribbon cable that accompanied your drive to connect to either the sound card or the SCSI adapter.

Connect the power supply cable to the drive.

Replace the system-unit cover and plug in and power on your PC.

Note: *If you are connecting the drive to a SCSI adapter, you might need to set the drive's SCSI address, as discussed in Lesson 14. Also, depending on the drive's location in the SCSI device chain, you might have to terminate the CD-ROM drive.*

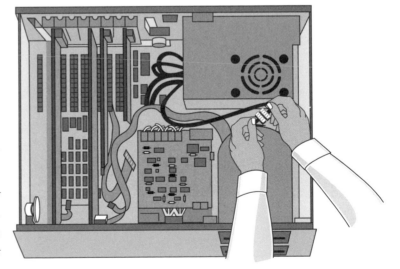

INSTALLING AN EXTERNAL CD-ROM DRIVE

Installing an external CD-ROM drive is actually quite simple. To begin, power off and unplug your PC system unit. Next, using the cable that accompanied the drive, connect the drive to the corresponding adapter (SCSI, USB, or parallel port). Next, you must plug in the drive to a power outlet.

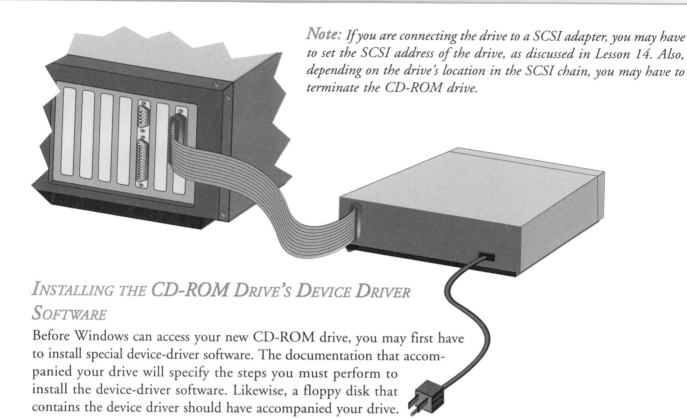

Note: If you are connecting the drive to a SCSI adapter, you may have to set the SCSI address of the drive, as discussed in Lesson 14. Also, depending on the drive's location in the SCSI chain, you may have to terminate the CD-ROM drive.

INSTALLING THE CD-ROM DRIVE'S DEVICE DRIVER SOFTWARE

Before Windows can access your new CD-ROM drive, you may first have to install special device-driver software. The documentation that accompanied your drive will specify the steps you must perform to install the device-driver software. Likewise, a floppy disk that contains the device driver should have accompanied your drive.

After the installation program ends, you might need to restart your system. In addition to providing an installation program, the floppy disk might include one or more test programs you can run to ensure that you have correctly installed the CD-ROM drive.

Note: If your CD-ROM drive connects to a sound card, first ensure that your sound card is properly working before you start troubleshooting the CD-ROM drive itself. Lesson 18 examines PC sound cards in detail.

Note: If you will use your CD-ROM within an MS-DOS environment, you must also install an MS-DOS-based device driver. Depending on your CD-ROM drive type, you may have to edit your AUTOEXEC.BAT or CONFIG.SYS files to install the driver.

USING A CD-ROM DRIVE WITH A NOTEBOOK PC

Over the past few years, the popularity of CD-ROM drives and sound cards has merged with popular notebook PCs to produce multimedia notebook PCs. If you are shopping for a notebook PC, you should consider a notebook that has a built-in CD-ROM drive.

To reduce their weight by reducing disk drives, many newer notebook PCs let you remove the CD-ROM drive and replace it with a floppy-disk drive, as your needs require.

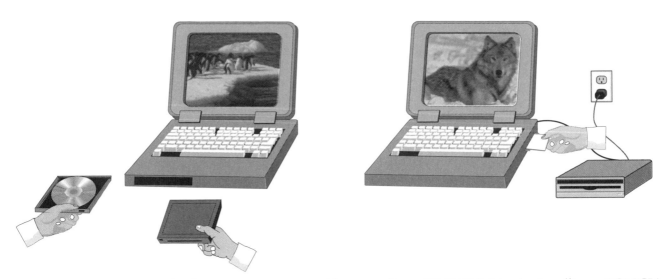

If you have an existing notebook computer, you can add support for a CD-ROM drive by installing a PCMCIA card that contains a SCSI interface. Then, you can connect an external CD-ROM drive to the SCSI port. Likewise, you may choose to purchase a USB-based CD-ROM drive that you connect to your notebook PC's universal serial bus.

UNDERSTANDING DIGITAL VIDEO DISCS (DVDs)

DVD is a data format that lets CD-ROMs store data in a more compact way, which lets a CD-ROM disc store up to 4.7GB of data! Today, the most common use of DVD discs is store movies, much like a VHS tape. In the future, as more drives support DVD, programs that today ship on multiple CD-ROMs, will ship on one DVD disc. As you shop for a new CD-ROM drive, make sure the drive is DVD compatible.

CD-ROM DRIVES AND CD-AUDIO

In addition to letting you access CD-ROMs that contain multimedia programs or electronic references, you can use your CD-ROM drive and sound card to play back audio CDs (the CDs you normally play in your car or with your home stereo). Figure 21, for example, illustrates the CD Player program that comes with Windows. Using the CD Player program, you can select the specific tracks you want to hear, play the CD's tracks in a specific order, or continuously repeat one or more specific songs. Also, most CD-ROM drives provide a port to which you can connect headphones, which let you play the music you desire without disturbing others near your workspace.

Figure 21 Using the Windows 95 CD Player program to play audio CDs.

UNDERSTANDING COMPACT DISC-RECORDABLE (CD-R)

The term CD-ROM, stands for compact disc read-only memory. The words read-only memory tell you that you can read the information a CD-ROM contains, but you cannot write (record) information on to the CD-ROM. A CD-ROM drive, therefore, can only read data from a CD.

You can buy, however, a device that lets you both read and record CDs. Users refer to such devices as a *CD burner* or a *CD-R drive*. To record your own CDs, you purchase special (writeable) discs, called *CD-R discs*. Using software that comes with your drive, you can use the CD-R drive to record data on to the CD-R disc. The drive records information by using a laser to burn microscopic pits into the surface of the disc (the presence of a pit on the disc's surface represents the value one, whereas the absence of the pit, signifies a zero).

CD-R drives read or record CDs. Normally, however, such drives are much slower than the fastest CD-ROM drive on the market. A CD-R drive, for example, might read data at 8X speed and write data at 4X. Whereas a fast CD-ROM drive can read data at 36X speed.

Many users (and companies) are finding it very convenient to record their file backups on a CD-R disc which costs less than $2.

WHAT YOU MUST KNOW

The vast amount of information that can fit on one CD-ROM makes it an excellent candidate for applications that require a lot of storage space, such as animation, detailed graphics, and sound. In this lesson, you have learned how to install a CD-ROM drive.

When you plug in your PC system unit, you actually plug in the PC's power supply which, in turn, disseminates power to the electronic components within your PC. Occasionally, a power supply will fail and you must replace it. In Lesson 22, "Replacing the PC's Power Supply," you will examine the steps you must perform to replace a power supply. Before you continue with Lesson 22, however, make sure that you have learned the following key concepts:

- ✓ CD-ROM drives can be internal or external.

- ✓ You connect a CD-ROM drive to either a sound card, SCSI adapter, parallel port, or to the universal serial bus, depending on the type of drive.

- ✓ Be wary of CD-ROM drives that connect to a sound card. If you ever change sound cards, you might not be able to use your CD-ROM drive.

- ✓ CD-ROM drives come in different speeds. The faster the CD-ROM drive, the more information the drive can provide the computer in a short period of time. If you are shopping for a CD-ROM drive, you should consider a triple-speed drive or faster.

Lesson 22

Replacing the PC's Power Supply

Every operation the PC performs is based on the presence or absence of electronic signals. When you plug your PC's power into your 120-volt AC (alternating current) wall socket, you actually plug in the PC's power supply. The power supply, in turn, transforms the voltage into the 5-volt DC (direct current) that the computer can use. Within your PC's system unit, in turn, other devices, such as the motherboard and disk drives, plug into the power supply. Occasionally, a power supply will fail, and you must replace it. This lesson covers the steps you must perform to replace a power supply. By the time you finish this lesson, you will understand the following key concepts:

- How to recognize when your PC's power supply has failed

- How to replace your power supply

- When and how you need to plug devices into your power supply

- How to determine your PC's power requirements

When the original IBM PC was released in 1981, the PC shipped with a small 63-watt power supply. Since many internal hardware devices require power, many users replaced their power supplies with a larger one. Today, most PCs ship with large power supplies (200 watts or more), which should more than meet your PC's needs.

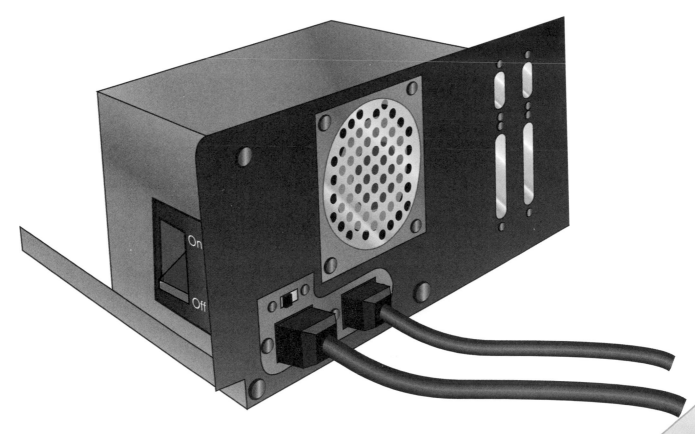

RECOGNIZING A FAILED POWER SUPPLY

When your PC's power supply does not work, your PC will not start. In addition, when the power supply fails, you will not hear the PC's fan whir. The PC's fan is contained within the power supply.

Do not jump to the assumption that your power supply is bad just because your system does not start and you cannot hear the fan whir. Instead, first double-check the PC's power plugs to ensure that they are plugged in correctly. Next, verify that the wall outlet into which the PC is plugged is working (you may have to plug a different device, such as a lamp into the outlet to verify the outlet is working).

If you are using a surge suppresser, as discussed in Lesson 1, "Getting Past Your Fears (You Can Do This)," remove the suppresser and plug your PC directly into a working wall outlet. When a surge suppresser captures an electrical spike, it will normally trip an internal breaker. Most surge suppressers have a reset button you can press to restore the suppressor's normal operation.

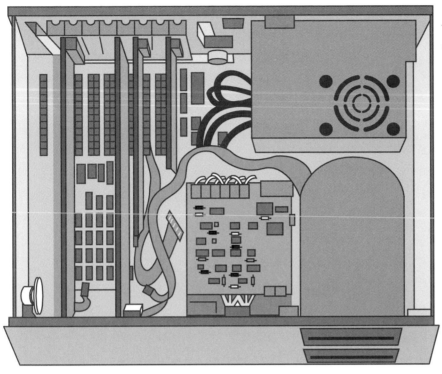

REPLACING YOUR POWER SUPPLY

To replace your PC's power supply, first power off and unplug the PC system unit. Next, remove the system unit cover, as discussed in Lesson 2, "Opening Your PC's System Unit." Place the screws you remove in a safe location.

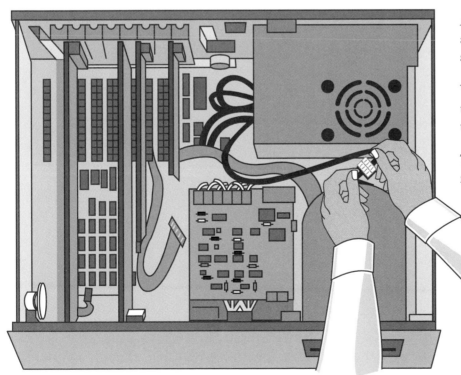

As discussed, the PC motherboard and disk drives plug into the power supply.

Within your system unit, locate the small power supply cables and their plugs.

To remove the plugs, you might need to rock the plugs gently from right to left. Be careful to grasp the plugs, not the wires attached to the plugs, or you might damage the power-supply cables.

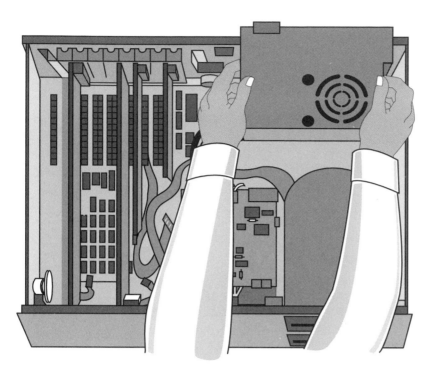

There are normally several screws that hold the power supply to the back of the system unit. Remove these screws and place them in a safe location.

The power supply should now lift out from your system unit easily. Be careful as you lift the power supply from the system unit. The power supply is heavier than it looks.

Make sure you do not set the power supply (or let it fall, in the case of a tower configuration) on top of any fragile components.

Place your new power supply into the system unit and replace the screws that attach the power supply to the system unit.

Next, plug in your motherboard, disk drives, and other devices you may have unplugged from the power supply.

Note that the power supply plugs are shaped so that they can be plugged in only one way.

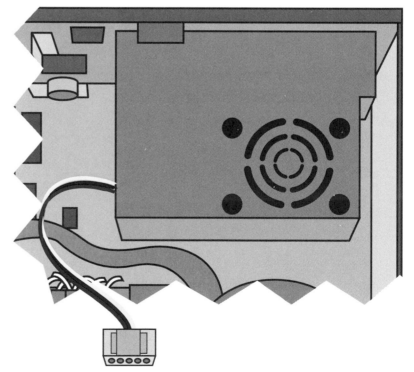

REPLACING A POWER SUPPLY

To replace a power supply, perform these steps:

1. Power off and unplug the system unit.

2. Remove the system unit cover, as discussed in Lesson 2.

3. Unplug devices attached to power supply cables, such as your motherboard and disk drives.

4. Remove the screws that attach the power supply to the system unit. Place the screws in a safe location.

5. Lift your old power supply from the system unit, replacing it with the new power supply.

6. Secure the power supply in the system unit by replacing the screws you previously removed.

7. Plug in the devices you previously unplugged from the power supply.

8. Replace and secure your system unit cover.

9. Plug in and power on your PC.

WHICH DEVICES PLUG INTO THE POWER SUPPLY

As you have learned, your PC's motherboard and your disk drives plug into the power supply. As you read through the lessons in this book, you might install other devices, such as a CD-ROM or tape drive, that you must also plug into the power supply. As a rule, you normally must plug in larger mechanical devices directly to the power supply. Cards such as a sound board or modem, on the other hand, do not need to be plugged in. Instead, these devices get their power directly from the expansion slot.

SPLITTING A POWER SUPPLY CABLE

Depending on the devices you install within your system unit, there may be times when you run out of power supply cables before the power supply runs out of available power.

In such cases, you can use a power cable splitter, which breaks one power cable into two.

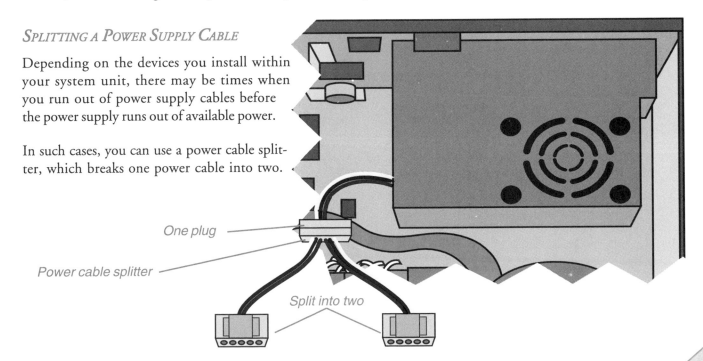

One plug

Power cable splitter

Split into two

HOW TO DETERMINE YOUR POWER REQUIREMENTS

As you have learned, most power supplies sold today provide 200 watts. To determine your PC's power requirements, use the device power needs listed in Table 22.

Device	Power Requirement
CD-ROM drive	20 to 25 watts
Expansion board (small card)	5 watts
Expansion slots (large card)	10 to 15 watts
Floppy drive (3 1/2-inch)	5 watts
Floppy drive (5 1/4-inch)	5 to 15 watts
Hard drive (3 1/2-inch)	5 to 15 watts
Hard drive (5 1/4-inch)	10 to 30 watts
Memory (per 8Mb)	1 watt
Motherboard	20 to 35 watts

Table 22 *Power requirements for common PC devices.*

WHAT YOU MUST KNOW

As the number of hardware devices in your computer increases, so too does the amount of power required of your power supply. In this lesson, you have learned how much power various devices use and how to replace your power supply. Today, all PCs ship with some type of mouse. Depending on your preferences, you may like a specific mouse type. Also, the mouse, like all mechanical devices, may eventually break. Lesson 23, "Upgrading Your Mouse," examines the different PC mouse types and the steps you must perform to upgrade your mouse. Before you continue with Lesson 23, however, make sure that you understand the following key concepts:

✓ When you plug in your PC, you actually plug in the PC's power supply. The power supply, in turn, disperses power throughout your PC's internal components.

✓ When your power supply fails, not only will your PC not start, you will not hear the power supply's built-in fan.

✓ Before you blame your PC's power supply, make sure you first double-check your power cables and surge suppressor, and ensure that the wall outlet is working.

✓ Power requirements are expressed in terms of watts. Today, most power supplies sold provide 200 watts of power.

Lesson 23

Upgrading Your Mouse

With the tremendous success and acceptance of Microsoft Windows, virtually every PC sold today ships with a mouse. Because a mouse is a mechanical device, it can eventually wear out. This lesson examines the steps you must perform to replace a mouse. In addition, this lesson presents several concepts you might want to consider when you shop for a mouse. By the time you finish this lesson, you will understand the following key concepts:

- There are two primary mouse types: a serial mouse and a bus mouse

- Mice differ by the number of buttons they support, their resolution, and how you attach the mouse to your PC

- A wireless mouse eliminates the mouse cable—an optical mouse eliminates the small track ball that rolls as you move your mouse across your desk

- A trackball is like a stationary, upside-down mouse with a large ball—very handy if desk space is limited

- The mouse's use and the functions it is capable of performing are defined by the mouse driver

WHAT YOU WILL NEED

Depending on your mouse type, you might have to open your system unit. If you are installing a bus mouse and bus mouse card, make sure you have the following readily available before you get started on this lesson.

1. A PC tool kit with a screwdriver

2. A container within which you can place the chassis screws

3. A well-lit workspace with room for you to place the chassis

UNDERSTANDING HOW YOUR MOUSE WORKS

As you know, when you move a mouse across your desk, a mouse cursor moves in the same direction across your screen.

If you turn the mouse over, you will find the mouse ball. As you move the mouse, this ball's movement causes the mouse to produce signals which, in turn, move the cursor.

For the computer to respond to mouse movements, the mouse must be connected to the computer. There are four ways to connect a mouse to your computer. These connection techniques correspond to the four mouse types: serial, bus, a proprietary bus, and the universal serial bus.

USING A SERIAL MOUSE

A *serial mouse* is a mouse that connects to one of your computer's serial ports, such as COM1 or COM2. The serial mouse is the most commonly used mouse. To replace a serial mouse, simply unplug your current mouse and plug in the new mouse. The advantage of a serial mouse is its simplicity. Windows and other software programs readily support most serial mice. In fact, most serial mice conform to the Microsoft mouse standard. Thus, when you tell your software that you are using a serial mouse, you might be able to use the Microsoft mouse type if your mouse is not listed in the supported mice.

The disadvantage of a serial mouse is that the mouse consumes a serial port that you might need to use for a modem, joystick, or other device.

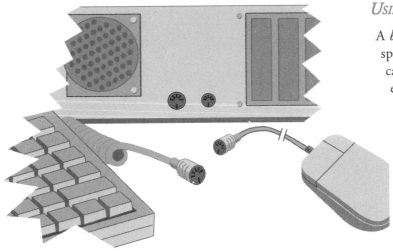

USING A BUS MOUSE

A *bus mouse* is a mouse that either connects to a special PC port or requires its own hardware card, which resides in one of your computer's expansion slots. Over the past few years, bus mice have grown in popularity. Today, most PCs provide a bus-mouse connector that resides on the back of the PC next to the keyboard port. The advantage of a bus mouse is the mouse does not consume a serial port. The disadvantage of the bus mouse, however, is that if your PC does not provide a bus-mouse connector, you must install a bus-mouse card that consumes an expansion slot.

USING A UNIVERSAL SERIAL BUS MOUSE

In Lesson 28, "Using a Universal Serial Bus (USB)," you will learn that a universal serial bus provides an easy way for you to connect up to 127 devices to your PC. When you use a universal serial bus to connect devices, you do not have to worry about device settings such as IRQs. Instead, you simply plug the device into the bus, install a device driver (software) and you are ready to go. Recently, several universal serial bus mice have entered the marketplace.

REPLACING OR INSTALLING A BUS MOUSE

If you are connecting a bus mouse to a PC bus-mouse port, perform these steps:

1. Power off your PC's system unit.

2. Connect the bus mouse to the bus-mouse port.

3. Power on your PC and update your mouse driver software.

If you must install a bus-mouse card, perform these steps:

1. Use the Windows Device Manager, as discused in Lesson 40, "Using the Windows Device Manager," or the MS-DOS-based MSD command, discussed in Lesson 39, "Troubleshooting with MSD," to determine the IRQ lines that are currently in use. Select an unused IRQ for use by the bus mouse. Use a jumper or DIP switch on the board to select the IRQ.

2. Power off and unplug the PC's system unit. Remove the system unit cover, as discussed in Lesson 2, "Opening Your PC's System Unit," and discharge any static from your body.

3. Remove your existing bus-mouse adapter or select the slot into which you want to install a new bus mouse. Install and secure the new bus-mouse adapter into an expansion slot.

4. Replace and secure the PC system-unit cover.

5. Plug in and power on your PC and update your software, as necessary.

UNDERSTANDING MOUSE RESOLUTION

As you shop for a mouse, you may encounter the term *mouse resolution*—which is measured in counts per inch. As you know, when you move your mouse, the mouse generates electronic signals and sends them to the computer. The higher a mouse's resolution, the more signals the mouse generates as you move it. In this way, you may not have to move your mouse as far to move your mouse cursor quickly across your screen. Also, if you must use your mouse to aim the mouse pointer at a specific (small) screen object, the higher your mouse resolution, the easier you will find the operations.

CLEANING YOUR MOUSE

If your mouse does not seem as responsive as it once was, your mouse might need to be cleaned. To clean your mouse, turn it over and remove the mouse ball. Using a lint-free cloth and some rubbing alcohol, clean the mouse ball. Next, blow out any dust that may reside in the mouse ball's container. If you look inside the cavity where the ball sits, you can see little disc-shaped rollers (mounted on little metal shafts) against which the ball sits.

When the ball rolls, so do the rollers, moving small metal pins across counters that indicate how far the mouse is moving. The dirt that the ball picks up from your desk or pad can get packed onto these rollers, so you must actually clean the rollers with alcohol too. If your mouse action feels "lumpy," even when you roll it across a clean surface, this might be the problem. Place the clean ball back into the mouse and secure the cover.

ALTERNATIVE MOUSE TYPES

As you shop for a mouse, you might encounter optical as well as wireless mice. An *optical mouse* is a mouse that uses a special mouse pad and a light instead of a ball. As you move the optical mouse across its special pad, the mouse uses special sensors to detect the movement.

A *wireless mouse* is a mouse that eliminates the mouse cable. As you move the mouse, the mouse transmits radio signals to a special adapter card.

If you work in an office with many users, don't worry. Like garage door openers, wireless mice use unique radio frequencies. The odds of two wireless mice conflicting are very low.

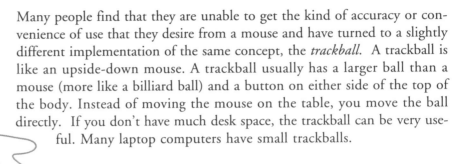

Many people find that they are unable to get the kind of accuracy or convenience of use that they desire from a mouse and have turned to a slightly different implementation of the same concept, the *trackball*. A trackball is like an upside-down mouse. A trackball usually has a larger ball than a mouse (more like a billiard ball) and a button on either side of the top of the body. Instead of moving the mouse on the table, you move the ball directly. If you don't have much desk space, the trackball can be very useful. Many laptop computers have small trackballs.

Understanding Touch Pads

Recently, a new mouse-like device called a *touch pad* is gaining popularity. Using the touch pad, the user slides a finger across the pad's surface to move the mouse pointer across the screen. To click the touch pad, the user can click buttons on the pad or simply tap their finger on the pad one time for a single-click or twice for a double-click. Like a mouse, you connect a touch pad to either a serial port or a bus-mouse connector.

Mice and Notebook PCs

Over the past few years, the use of notebook PC's has exploded. As you examine notebook PCs, you will find a wide variety of mouse configurations. For example, you might find notebook PCs that include a built-in trackball, a keyboard-based mouse button, or even a touch pad.

In addition, if a user really enjoys the feel and responsiveness of a standard mouse, most notebook PCs provide a bus-mouse adapter to which the user can connect the mouse. Also, a user can almost always connect a serial mouse to a notebook's serial port.

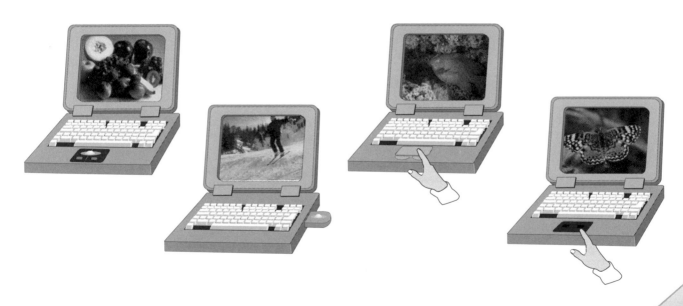

SWAPPING MOUSE BUTTONS

By default, mice normally come configured for right-handed users. Many software programs, however, let you switch the mouse buttons. If you are using Windows 95 or 98, you can use the Mouse Properties dialog box, as shown in Figure 23.1, to swap your mouse buttns and to fine tune the responsiveness of your mouse.

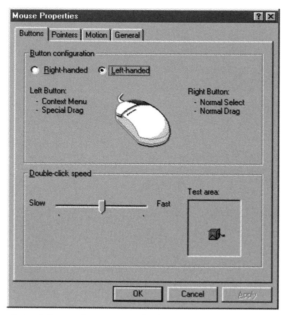

Figure 23.1 *The Windows 95 and 98 Mouse Properties dialog box.*

If you are using Windows 3.1, you can switch the mouse buttons using the Control Panel Mouse dialog box, as shown in Figure 23.2.

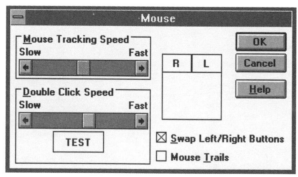

Figure 23.2 *The Control Panel Mouse buttons.*

UPDATING THE MOUSE DEVICE DRIVER

A *device driver* is special software that lets your computer use a device—in this case, it's the mouse driver. When you upgrade your mouse, you may need to update the device driver as well, since it's the driver, not the physical mouse, that defines the functions the mouse can perform. The documentation that accompanies your mouse should include instructions for the steps you must perform to use the mouse. If, after you install a new mouse, the mouse appears not to work, the problem might be your software. Normally, most software programs only respond to the mouse-select button. Some mice, however, come with software that lets you take advantage of the second or even a third mouse button.

UNDERSTANDING IRQ CONFLICTS

One of the first problems many users experience when they add a modem is a conflict between their mouse and modem. For example, when the user starts using the modem, his or her mouse won't respond. Likewise, in some cases, when they move their mouse, the modem may hang up, ending the current call. If you experience such errors, the problem is not your mouse or your modem. Instead, the problem is an IRQ conflict, as discussed in Lesson 8, "Understanding Common Conflicts." If you suspect an IRQ conflict, use the MSD command, as discussed in Lesson 36, to determine your system's current IRQ settings.

TROUBLESHOOTING YOUR MOUSE

If you experience problems with your mouse, your mouse might not be the culprit. Before you condemn your mouse, perform the following troubleshooting steps:

1. Make sure the mouse cable is correctly connected to its port.

2. Turn your PC's system-unit power off and back on and see if the error disappears.

3. If you have a second mouse available, turn off your PC's power and connect the new mouse. Power the PC back on to see if the error disappears.

4. Some software programs do not support a mouse. Try your mouse with a program, such as Windows, that is known to support the mouse.

5. Make sure the mouse device-driver is in use, and that it is the correct one.

6. If you are using a serial mouse, try using a second serial port. You might need to update the mouse device-driver to use the second serial port.

7. If you are using a bus mouse, make sure that the mouse-adapter card is properly seated in its expansion slot.

WHAT YOU MUST KNOW

If your PC didn't have a mouse when you bought it, or the mouse has been broken beyond reasonable repair, you might find that you need to install a new mouse. In this lesson, you learned how to troubleshoot your existing mouse and how to install a new one.

As more users establish home offices, the need for users to perform disk backups becomes more important. As hard disk capacities continue to increase, backing up a hard disk to floppy disks is becoming less common. Instead, many users are finding that tape backups are very easy and time effective. Lesson 24, "Installing a Tape Backup Unit," discusses the steps you must perform to install a tape drive. Before you continue with Lesson 24, however, make sure that you have learned the following key concepts:

✓ The PC supports four different mouse types: serial, bus, proprietary, and universal serial bus mice.

✓ A serial mouse is a mouse that connects to one of your computer's serial ports, such as COM1 or COM2. The serial mouse is the most commonly used mouse. The advantage of a serial mouse is its simplicity. The disadvantage of a serial mouse is that the mouse consumes a serial port, which you might need to use for a modem, printer, or other device.

✓ Depending on your PC's type, you may connect a bus mouse to a port on the back of your PC or the mouse may require its own hardware card, which resides within one of your computer's expansion slots. The advantage of a bus mouse is the mouse does not consume a serial port. The disadvantage of the bus mouse, however, is that it may consume an expansion slot.

✓ You can remove the ball from your mouse, and clean the ball and the rollers the ball contacts.

✓ There are several alternative mouse types: the optical mouse, which doesn't use a ball; the cordless mouse, which doesn't use a cord to the computer; the trackball, which is like a stationary, upside-down mouse with a large ball that you manipulate directly; and the touch pad with which you move the mouse pointer by moving your finger across the pad.

✓ Before you can use a mouse, you normally need to install a mouse device driver.

✓ If, when you use your mouse, you experience difficulties with other devices, your system is experiencing an IRQ conflict, as discussed in Lesson 8.

Lesson 24

Installing a Tape Backup Unit

As the size of PC hard disks has rapidly grown over the past few years, users no longer have to pay quite as much attention to their hard-disk contents. When hard disks were smaller, users often struggled to find disk space. As a result, they often shuffled programs off of and onto their hard disk. Many disks today, in contrast, hold all the programs a user needs.

Because users now pay less attention to their hard disks, many users also pay less attention to making backups of their files. In addition, because hard disks are becoming so large, performing floppy disk-based backups is becoming unreasonable. Today, all PCs should ship with a tape-backup unit. Unfortunately, most do not. As a result, you should place a tape drive on your PC upgrade list.

This lesson examines the steps you must perform to install a tape backup unit. By the time you finish this lesson, you will understand the following key concepts:

- The advantage of performing tape-based backups over backups that use floppy disks
- How to install an internal or external tape unit
- Why you want to purchase formatted tapes

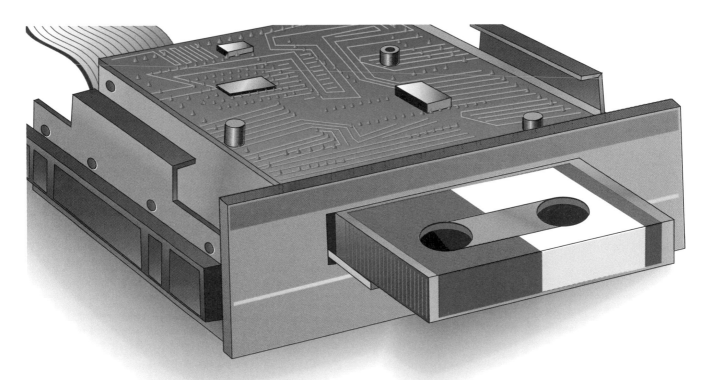

WHAT YOU WILL NEED

Before you get started on this lesson, make sure that you have the following readily available:

1. A PC tool kit with a screwdriver

2. A container within which you can place the chassis screws, and a second container to hold the screws that hold the tape drive to the chassis

3. A well-lit workspace with room for you to place the chassis and tape drive

---

INSTALLING A TAPE BACKUP UNIT

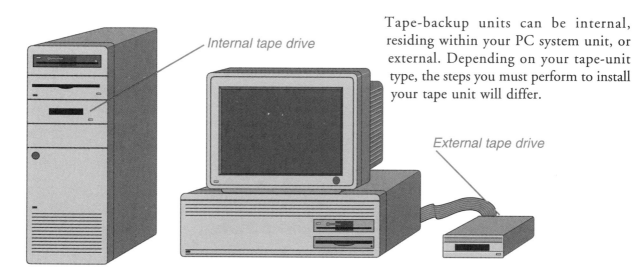

Internal tape drive

External tape drive

Tape-backup units can be internal, residing within your PC system unit, or external. Depending on your tape-unit type, the steps you must perform to install your tape unit will differ.

INSTALLING AN INTERNAL TAPE DRIVE

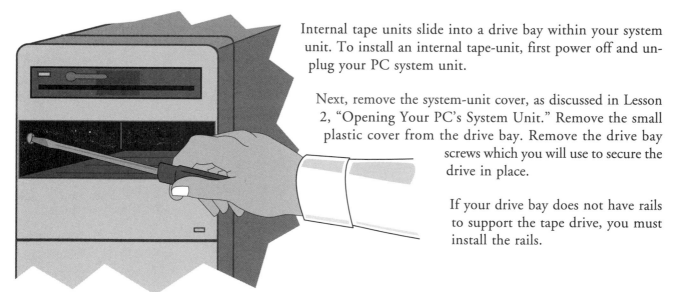

Internal tape units slide into a drive bay within your system unit. To install an internal tape-unit, first power off and un-plug your PC system unit.

Next, remove the system-unit cover, as discussed in Lesson 2, "Opening Your PC's System Unit." Remove the small plastic cover from the drive bay. Remove the drive bay screws which you will use to secure the drive in place.

If your drive bay does not have rails to support the tape drive, you must install the rails.

Most tape units ship with rails you can use. If you do not have proper rails, you may find it more convenient to have your computer retailer perform the installation for you. Slide the tape drive into the drive bay. Secure the tape unit in place with the screws you previously removed from the system-unit rails. Next, attach a power cable from the PC's power supply to the tape unit.

Internal tape-drives connect to the PC in one of three ways. First, the tape unit might use its own controller card. If this is the case, use the MSD command or the Windows Device Manager to determine a proper IRQ setting for the card. Change the board settings if necessary. Insert the card into an expansion slot and use the tape drive's ribbon cable to connect the controller and tape unit.

Second, the tape unit might connect to a SCSI adapter. In this case, connect the tape-drive cable to a SCSI adapter or to a device in the SCSI device chain (see Lesson 14). Finally, some tape drives connect to the floppy-disk controller using a special cable. The documentation that accompanied your tape unit will tell you the steps you must perform. After you connect the tape unit to a controller, replace the system-unit cover and plug in and power on your PC.

INSTALLING AN EXTERNAL TAPE DRIVE

External tape drives connect to the PC in one of four ways. First, the drive might connect to its own controller card. If you must install a controller card, power off and unplug your PC. Follow the steps discussed in Lesson 4, "Understanding the PC's Expansion Slots," to install the card. After you install the card and the system unit cover is in place, connect the tape drive to the card and plug in the tape drive. Next, plug in and power on your PC system unit.

Second, an external tape drive might connect to a SCSI adapter. If you must install the SCSI adapter card, follow the steps presented in Lesson 14, "Installing a SCSI Adapter." If the SCSI card is already in place, power off your PC and SCSI peripherals. Connect the tape unit to the adapter or the SCSI daisy chain. Plug in your tape-drive unit, the system unit, and your SCSI peripherals. Some tape drives connect to a PC parallel port, which is very convenient when you must move the tape drive from one system to another. To connect a tape drive to a parallel port, power off your PC. If necessary, remove the cable for a device currently connected to the parallel port (normally your printer). Next, connect the tape unit to the parallel port. Plug in the tape unit and power on the PC. Finally, as discussed in Lesson 28, "Using a Universal Serial Bus (USB)," some newer tape drives connect to the universal serial bus.

USING TAPE-DRIVE SOFTWARE

Tape drives normally come with software that lets you test the tape drive and perform backup operations. The documentation that accompanied your tape drive should discuss the software in detail. In addition, there are several third-party tape-drive backup programs available on the market that you might find easier to use. One of the primary advantages of using a tape drive for your backup operations is that you can perform the backup operation without being present (because you do not have to insert and remove floppy disks).

TAPE BACKUPS USING WINDOWS

Because hard-disk drives have become so large, floppy disk-based backup operations are no longer reasonable. For example, to backup a 300Mb hard disk, you would need over 200 floppy disks! All systems should ship with a tape drive. Unfortunately, they do not. The fact that so many systems ship without tape drives shows the low importance that users associate with performing backup operations. To simplify backup operations, Windows includes backup software that lets you backup your disk to a tape drive. Figure 24, for example, illustrates the Windows backup software.

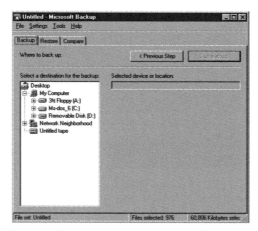

Figure 24 *The Windows backup software fully supports tape-drive backups.*

WHAT YOU MUST KNOW

The dramatic increase in hard disk sizes has made floppy disk-based backup impractical. In this lesson, you have learned how to install a tape drive into your system. Most users make extensive use of their printers. However, most never think about upgrading their printers. As you will learn in Lesson 25, you can improve your system performance by upgrading your printer. Before you continue with Lesson 25, however, make sure you understand the following key concepts:

✓ Tape drives make it easy to perform disk backups. In addition, you can normally perform an unattended tape backup in much less time than a floppy disk-based backup.

✓ Tape drives can be internal or external devices.

✓ You can connect an internal tape drive to a SCSI adapter, a proprietary card, or a floppy-disk controller card. External tape drives connect to a SCSI adapter, a proprietary card, a parallel port, and the unversal serial bus.

✓ Most tape drives come with software that you can use to test your tape drive installation and to backup the files on your disk.

Lesson 25

Upgrading Your Printer

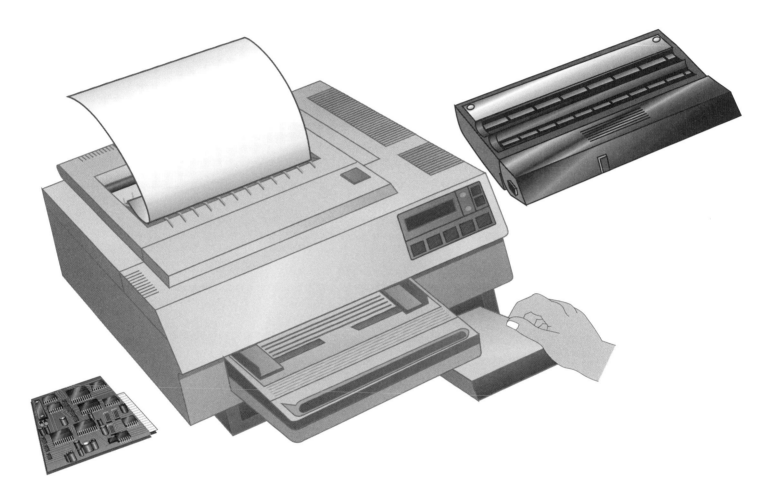

Because of the large number of printer types, it is difficult, at best, to list the exact steps you must perform to upgrade different parts of your printer. Instead, this lesson examines several common printer upgrades and the benefits each offers. By the time you finish this lesson, you will understand the following key concepts:

- To improve your print speed, connect your printer to a parallel port or universal serial bus as opposed to a serial port
- Adding memory to your printer improves your system performance
- Printers use hard (hardware-based) and soft (software-based) fonts
- PostScript is a programming language for printers
- Windows provides software you can use to manage your printers and print jobs

CHOOSING A SERIAL OR PARALLEL PORT

As you have learned, most PCs provide at least one serial port and and one parallel port. You normally use serial ports to connect slower devices that do not transmit very large amounts of data, such as a mouse. Serial ports transmit data 1-bit (binary digit) at a time over a single wire. Parallel ports, on the other hand, transmit data over eight wires at the same time. As a result, parallel ports are much faster.

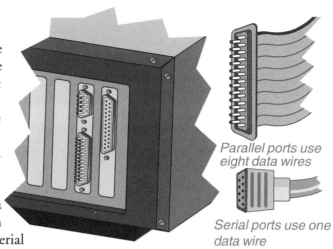

Parallel ports use eight data wires

Serial ports use one data wire

If you examine your printer closely, you should find a serial port and a parallel port with which you can connect a printer to your PC. If you are using the serial port to connect your printer, you will improve your system performance by upgrading to a parallel port connection.

*Note: If you change your printer connection from a serial port to a parallel port, you must tell Windows that you are now using a parallel port. For information on changing the Windows printer settings, turn to the book 1001 **Windows 98 Tips**, Jamsa Press, 1998.*

WHY PARALLEL PORTS IMPROVE YOUR SYSTEM PERFORMANCE

If you are using a serial port to connect your printer to your PC, your computer transmits data to the printer 1-bit at a time, a slow process. Parallel ports, on the other hand, transmit data 8-bits at a time, a much faster process. By reducing the amount of time it takes for your programs to send information to the printer, your programs become more responsive. As a result, your system performance improves.

CONNNECTING YOUR PRINTER TO A UNIVERSAL SERIAL BUS

In Lesson 28, "Using the Universal Serial Bus (USB)," you will learn that you can connect up to 127 devices to your PC using the universal serial bus. The advantage of using the universal serial bus to connect devices is simplicity. You simply connect the device to a bus port (or hub), install a device driver, and the device is ready to use. You do not have to worry about IRQ or other settings. By connecting a printer to a universal serial bus, you can improve your system performance because the bus offers higher speed than a parallel port. However, your printer must support a universal serial bus connection.

CONNNECTING YOUR PRINTER TO A NETWORK

If you work in an office that uses a local-area network, you may share a printer with other users. Depending on the printer type and the network configuration, the printer may connect to a PC or to the network itself. The advantage of connecting a printer to the network itself is speed (the printer can receive data at the speed of the network, which may be 100 megabits per second (100Mbs). To connect a printer directly to the network itself, the printer must support a network card (such as an Ethernet card) and have considerable memory (some network printers even have a built-in hard disk to which the printer can spool incoming data).

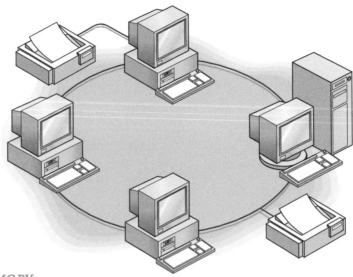

ADDING PRINTER MEMORY

When you print a document, your application program sends the document to the printer which, in turn, places the document into its own memory. The printer then prints the information its memory contains. If your document is small, the entire document will fit into your printer's memory. In this way, the application does not have to wait for the entire document to print before it can continue. After the printer's memory contains the document, the application considers the printing complete and can continue other operations. If the document you are printing is larger than the printer's memory, the application must wait for the printer to print part of the document so that it can send more data to the printer. This waiting and sending process continues until the last of the document is in the printer's memory.

By adding memory to your printer, you increase the likelihood that your documents can fit into the printer's memory. In this way, you reduce the amount of time your applications spend waiting on the printer. Depending on your printer type, the steps you must perform to install memory will differ. If you are using an older printer, the printer memory very likely resides on a hardware card. Newer printers, on the other hand, use SIMM or DIMM chips similar to those discussed in Lesson 12, "Adding Memory to Your PC."

To install the printer's memory, power off and unplug your printer. Next, follow the steps specified in your printer manual to install the printer memory board or memory chips. Do not forget to discharge all static from your body before you handle the cards or chips.

Note: *Most printers provide a menu option or button combination that lets you print a status-report page specifying the amount of memory the printer contains, a list of built-in fonts, and even the number of pages the printer has printed to date. For specifics on printing your printer's status page, refer to the documentation that accompanied your printer.*

ADDING PRINTER MEMORY

By adding memory to your printer, you increase the likelihood that your printer can hold the documents you print. In this way, you decrease the amount of time your programs spend waiting on the printer. To install memory within your printer, perform these steps:

1. Power off and unplug your printer.

2. Follow the steps specified in the manual that accompanied your printer to install the memory board or memory chips.

3. Plug in and power on your printer.

ADDING PRINTER FONTS

Most printers come with a collection of built-in fonts. Using an option on a printer menu, or by pressing a button combination on your printer, you should be able to display the printer's current fonts. For specifics on printing a font sample, refer to the documentation that accompanied your printer.

Printer fonts are classified as hard or soft. *Hard fonts* are either built into the printer or reside in an add-on font cartridge. *Soft fonts*, on the other hand, are provided on disk, much like software. When you use a soft font, your program loads the font into the printer's memory (another good reason to install more memory into your printer—to make room for documents that use many soft fonts). Today, most users make extensive use of soft fonts, such as the TrueType fonts provided with Windows.

The most common way to increase the number of hard fonts in your printer is to install a font cartridge. A font cartridge is just that—a small memory-board cartridge that you insert into a socket in your printer. Each cartridge contains one or more font families. In most cases, you cannot use the font cartridge made for one type of printer in a second printer type.

USING AN INK-JET PRINTER

Over the past few years, inexpensive ink-jet printers have become very popular as the printers' quality has improved. Ink-jet printers are so named because they spray a very precise stream of ink onto the paper to create characters or images. Ironically, as the cost of ink-jet printers has decreased, the quality the ink-jet printers produce has increased. As a result, ink-jet printers provide reasonable quality at an affordable price. Recently, ink-jet printers that let users print in full color have become very popular. To print a color image, the ink-jet printer uses a special ink cartridge that holds cyan (blue), (yellow), magenta (red), and black inks. By combining these four colors on a page, ink-jet printers can produce a large variety of colors.

A key to achieving quality color images using a color ink-jet printer is to use the correct paper. Because color ink-jet printers place a large amount of ink on the page, they can quickly saturate many papers. Before you complain about the quality of your color printouts, make sure you are using the correct paper type. In addition to printing on paper, you can use an ink-jet printer to print on transparencies. However, as before, you need to ensure you are using the correct transparency type. Also, many ink-jet printers use a special cleaning sheet that you send through the printer just as you would a piece of paper. As the cleaning sheet moves through the printer, it will remove built-up ink residue.

Currently, the primary shortcoming of ink-jet printers is that they do not support the PostScript printer language discussed next. However, as you will learn, several software packages are now available that you can use to let you print PostScript output to an ink-jet printer.

UNDERSTANDING POSTSCRIPT

As you have learned, a computer program is simply a list of instructions the computer executes. Computer programs are written in a programming language, such as C++, BASIC, Pascal, and so on. In a similar way, PostScript is a programming language for printers. Using PostScript, you can create powerful effects, such as a gradation. If you have a PostScript printer, many applications will take advantage of PostScript's programming capabilities behind the scenes. If you perform considerable desktop publishing, or if you create computer-based illustrations, you will probably work with PostScript files on a regular basis, and you will want a PostScript printer. If you only use your printer to print word-processing or spreadsheet documents, you probably do not need PostScript capabilities. In the past, PostScript printers were very expensive. Thus, some users would add special hardware to their printer that gave the printer PostScript capabilities. With PostScript printers becoming more affordable, you should buy a new printer if you need PostScript support. In most cases, a newer printer will provide faster output (print more pages per minute) and give you higher resolution (sharper images). In the short term, however, you can run software on your PC that will let your printer support PostScript, as discussed next.

SOFTWARE SUPPORT FOR POSTSCRIPT

As you have just learned, most inexpensive printers (such as an ink-jet) do not support the PostScript printer language. However, because PostScript is very powerful and used extensively by many drawing packages, a printer's ability to print PostScript is very important. Luckily, several software programs now exist that convert PostScript commands into information a non-PostScript printer can understand. Using this software, even the most inexpensive printers can print PostScript. Best of all, in most cases, after you install the software, you do not have to do anything else—you simply print to your printer.

UNDERSTANDING PRINT SPOOLING

When you print information to your printer, Windows has two ways of getting the information to your printer. First, Windows can let the program print directly to the printer. Normally, when a program prints to the printer in this way, you cannot use the program to perform other tasks while the program is printing. In addition, if you run a second program, that program cannot print until the first program finishes with the printer.

The second way that Windows lets programs print is to spool (temporarily place) the printer output on disk. In other words, rather than sending the information to the slow printer, the program sends the information to a file on disk, which is a much faster process. Then, Windows runs a second program (behind the scenes) that prints the spooled data for the program. In this way, the program that has spooled its output is free to perform other tasks while its output prints. In addition, should you run a second program, you can print other information using that program. Because the program is not printing to the printer, but rather to a file on disk, several programs can spool printer output at the same time. When the software finishes printing the first program's spooled output, it can start printing the output of the next program that has spooled data to disk.

To spool data to disk in this way, your disk must have enough space to hold the data. If you are low on disk space and need to print a large document, you can direct Windows to print directly to the printer as opposed to spooling the output on disk. Normally, however, you will find that having Windows spool your program's printer output to disk is convenient and fast.

When Windows spools printer output to disk, Windows will create a temporary file on your disk within which it places a print job. Windows will create the temporary file within the folder that corresponds to the TEMP environment entry that you define within your *AUTOEXEC.BAT* file. To improve your system performance, you should use the TEMP entry to direct Windows to spool its printer output to your fastest disk. For more information on Windows print spooling operations, turn to the book *1001 Windows 98 Tips*, Jamsa Press, 1998.

MANAGING PRINT JOBS WITHIN WINDOWS 95 AND 98

As you have learned, when you print a job within Windows 95 or 98, Windows spools your program's printer output to a file on disk. After Windows spools the output, Windows will then run a program that prints the output. If you spool multiple jobs to a printer, you can use Windows to manage your output, by performing these steps:

1. Select the Start menu Settings option and choose Control Panel. Windows, in turn, will open the Control Panel window.

2. Within the Control Panel window, double-click your mouse on the Printers icon. Windows will open the Printers window that displays an icon for each printer connected to your system.

3. Within the Printers window, double-click your mouse on the printer you desire. Windows, in turn, will open a window, similar to that shown in Figure 25, that lists the jobs the printer is currently printing. Within the printer window, you can stop one or more jobs from printing, or change the order in which jobs print.

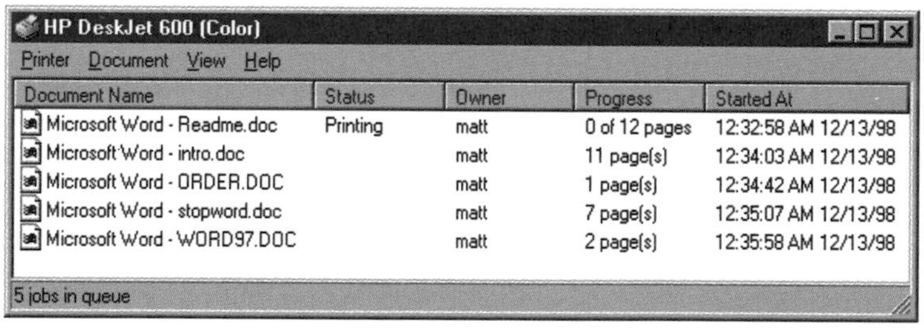

Figure 25 *Displaying the jobs a printer is currently printing.*

WHAT YOU MUST KNOW

Printing is a process that almost every computer user does. As a result, almost every user can benefit by a printer upgrade of some kind. In this lesson, you have learned several ways to improve your printer performance. In a similar way, to many users, the keyboard has become an extension of their fingertips. However, few users think about upgrading their keyboards. In Lesson 26, "Upgrading Your Keyboard," you will examine different keyboard upgrades. Before you continue with Lesson 26, however, make sure that you understand the following key concepts:

✓ You can connect most printers to either a serial or parallel port. In addition, you may also be able to connect a new printer to a universal serial bus as well as a network.

✓ Just as you can improve your PC performance by adding memory to your PC, you can also improve your system performance by adding memory to your printer.

✓ Depending on your printer type, its memory can come on a hardware card or on SIMM or DIMM chips. Refer to the documentation that accompanied your printer to determine the steps you must perform to install additional memory.

✓ Printers can use hard or soft fonts. Hard fonts are either built into your printer or a font cartridge. Soft fonts, on the other hand, come on disk. When a program uses soft fonts, the program downloads the font into the printer's memory.

✓ PostScript is a printer programming language. If you perform considerable desktop publishing or create computer-based illustrations, you will probably work with PostScript files on a regular basis and will want a PostScript printer—otherwise, you probably will not need PostScript capabilities.

✓ When you print from within a Windows-based program, Windows will run special software that spools the output to a file on your disk and then oversees the spooled data's printing.

Lesson 26

Upgrading Your Keyboard

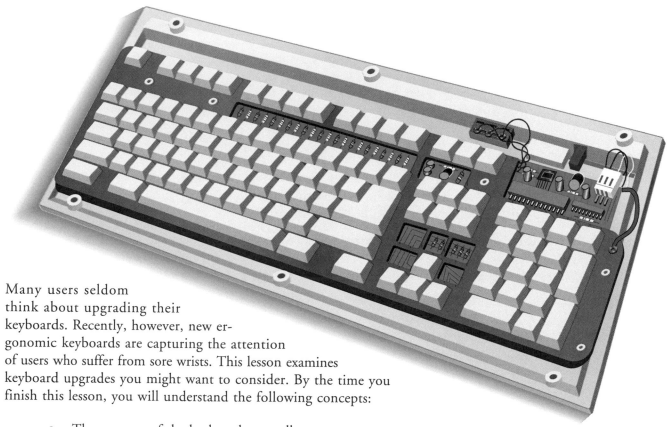

Many users seldom think about upgrading their keyboards. Recently, however, new ergonomic keyboards are capturing the attention of users who suffer from sore wrists. This lesson examines keyboard upgrades you might want to consider. By the time you finish this lesson, you will understand the following concepts:

- The purpose of the keyboard controller
- How the keyboard controller simplifies a keyboard upgrade
- The advantage of ergonomic keyboards
- How keyboard pads can reduce wrist strain
- If you are using a notebook PC, you may want to attach a standard PC keyboard

UNDERSTANDING THE KEYBOARD CONTROLLER

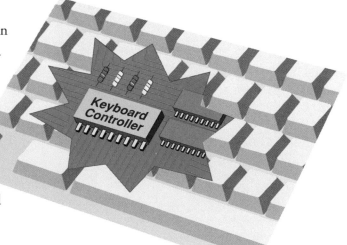

A keyboard controller is the electronic chip that converts the keystrokes you type into the electronic signals the PC understands. The keyboard controller resides within the keyboard itself.

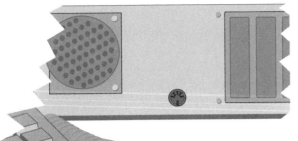

Because keyboards essentially "bring their own electronics," it is very easy for you to upgrade your keyboard. In short, to upgrade your keyboard, you simply unplug your existing keyboard and plug in your new keyboard.

UNDERSTANDING KEYBOARD ERGONOMICS

For most users, the keyboard has become an extension of their fingers. Unfortunately, for many users, existing keyboard designs have led to sore wrists, tendonitis, and even carpal-tunnel syndrome. As a result, newer keyboard designs have emerged that reduce the stress on your wrists and hands.

As the price of these ergonomic keyboards continues to drop, more users will make the switch.

To take advantage of these keyboards, you simply power off your PC, unplug your existing keyboard, and replace it with the new keyboard.

PUTTING A WRIST PAD TO WORK

If you are not quite ready to spring for an ergonomic keyboard, you should consider the addition of a keyboard wrist pad.

As you can see, the position of the wrist pad reduces the stress on your wrist by elevating your hands to the keyboard height.

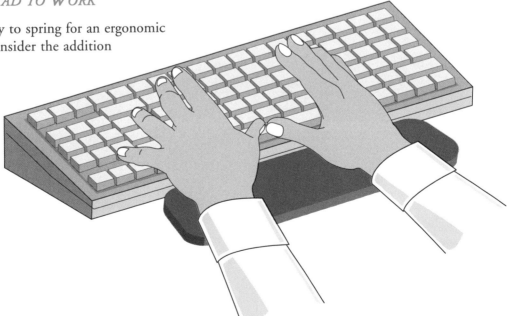

ENHANCING YOUR NOTEBOOK PC

If you work with a notebook PC, you are probably well aware that the notebook's small keyboard takes a little getting used to. As you travel, you are probably constrained to using the notebook's built-in keyboard (few of us have space in our suitcase for a standard keyboard). However, when you use your notebook PC at home or in the office, you may find that attaching a standard keyboard to your notebook is very convenient.

If you examine the back of your notebook PC, you should find a keyboard port into which you can plug a standard keyboard. As you shop for keyboards, you will be surprised by their low price.

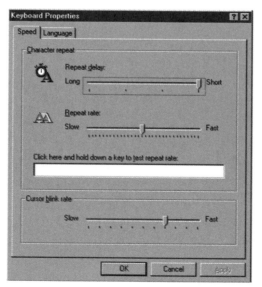

IMPROVING YOUR KEYBOARD RESPONSIVENESS

If you spend considerable time editing word-processing documents, you may want to fine tune your keyboard's responsiveness using the Keyboard Properties dialog box shown in Figure 26.

Figure 26 *The Keyboard Properties dialog box.*

Within the Keyboard Properties dialog box, you can control your keyboard's repeat rate which specifies how fast your keyboard repeats a keystroke when you hold down a key, such as your keyboard arrow keys. Within the Keyboard Properties dialog box, the Repeat delay field specifies how long your keyboard waits, when you first hold down a key, before it starts to repeat the keystroke. To maximize your keyboard's responsiveness, you want to minimize the repeat delay. Next, using the Repeat rate field, you can control how fast your keyboard repeats the keystroke (following the initial repeat delay). To maximize your keyboard's repsonsiveness, you want a fast repeat rate. To display the Keyboard Properties dialog box, perform these steps:

1. Click your mouse on the Start menu Settings option and choose Control Panel. Windows will open the Control Panel window.

2. Within the Control Panel window, double click your mouse on the Keyboard icon. Windows will display the Keyboard Properties dialog box.

WHAT YOU MUST KNOW

All PCs come with keyboards, and now thousands of people are showing signs of stress on their wrists. In this lesson, you have learned about the advantages of upgrading to an ergonomic keyboard and why it is so easy to upgrade your keyboard.

As you work with or upgrade your computer, you will eventually encounter different error messages or system problems. To help you resolve common errors, Lesson 27, "Upgrading Your Notebook PC" examines ways you can upgrade a notebook PC. Before you continue with Lesson 27, however, make sure that you understand the following key concepts:

✓ Keyboard upgrades are very simple—you simply turn off your computer, unplug your existing keyboard, and plug in the new keyboard.

✓ If you have experienced sore wrists due to long hours at the keyboard, you might want to upgrade to a new ergonomic keyboard.

✓ If the price of an ergonomic keyboard exceeds your budget, you should consider a keyboard wrist pad.

✓ Depending on your notebook PC type, you may be able to attach a standard keyboard to your notebook PC.

Lesson 27

Upgrading Your Notebook PC

If you examine the PC market, you will find that the fastest growing segment is the notebook PC. In fact, if you simply perform an "airport survey," you will find that almost all business travelers carry a notebook PC. For years, the high price of notebook PCs limited their use. Today, however, for less than two thousand dollars, users can buy a Pentium-based multimedia PC, with 32MB or RAM, a 4GB hard drive, and a CD-ROM that fits in a briefcase! Unfortunately, the day users buy their notebook PC, the PC is already on its way to being obsolete. This lesson, therefore, examines ways you can upgrade a notebook PC. By the time you finish this lesson, you will understand the following key concepts:

- The importance of PCMCIA cards
- The difference between PCMCIA slot types
- Why docking stations are popular

GETTING TO KNOW YOUR NOTEBOOK PC

Despite its small size, a notebook PC is quite similar to your desktop PC. A notebook has a processor, RAM, a hard drive, an internal or external floppy drive, and possibly a CD-ROM and sound card for multimedia applications. In addition, if you turn your notebook PC around, you will find serial and parallel ports as well as a connector for a standard keyboard, monitor, and possibly a docking station.

The ports that you will find at the back of the notebook PC are no different than those you have examined throughout this book. To connect a printer to your notebook PC, for example, you simply connect the printer to the notebook PC's parallel port. With respect to other ports, the primary difference between a desktop PC and a notebook PC is that you can't add ports to a notebook PC. Unlike a desktop PC that provides you with expansion slots into which you can insert hardware cards, you can expand a notebook PC using PCMCIA cards or a universal serial bus, which are discussed later in this lesson.

UPGRADING A NOTEBOOK PC'S PROCESSOR AND RAM

As you might guess, the faster a notebook PC's processor, the better the PC's performance. As is the case with a desktop PC, the more RAM you add to your notebook PC, the faster your programs will run. Within your notebook PC, the processor and RAM chips are identical to those you would find in a desktop PC. Like a desktop PC, you increase a notebook PC's RAM by installing SIMM (or DIMM) chips. Because of its compact size, it can be very difficult to work inside a notebook PC. Therefore, if you plan to upgrade the processor or add RAM to your notebook PC, you should strongly consider letting your retailer perform the upgrade for you. In the long run, letting a technician, who works on notebook PC's regularly, perform your upgrade will save you time and aggravation.

UPGRADING A NOTEBOOK PC'S HARD DRIVE

Over the past year, the size and cost of hard drives has dropped considerably. As such, it is not unusual to find notebook PCs with 4GB hard disk, or larger! Before you upgrade your notebook PC's hard drive, make sure the drive will fit into your notebook. As before, should you decide to upgrade your notebook PC's hard disk, consider letting your retailer perform the upgrade operation for you.

Before you buy and install a hard drive for your notebook PC, consider how you will use the drive. You may, for example, decide that a SCSI-based external drive is very convenient. Using the external drive, you can connect the drive to your notebook as you need, and later, connect the drive to your desktop PC. In this way, you will simplify your exchange of files.

UNDERSTANDING *PCMCIA* CARDS

PCMCIA cards are your key to upgrading your notebook PC. The PCMCIA card is a small credit-card sized card that contains the electronics for a specific device. For example, one PCMCIA card might provide modem electronics while a second card provides a network adapter or a SCSI adapter. Users often call PCMCIA cards PC cards. Most notebook PCs provide one or more PCMCIA slots into which you can insert the cards as you need them.

UNDERSTANDING *PCMCIA*-CARD TYPES

As you shop for a notebook PC, you will find that the PC's PCMCIA slot may support three types of PCMCIA cards: Type I, II, or III cards. In short, the only difference between the card types are the card's thickness: 3.3, 5.0, and 10.5 millimeters.

Depending on the card's purpose, the electronics on the card will differ. A PCMCIA card that contains RAM may fit in a thin Type I card, whereas a PCMCIA card that contains a small disk-storage device may require a thick Type III card. Most notebook PCs will provide PCMCIA slots that let you use two Type I and II cards at the same time or one Type III card. In this way, you might plug a PCMCIA card that contains a modem into the top slot and a SCSI adapter card wihtin the bottom slot. Because PCMCIA cards support plug-and-play, they make it very easy for you to install new hardware.

UNDERSTANDING THE UNIVERSAL SERIAL BUS

In Lesson 28, "Using the Universal Serial Bus (USB)," you will learn how the universal serial bus simplifies the process of connecting devices to a notebook or desktop PC. In general, the universal serial bus eliminates the user's need to configure interrupt-request, DMA, or other hardware settings. Instead, the user simply plugs a USB-based device into the bus by creating a device chain similar to a SCSI chain.

Today, most notebook PCs ship with a universal serial bus connector, and you can purchase USB-based tape drives, modems, monitors, scanners, Zip drives, and more. In the near future, the USB will replace the user's need to install cards into a desktop PC's expansion slots or PCMCIA cards into a notebook PC.

LET PEOPLE KNOW THE NOTEBOOK PC IS YOURS

If you travel with your notebook PC, make sure that you have a name-and-address tag on your notebook PC's carrying bag. In addition, create a text file named REWARD that you place in your disk's root directory. Place text similar to the following within the file:

```
************************* R E W A R D *************************

Please call John Smith at the phone number below to claim your
reward for locating this PC:

        John Smith              702-555-1212
        115 Main Street         Fax: 702-555-1212
        Las Vegas, NV 89105     Email: jsmith@provider.com


Thank you very much for your prompt response. John Smith

*************************************************************
```

USING A DOCKING STATION

Notebook PCs are wonderful because they let you take your work with you anywhere you go. The disadvantage of a notebook PC is the small size of the screen and keyboard. Because users who work at a PC all day want to work with a larger screen and keyboard, many turn to a docking station as a less expensive alternative than buying a second PC.

In short, a docking station provides users with a way to use their notebook PC as the system unit to which they can attach a larger monitor, keyboard, and even multimedia devices. To access these devices, the user simply attaches his or her notebook PC to the docking station. After the notebook PC is connected, the user can work using the larger keyboard and screen. When the user is done working for the day, he or she simply unplugs the notebook PC from the docking station and takes the work with them. Because all the user's work is performed on the notebook PC, the user eliminates his or her need to transfer files between systems. More importantly, because a docking station costs much less than a second system unit, the user saves considerable money.

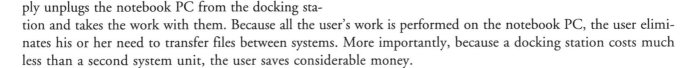

Unfortunately, you cannot connect just any notebook PC to any docking station. Normally, you must purchase a docking station that was designed specifically for your notebook PC. If you are shopping for a notebook PC, take a look at the system's docking bay capabilities.

WHAT YOU MUST KNOW

Although the steps you will perform using a notebook PC will differ from the steps you perform on a desktop PC, most of the upgrade operations this book discusses apply to notebook PCs as well as desktop systems. In Lesson 28, "Using a Universal Serial Bus (USB)," you will examine how the univeral serial bus will eliminate most of the difficulties users face when they install new hardware. Before you continue with Lesson 28, however, make sure that you have learned the following key concepts:

- ✓ At the back of your notebook PC, you will find parallel and serial ports which are identical to those of a desktop PC.

- ✓ Depending on your notebook PC type, you may also find ports that let you connect a mouse, standard keyboard, and monitor to your notebook.

- ✓ To upgrade your notebook PC, you will make extensive use of PCMCIA cards which contain the electronics for a specific device.

- ✓ PCMCIA cards are classified as Type I, II, or III cards based on their thickness.

- ✓ Most notebook PCs provide a PCMCIA slot that can hold two Type I or II cards at the same time or one Type III card.

- ✓ In the near future, notebook PC users will make extensive use of the universal serial bus to connect a variety of devices to their PCs.

- ✓ Using a docking station, you can use your notebook PC as a system unit to which you connect a larger keyboard and monitor.

Lesson 28

Using a Universal Serial Bus (USB)

In Lesson 8, "Understanding Common Conflicts," you learned that when you install hardware devices within your system, you must be concerned about each device's IRQ and memory settings, otherwise, your devices might conflict and not work. In Lesson 14, "Installing a SCSI Adapter," you learned that by connecting high-speed devices to a SCSI device chain, you could minimize many hardware conflicts. However, when you use SCSI devices, you must still consider each device's SCSI address, and each time you install or move a device, you must shutdown and restart your system.

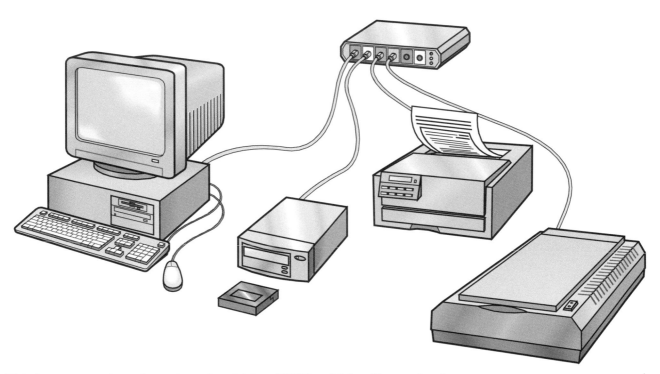

This lesson, examines the universal serial bus (USB), which will soon be the way most users connect most devices to their PC. To connect a device to the universal serial bus, you simply plug the device into a USB port. You do not have worry about device settings and you do not have to shutdown and restart your system. Instead, you can "hot swap" devices, plugging and unplugging devices into and from the bus without affecting your PC or other devices on the bus. By time you finish this lesson, you will understand the following key concepts:

- The universal serial bus is a new PC bus to which you can connect USB-based hardware devices.

- The universal serial bus has sufficient speed (12Mbs) to support most devices.

- If your PC does not have a universal serial bus, you can install a USB port for less than $50.

- Today, users can purchase USB-based mice, keyboards, Zip drives, tape drives, scanners, and more.

- To connect a device to the universal serial bus, you simply plug the device into a USB port. You do not have to worry about device settings such as an interrupt request (IRQ) line. Also, you can plug devices into the universal serial bus without shutting down and restarting your PC.

- Before your PC can use a USB-based device, you must install device-driver software on your system.

- Using the universal serial bus, you can attach up to 127 devices to your PC.

CONNECTING A DEVICE TO A UNIVERSAL SERIAL BUS

The universal serial bus lets you form a device chain, much like the SCSI device chain discussed in Lesson 14. If you are using a newer notebook PC, your PC quite likely has one or more universal serial bus ports. Using your PC's universal serial bus port, you can directly connect a device such as a USB-based scanner to your PC. If you examine external devices the next time you are at the computer store, you will find that you can now buy USB-based Zip drives, printers, tape drives, scanners, mice, and much more. If you are using a newer desktop PC, your PC may also have two USB ports. If your desktop PC does not have USB ports, you can install a USB-adapter card (which you can buy for less than $50) into your PC.

Using a universal serial bus, you can connect up to 127 devices to your PC. If you have more USB-based devices than you have USB ports on your PC, you can buy a USB hub, which you connect to your PC's USB port and then to each device.

To connect a device to a universal serial bus, you simply plug in the device. You do not have to shutdown and later restart your system as you do with a SCSI device. Likewise, you do not have to worry about configuring the device's IRQ and memory settings. Instead, you simply plug the device in. Then, you must install a device-driver for the device on your PC. When you purchase a USB-based device, the device should come with a floppy disk or CD-ROM that contains the device driver you must install.

HOW THE UNIVERSAL SERIAL BUS WORKS

The universal serial bus lets you create a device chain by connecting devices to USB hubs and then hubs

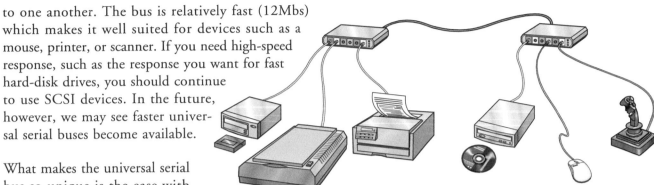

to one another. The bus is relatively fast (12Mbs) which makes it well suited for devices such as a mouse, printer, or scanner. If you need high-speed response, such as the response you want for fast hard-disk drives, you should continue to use SCSI devices. In the future, however, we may see faster universal serial buses become available.

What makes the universal serial bus so unique is the ease with which you can connect devices to the bus—you simply plug the device in. If you need to move a device from one PC to the next, you can simply unplug the device from one PC's USB and then plug the device into the second PC's USB, while both systems are running! (You must have previously installed the device's device driver on both systems.)

The universal serial bus uses software to manage devices on the bus. When your PC needs to send a request to a device, your PC sends a packet down the bus to the device. Although the packet may pass by other devices that are connected to the bus, only the device to which the packet was sent responds to the packet. In other words, to communicate with devices, the universal serial bus relies on software protocols and packets, in much the same way information moves across the Internet.

WHAT YOU MUST KNOW

Throughout this book, you have learned ways to install hardware devices within your PC. In the future, hardware installations will become much easier as users take advantage of the universal serial bus. This lesson introduced the universal serial bus, which lets your PC connect up to 127 devices.

In Lesson 29, "Using Infrared (IR) Devices," you will examine various wireless devices. Before you continue with Lesson 29, however, make sure you understand the following key concepts:

✓ The universal serial bus is a new PC bus to which you can connect USB-based hardware devices. Using a universal serial bus, you can attach up to 127 devices to your PC.

✓ Most newer PCs (both notebook and desktop PCs) provide two universal serial bus ports. To attach a USB-based device, you simply plug the device into the port.

✓ The advantage of the universal serial bus is its ease of use. The universal serial bus eliminates your need to worry about device settings such as IRQs.

✓ You can attach devices to the universal serial bus without shutting down and restarting your PC. To use a device, however, you must install a device driver for the device on your PC.

✓ The universal serial bus supports a variety of devices that include mice, keyboards, Zip drives, tape drives, and scanners.

Lesson 29

Understanding Infrared (IR) Devices

If you are like most users, one side of your desk hides the myriad of cables that connect devices to your PC. For many users, their ability to cable their PC devices dictates where they can position their desk. Then, after they put the PC on their desk, the PC's mouse and keyboard cables contribute to the desk's clutter. In this lesson, you will examine wireless devices that communicate using an infrared (IR) signal or radio waves. By the time you finish this lesson, you will understand the following key concepts:

- One way to remove clutter from your desk is to use an infrared keyboard and mouse.

- If you must regularly exchange files between two PCs, and the PCs are not connected to a network, you may find it convenient to use an infrared link between the devices.

- Many notebook PCs provide built-in infrared receivers and transmitters. You can also buy a printer that supports infrared communication.

- If you need to share devices within a small office or in your home, you can create a simple wireless network using devices that communicate using radio-wave transmissions.

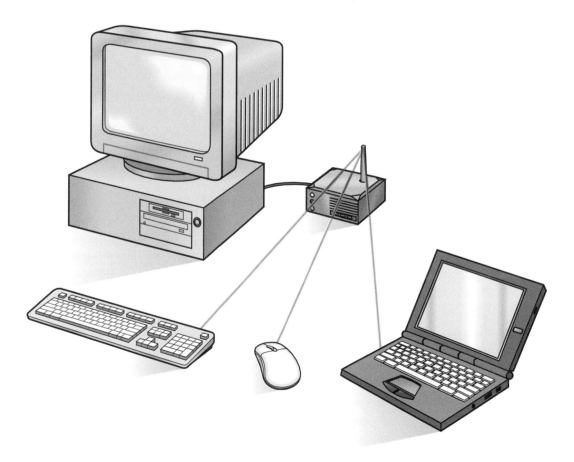

GETTING STARTED WITH IR DEVICES

Possibly without realizing they are using an infrared device, most users take advantage of the infrared technology each time they turn on their TV or change the TV's channel using the remote control. Infrared devices transmit and receive information using a beam of infrared light. To use an infrared device with your PC, your PC must have an infrared receiver. Many users, for example, eliminate the mouse cable from their desk by using an infrared mouse.

Normally, most infrared devices can send and receive data up to a distance of about 20 feet. Like your TV's remote control, you must use batteries to power infrared devices such as a mouse or keyboard. When you purchase an infrared keyboard or mouse (you can buy both for less than $100), you will get a small receiver that you will attach to your PC. If you are using a notebook with a built-in infrared port, you may be able to use that port to send and receive infrared data to or from a device. In fact, depending on your notebook PC type, you may have an infrared serial port and an infrared parallel port (which you can use to send data to a printer that supports an infrared interface).

USING THE CONTROL PANEL INFRARED ICON

If you are using Windows 98, you can use Control Panel Infrared icon to configure your PC's infrared ports. When you double-click your mouse on the Infrared icon, Windows will display the Infrared Monitor dialog box, as shown in Figure 29.1.

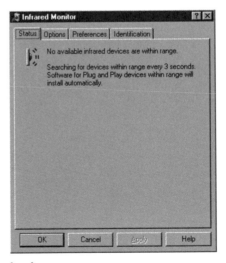

Figure 29.1 *The Infrared Monitor dialog box.*

Within the Infrared Monitor dialog box, click your mouse on the Options tab. Windows, in turn, will display the Options sheet, that you can use to configure your system's infrared settings. For example, if you do not plan to use infrared devices, you can disable Windows 98 infrared support (which will improve your system performance because Windows will not spend time searching for infrared devices). You can also use the Infrared Monitor dialog box to control whether or not Windows 98 displays an icon for the Infrared Monitor on your taskbar and you can use it to define your network identification. Using infrared connections, you can create a simple network.

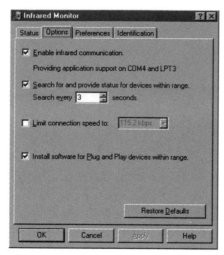

Figure 29.2 *The Infrared Monitor dialog box Options sheet.*

EXCHANGING FILES USING AN INFRARED LINK

Many users have a desktop PC that is home to many of their files and a notebook PC they use when they travel. Often, users must exchange files between such systems. If each system has a network card, you can exchange files across the network. Likewise, if you have external Zip drive, you may connect the drive to one system, copy files to the Zip disk, and then move the drive to the second system, as discussed in Lesson 16, "Installing a Zip

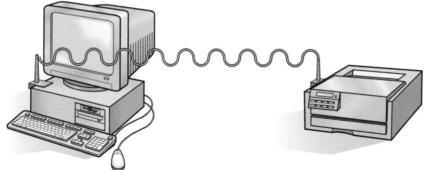

Drive." However, if your notebook and desktop PC support infrared operations, you can use the Windows Direct Connection utility to create an infrared link between the systems, over which you can exchange files. For more information on the Windows Direct Connection utility, turn to the book *1001 Windows 98 Tips*, Jamsa Press, 1998.

TAKING ADVANTAGE OF OTHER WIRELESS DEVICES

Infrared devices are ideal for situations for which the devices reside in the same room (infrared devices must see one another to communicate). If you are in a small office or house, you can use wireless devices (radio-wave-based devices as opposed to infrared devices) to create a simple network. Such devices use radio waves to communicate and can even do so through walls and ceilings. In most cases, the devices can send data up to 150 feet (which means the devices will work well in most houses). Depending on your needs, you can use a radio-based device to share a printer (such as a fast laser printer), or you can install a wireless local-area network, which you can use to share files and other resources. In the near future, many households will take advantage of wireless network technologies.

What You Must Know

In this lesson, you examined how using infrared ports, your PC can communicate with devices such as mouse, keyboard, printer, and even another PC. You also learned how to use radio-wave-based devices to share resources within a small office or a house.

In Lesson 30, "Understanding Device Drivers," you will learn that when you install a hardware device, you normally must install special software on your system called a device driver that lets your operating system (Windows or MS-DOS) communicate with the device. Before you continue with Lesson 30, however, make sure you have learned the following key concepts:

✓ Using infrared devices, such as a keyboard or mouse, you can reduce cable clutter from your desk.

✓ In addition to using infrared links with a keyboard, mouse, and printer, you can use an infrared connection to establish a simple network between two PCs.

✓ Infrared devices require a line of sight with one another. In other words, they must see one another in order to communicate.

✓ Many notebook PCs provide built-in infrared receivers and transmitters. Your notebook PC, for example, might have both an infrared serial and parallel port.

✓ If you need to share devices within a small office or in your home, you can create a simple wireless network using devices that communicate using radio-wave transmissions.

Section Four

SOFTWARE UPGRADES

Software upgrades are often more subtle than hardware upgrades. While it is easy to see (or hear) a new hard drive, for example, it is more difficult to notice the doubling of your disk's storage capacity through a program such as DBLSPACE, even though you might actually get more storage space from the software upgrade. You will find that software upgrades are generally less expensive than hardware upgrades, and they have no moving parts! Software upgrades are necessary for you to take full advantage of the power of your computer—without software, hardware isn't very useful. The lessons presented in this section include the following:

Lesson 30 *Understanding Device Drivers*

Lesson 31 *Telling Windows about Your Upgrade*

Lesson 32 *Installing New Software*

Lesson 33 *Improving Disk Performance with a Disk Cache*

Lesson 34 *Doubling Your Disk's Storage Capacity*

Lesson 35 *Installing MS-DOS Memory Management Software*

Lesson 36 *Defragmenting Your Hard Disk*

Lesson 37 *Fine-Tuning Windows' Memory Use*

Lesson 38 *Cleaning Up Your Existing Disk Space*

Lesson 39 *Troubleshooting with MSD*

Lesson 40 *Using the Windows 95 Device Manager*

Lesson 41 *Monitoring Windows 95 Performance*

Lesson 42 *Basic Troubleshooting Tips*

Lesson 30

Understanding Device Drivers

When you install different hardware components, you often must install special software, called a *device driver*, which must be in place before Windows or MS-DOS can recognize and use the device. If your hardware requires a special device driver, you will normally receive software on a floppy disk or CD-ROM in that box that accompanies your device. This lesson examines the steps you must perform to install and update a device driver under Windows 95 and 98 as well as MS-DOS. If you are using MS-DOS, you direct MS-DOS to load device-driver software into your computer's memory each time your computer starts using a special file named *CONFIG.SYS*. If you are using Windows 95 or 98, you can normally ignore the *CONFIG.SYS* file. (The only time Windows uses the file is when you open an MS-DOS window.)

By the time you finish this lesson, you will understand the following:

- A device driver is special software that lets your operating system (Windows or MS-DOS) recognize and use a hardware device.

- Before you can use a device, your operating system must load device-driver software into your computer's memory.

- To load device-driver software using MS-DOS, you place special entries in the *CONFIG.SYS* file.

- If you change the *CONFIG.SYS*, you must restart MS-DOS for the changes to take effect.

- If you are using Windows 95 or 98, you can normally ignore the *CONFIG.SYS* file.

INSTALLING DEVICE-DRIVER SOFTWARE UNDER WINDOWS 95 OR 98

If you are using Windows 95 or 98, the easiest way for you to install your device-driver software is to use the Add New Hardware Wizard discussed in Lesson 31, "Telling Windows About Your Hardware Upgrade." The Windows installation CD-ROM contains a very large number of device drivers for a myriad of devices. In most cases, the Windows CD-ROM will contain the device-driver files you need for your common devices, such as your keyboard, mouse, and printer.

When you purchase a new hardware device (such as a modem or scanner), you will normally find a CD-ROM, in the box which accompanies your device, that contains a Windows device driver. In such cases, the documentation that accompanies your device will specify the steps you must perform to install the driver.

VIEWING DEVICE DRIVER INFORMATION UNDER WINDOWS 95 OR 98

As you troubleshoot system errors, there will be times when you must determine which version of a device driver you are currently running. Within Windows 95 and 98, you can use the Device Manager, discussed in Lesson 40, "Using the Windows Device Manager," to display specifics about a device driver, by performing these steps:

1. Select the Start menu Settings option and choose Control Panel. Windows, in turn, will open the Control Panel folder.

2. Within the Control Panel folder, double-click your mouse on the System icon. Windows will display the System Properties dialog box.

3. Within the System Properties dialog box, click your mouse on the Device Manager tab. Windows will display the Device Manager.

4. Within the Device Manager, click your mouse on the device you desire and then click your mouse on Properties. Windows, in turn, will display the Properties dialog box.

5. Within the Properties dialog box, click your mouse on the Drivers tab (if one is present). Windows will display specifics about the device driver software.

UPDATING A DEVICE DRIVER UNDER WINDOWS 95 OR 98

When you experience device errors, there may be times when you must update the device's device-driver software. In some cases, you will receive a floppy disk that contains a setup program that you can run to install the device. At other times, you can download a new driver from the device manufacturer's Web site. In addition, if you are using Windows 98, you may be able use the Windows Update Wizard (depending on the driver you are trying to update) to download a new driver from the Microsoft Web site. To use the Windows Update Wizard, you first connect your PC to the Internet. Then, you can normally select the Windows Update option from your Start menu. Windows, in turn, will launch your Web browser and will connect you to the Microsoft Web site. The Windows Update Wizard will then examine the software on your system to determine if the Web site contains newer versions. If a newer version is avaiable, you can download the version from across the Web.

In addition, in the previous section, you learned how to view device-driver information within the Windows Device Manager. If you are using Windows 98, you can direct the Device Manager to update using Windows Update. For more information on Windows Update, turn to the book *1001 Windows 98 Tips*, Jamsa Press, 1998.

VIEWING A LIST OF THE WINDOWS 95 OR 98 DEVICE DRIVERS

Each time Windows 95 or 98 starts, it creates a log file within your disk's root directory named *Bootlog.TXT* within which it records a list of the device drivers it is loading. The file is a hidden file, which means, it does not normally appear within a directory listing. To view the file's contents, you can use the Notepad editor or you can simply use the TYPE command from the MS-DOS prompt. Should your system fail to start, you can use the log file to determine which driver is causing the error:

```
C:\> TYPE  \Bootlog.TXT <ENTER>
```

VIEWING THE CONTENTS OF YOUR MS-DOS CONFIG.SYS FILE

Each time MS-DOS starts, it searches your disk's root directory for a special file named *CONFIG.SYS*. If MS-DOS locates the file, it uses the entries the file contains to configure your system. If MS-DOS does not find the file, it uses its default settings. To display the contents of your *CONFIG.SYS* file, first select the root directory using the DOS CHDIR command, as follows:

```
C:\WINDOWS> CHDIR  \  <ENTER>
C:\>
```

Next, use the EDIT command to display your file's contents:

```
C:\> EDIT  CONFIG.SYS  <ENTER>
```

In most cases, EDIT will display a screen full of entries, similar to those shown in Figure 30.

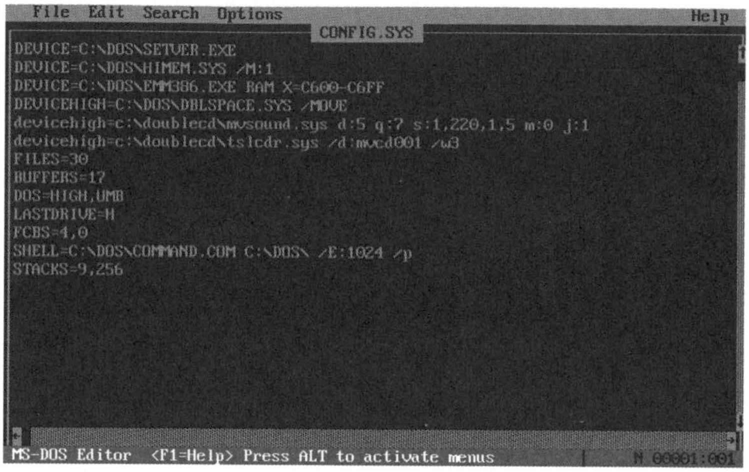

```
   File Edit  Search  Options                                    Help
                              CONFIG.SYS
   DEVICE=C:\DOS\SETVER.EXE
   DEVICE=C:\DOS\HIMEM.SYS /M:1
   DEVICE=C:\DOS\EMM386.EXE RAM X=C600-C6FF
   DEVICEHIGH=C:\DOS\DBLSPACE.SYS /MOVE
   devicehigh=c:\doublecd\mvsound.sys d:5 q:7 s:1,220,1,5 m:0 j:1
   devicehigh=c:\doublecd\tslcdr.sys /d:mvcd001 /w3
   FILES=30
   BUFFERS=17
   DOS=HIGH,UMB
   LASTDRIVE=H
   FCBS=4,0
   SHELL=C:\DOS\COMMAND.COM C:\DOS\ /E:1024 /p
   STACKS=9,256



   MS-DOS Editor  <F1=Help> Press ALT to activate menus        N 00001:001
```

Figure 30 *Viewing CONFIG.SYS entries with EDIT.*

If your system has a *CONFIG.SYS* file, use EDIT's File menu Print option to print the file's contents. Then, place the printout in a safe location. If a new entry in your *CONFIG.SYS* file one day keeps your system from starting, you can use this printout of the file's contents to restore working entries. For now, leave the file's contents unchanged. Use the File menu's Exit option to exit EDIT to the MS-DOS prompt. As you will learn, when you install different hardware components, there may be times when you must load special software, called a device driver, into your computer's memory, before MS-DOS can use your devcie. To load the device driver, you normally place an entry in your *CONFIG.SYS* file. Device drivers are stored in files on disk, much like programs. Most device drivers use the *SYS* extension, such as *MOUSE.SYS*.

UNDERSTANDING *MS-DOS CONFIG.SYS* ENTRIES

When you examine your CONFIG.SYS file, you may find that the *CONFIG.SYS* file consists of several single-line entries, as shown here:

```
DEVICE=C:\DOS\HIMEM.SYS
DEVICE=C:\DOS\EMM386.EXE NOEMS
DOS=HIGH,UMB
BUFFERS=4
FILES=40
LASTDRIVE=Z
PROMPT $P$G
DEVICEHIGH=C:\DOS\ANSI.SYS
DEVICEHIGH=C:\DOS\DBLSPACE.SYS /MOVE
SHELL=C:\DOS\COMMAND.COM C:\DOS\   /p
```

For now, do not worry about each entry's purpose. Instead, keep in mind that each entry uses a single line. When MS-DOS starts, it reads these entries and uses their settings to configure itself in memory.

INSTALLING A DEVICE DRIVER UNDER MS-DOS

In most cases, the documentation that accompanies your hardware board will include instructions that specify the steps you should perform to install the corresponding MS-DOS device driver. To begin, you will normally edit your *CONFIG.SYS* file and place a DEVICE (or DEVICEHIGH) entry within the file. Assume, for example, that you want to install the *ANSI.SYS* device driver file, which resides in the *DOS* directory. To install this driver, you would place the following entry in your *CONFIG.SYS* file:

```
DEVICE=C:\DOS\ANSI.SYS
```

As you can see, the DEVICE entry specifies the complete directory path to the device driver file which, in this case, is *C:\DOS*.

Note: *When you edit your CONFIG.SYS file, do not use a word processor. As you know, word processors let you format text, possibly using* **bold,** *underlined,* *or justified text. To perform these operations, word processors embed special hidden characters within your document. Although these characters are meaningful to your word processor, they will not be meaningful to DOS within your CONFIG.SYS file. As a result, errors will occur when DOS tries to read the file's contents. To edit your CONFIG.SYS file, use an ASCII text editor, such as the EDIT command provided with DOS.*

In some cases, your instructions may tell you to copy the device driver from a floppy disk to your hard disk. To simplify their instructions, some vendors will tell you to copy the file to your hard disk (usually your root directory, DOS directory, or a separate sound-card driver directory). For example, assume that you are installing a new mouse. Your installation notes tell you to copy the file *MOUSE.SYS* from the floppy disk in drive A to the root directory of your hard disk. To do so, you would use the COPY command, as follows:

```
C:\> COPY    A:MOUSE.SYS   *.*    <ENTER>
```

After the COPY command completes, you could install the device driver in your *CONFIG.SYS* file using the following entry:

```
DEVICE=MOUSE.SYS
```

Because the device driver resides in the hard disk's root directory, you did not need to precede the filename with a directory path.

Most users, however, like to keep their disk's root directory relatively clutter-free. Rather than copying the file to your disk's root directory, you should first create a directory to hold the driver file (or you may have a directory for drivers). In this case, for example, you might create a directory named *MOUSE* using the MKDIR command, as follows:

```
C:\> MKDIR   \MOUSE   <ENTER>
```

Next, you can copy the file from the floppy disk in drive A to the directory using this COPY command:

```
C:\> COPY   A:MOUSE.SYS   C:\MOUSE\*.*   <ENTER>
```

Within your *CONFIG.SYS* file, you would use the following DEVICE entry to install the device driver:

```
DEVICE=C:\MOUSE\MOUSE.SYS
```

As you can see, the entry specifies the complete pathname to the file. After you place the DEVICE entry into your *CONFIG.SYS* file, you must restart your system for the change to take effect (make sure you have saved all work in progress and exited any running programs). To restart MS-DOS, exit all programs and press the CTRL-ALT-DEL keyboard combination.

UNDERSTANDING *DEVICE* VERSUS *DEVICEHIGH*

If you examine the *CONFIG.SYS* entries presented earlier in this lesson, you will find that some entries use the DEVICE entry, while others use DEVICEHIGH:

```
DOS=HIGH,UMB
DEVICE=C:\DOS\HIMEM.SYS
DEVICE=C:\DOS\EMM386.EXE  NOEMS
BUFFERS=4
FILES=40
DEVICEHIGH=C:\DOS\ANSI.SYS
DEVICEHIGH=C:\DOS\DBLSPACE.SYS  /MOVE
SHELL=C:\DOS\COMMAND.COM C:\DOS\   /p
```

Both the DEVICE and DEVICEHIGH entries let you install a device driver. The difference between the two entries is the location in memory that MS-DOS uses to install the driver. Lesson 35, "Installing MS-DOS Memory Management Software," discusses MS-DOS memory management in detail. Within Lesson 35, you will learn that the DEVICEHIGH entry lets you install a device driver into the upper-memory area, which MS-DOS normally reserves for your hardware devices. By installing device drivers into this area, you can free up memory for use by your MS-DOS-based programs. Before you can use the DEVICEHIGH entry, you must configure MS-DOS to support the upper-memory area. For more information on memory management, turn to Lesson 33.

INSTALLING AN *MS-DOS* DEVICE DRIVER USING *AUTOEXEC.BAT*

Most of the device drivers you will install will use DEVICE entries within the *CONFIG.SYS* file, as just discussed. In some cases, however, a device driver is installed using a MS-DOS command (a program). In such cases, you will install the device driver command (or the installation program might do this for you automatically) within the special batch file named *AUTOEXEC.BAT*.

Like the *CONFIG.SYS* file, *AUTOEXEC.BAT* resides in your disk's root directory. Using the following TYPE command, you can display the file's contents:

```
C:\> TYPE   AUTOEXEC.BAT   <ENTER>
```

To place an entry within the *AUTOEXEC.BAT* file, you can use the EDIT command as previously discussed. You can also use EDIT to print a copy of the file's contents. Prior to each change you make to the *AUTOEXEC.BAT* file (or each software installation), you should print a copy of the file's contents. In this way, should your system fail to start following the installation, you can quickly determine the new entries within the file.

UNDERSTANDING THE AUTOEXEC.BAT FILE

Each time your system starts, MS-DOS searches your disk's root directory for a special batch file named AUTOEXEC.BAT, which contains a list of commands you want MS-DOS to automatically (AUTO) execute (EXEC). Commands commonly found in AUTOEXEC.BAT include the PROMPT command, which defines your system prompt; the PATH command, which tells MS-DOS where to locate your program files (within which directories); and device driver entries.

RECOVERING FROM A CONFIG.SYS OR AUTOEXEC.BAT ERROR

When you add a device driver entry to your *CONFIG.SYS* or *AUTOEXEC.BAT* files, there may be times when the driver does not work. Unfortunately, because MS-DOS loads the driver before it displays your system prompt, an errant device driver can sometimes prevent your system from starting. Should you encounter a device driver error that prevents your system from starting, you must start without loading the device driver so that you can edit the corresponding file to correct or remove the device driver entry.

If you are using a version of MS-DOS previous to MS-DOS 6, you must reboot from a floppy disk and then edit your *CONFIG.SYS* or *AUTOEXEC.BAT*.

If you are using MS-DOS 6 or later, you can direct MS-DOS to alter its normal system startup operations by pressing the F5 or F8 function keys immediately after MS-DOS displays the following message on your screen display:

```
Starting MS-DOS . . .
```

If, when this message appears, you press the **F5** function key, MS-DOS will bypass the *CONFIG.SYS* and *AUTOEXEC.BAT* processing, displaying instead, the DOS prompt.

When you bypass *CONFIG.SYS* and *AUTOEXEC.BAT* processing by pressing F5, MS-DOS will start a minimal system. You will not have a complete command path defined. Likewise, you cannot open more than three files at any given time. Bypassing the system startup in this way provides you with an opportunity to correct errors within *CONFIG.SYS* or *AUTOEXEC.BAT*.

Assume, for example, that an entry in your *CONFIG.SYS* file is causing an error that hangs your system. To correct the error, restart your system. When MS-DOS displays its starting message, press the F5 function key. MS-DOS will start, displaying its prompt. Next, use the following command to edit the contents of your *CONFIG.SYS* file:

```
C:\> \DOS\EDIT  CONFIG.SYS   <ENTER>
```

You should note that the command includes a complete pathname for the MS-DOS EDIT command. When you bypass *CONFIG.SYS* and *AUTOEXEC.BAT* processing, you bypass your PATH command (in *AUTOEXEC.BAT*), which establishes a command path. In this case, if you use an editor other than EDIT, you will need to first change to the directory that contains the editor or you must specify a complete pathname. After you correct the *CONFIG.SYS* entry, restart your system using the CTRL-ALT-DEL keyboard combination.

Note: *When you bypass your CONFIG.SYS and AUTOEXEC.BAT files using the F5 function key, DOS will set your command prompt to display the current drive and directory. Your default PATH will be set to the directory that contains your DOS command files (normally C:\DOS).*

PROCESSING SPECIFIC *CONFIG.SYS* AND *AUTOEXEC.BAT* ENTRIES

As you just learned, pressing the **F5** function key when your system starts directs MS-DOS 6 and later versions not to process *CONFIG.SYS* and *AUTOEXEC.BAT*. In a similar way (in MS-DOS 6 and later), by pressing the **F8** function key when your system starts, you can select specific *CONFIG.SYS* and *AUTOEXEC.BAT* entries for processing. For example, assume that your *CONFIG.SYS* file contains the following entries:

```
FILES=20
BUFFERS=30
DEVICE=C:\DOS\HIMEM.SYS
```

If, when your system starts, you press the **F8** function key, MS-DOS will display a prompt for each entry, asking you if you want to process the entry, as shown here:

```
FILES=20 [Y,N]?
```

If you press **Y**, MS-DOS will process the FILES entry. If you instead press **N**, MS-DOS will ignore the entry, just as if the entry were not in the file. Next, MS-DOS will display a similar prompt for the BUFFERS entry:

```
BUFFERS=30 [Y,N]?
```

MS-DOS will perform this processing for each entry in the *CONFIG.SYS* file. Next, MS-DOS will display the following message asking you if you want to process the *AUTOEXEC.BAT* entries:

```
Process AUTOEXEC.BAT [Y,N]?
```

If you press **Y,** MS-DOS will display a prompt for each command in the *AUTOEXEC.BAT* file, letting you select the commands you want to execute. If you instead press **N**, MS-DOS will not process any of the commands in the *AUTOEXEC.BAT* file.

INSTALLING A DEVICE DRIVER FOR WINDOWS 3.1

If you are using Windows 3.1, you may need to install Windows specific device-driver software beyond the software you installed for MS-DOS. Normally, when you purchase a new hardware device such as a modem or printer, the device will come with a floppy disk that contains a Windows device driver. To install the device driver, you will normally run an installation program that resides on the floppy disk. The installation program, in turn, wil load the software you need. The documentation that accompanied your device will provide you with the instructions you need to perform to install the device driver.

WHAT YOU MUST KNOW

Many hardware devices require you to install device-driver software so that the operating system, Windows or MS-DOS, can recognize and use the device. In this lesson, you learned how to install device drivers within Windows 95 and 98 as well as MS-DOS.

When you install new hardware, there will be times when you will must tell Windows about the new device. In Lesson 31, "Telling Windows About Your Hardware Upgrade," you will examine the steps you must perform to notify Windows of your hardware. Before you continue with Lesson 31, however, make sure you have learned the following key concepts:

✓ A device driver is a special software program that lets the operating system communicate with a specific device. When you install a new card within your computer, such as for a scanner or mouse, you must install device driver software before your computer can use the device.

✓ Within Windows 95 or 98, you can install a device driver by running a special setup program that comes on a disk (floppy or CD-ROM) that accompanies your device or you can use the Windows Add New Hardware Wizard, discussed in Lesson 31.

✓ If you are using Windows 98, you can use the Windows Update Wizard to download and install drivers from the Microsoft Web site.

✓ To install device-driver software under MS-DOS, you either place a DEVICE entry within the *CONFIG.SYS* file or a command within the special batch file *AUTOEXEC.BAT*. In many cases, the installation program that accompanies your card will perform these operations for you.

✓ If you make a change to your *CONFIG.SYS* or *AUTOEXEC.BAT* file that causes an error that prevents your system from starting, you can press the **F5** function key when you first start your system to direct MS-DOS 6 or later to ignore *CONFIG.SYS* and *AUTOEXEC.BAT*. Earlier versions of MS-DOS require you to reboot from a boot floppy.

Lesson 31

Telling Windows about Your Hardware Upgrade

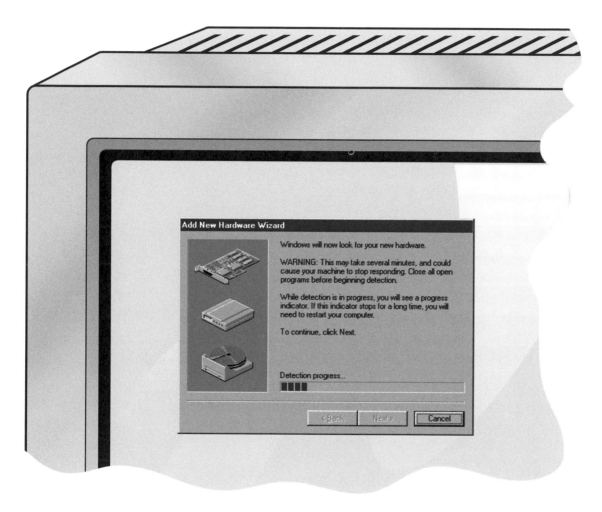

As you have learned, a device driver is a special software program that lets your operating system (Windows or MS-DOS) communicate with (use) a hardware device. In Lesson 30, "Understanding Device Drivers," you learned how to install Windows and MS-DOS device drivers. This lesson examines the steps you must perform to notify Windows about your hardware upgrades. By the time you finish this lesson, you will understand the following key concepts:

- Windows 95 and 98 will often recognize your hardware upgrade immediately after you restart your system

- If Windows 95 or 98 does not recognize that you have installed new hardware, you must run the Add Hardware Wizard

- How to use the Setup program to inform Windows 3.1 of a change to your video, keyboard, mouse, or network

- How to use the Windows 3.1 Control Panel Drivers icon to install device drivers for use with a sound card or video player

TELLING WINDOWS 95 AND 98 ABOUT NEW HARDWARE

Normally, Windows 95 and 98 makes it very easy for you to install the software they need to support new hardware. In fact, normally, when you restart your system, Windows will recognize your new hardware and will start a Wizard which will walk you through the software installation process. If, for some reason, Windows does not recognize your new hardware, you can use the Add New Hardware Wizard to walk you through the installation of your software. To run the Add New Hardware Wizard, perform these steps:

1. Select the Start menu Settings option and choose Control Panel. Windows, in turn, will open the Control Panel window.

2. Within the Control Panel window, double-click your mouse on the Add New Hardware icon. Windows will start the Add New Hardware Wizard, which, in turn, will display a dialog box that describes its purpose briefly.

3. Click your mouse on the Next button. The Wizard will display a dialog box asking you if you want it to detect new hardware devices.

4. Select Yes and click your mouse on the Next button. The Wizard, in turn, will display a dialog box that states its processing may take several minutes.

5. Select Next. The Wizard will start its hardware detection, examining your system's hardware as shown in Figure 31.1.

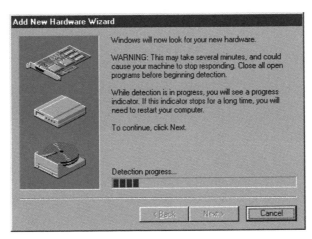

Figure 31.1 *The Add New Hardware Wizard's hardware detection process.*

6. When the Wizard completes its detection process, it will display a dialog box within which you can view a list of the devices the Wizard detected by clicking your mouse on the Details button.

7. To direct the Wizard to install support for the devices, select Finish. Depending on the hardware the Wizard detected, the Wizard may prompt you to install the Windows CD-ROM or the program's setup disks.

8. After the Wizard installs the software, the Wizard may display a message telling you that it must restart your system for the changes to take effect. Select Yes to restart your system.

USING THE WINDOWS 3.1 SETUP COMMAND

If you are using Windows 3.1 and you have upgraded your video card, keyboard, or mouse, or added a network, you inform Windows 3.1 of the change using the Setup program. As Figure 31.2 shows, the Setup program icon resides within the Program Manager's Main window.

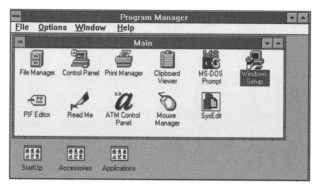

Figure 31.2 *The Setup icon resides in the Program Manager's Main window.*

When you double-click your mouse on the Setup icon, Windows will display the Windows Setup dialog box, as shown in Figure 31.3.

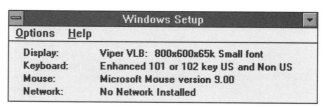

Figure 31.3 *The Windows Setup dialog box.*

The Setup dialog box displays your current display, keyboard, mouse, and network settings. To change a setting, select the Options menu and choose the Change System Settings option. Windows, in turn, will display the Change System Settings dialog box, as shown in Figure 31.4.

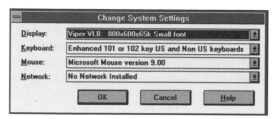

Figure 31.4 *The Change System Settings dialog box.*

The Change System Settings dialog box presents four pull-down lists. To display a pull-down list of setting options, click your mouse on the down arrow:

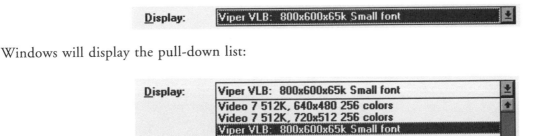

Windows will display the pull-down list:

Using your keyboard arrow keys, or by clicking your mouse on the scroll bar, you can scroll through the available options. If you find the option that matches your new hardware, highlight the option and click on the OK button.

Depending on the maker of the hardware board you installed, there may be times when you cannot find a matching item within the options list. In such cases, you must install a software driver which your hardware manufacturer should have provided on floppy disk. To do so, scroll through the list of options until you encounter the option that requires a floppy from the OEM:

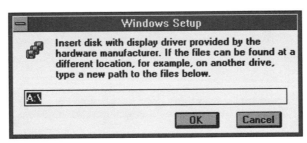

When you select this option, Windows will display the Windows Setup dialog box shown in Figure 31.5, which prompts you to insert the floppy in drive A.

Figure 31.5 *The Windows Setup dialog box prompting for a floppy.*

Insert the disk that contains the driver and select OK. Windows, in turn, will load the corresponding device driver.

Note: If the disks you received from the manufacturer are not labeled, search each disk's directory for a file named OEMSETUP.INF. The file contains the information Windows needs to install the driver.

USING THE WINDOWS 3.1 CONTROL PANEL'S DRIVERS PROGRAM

If you install a sound card, you will need to use the Control Panel Drivers icon, shown in Figure 31.6, to tell Windows 3.1 about your installation.

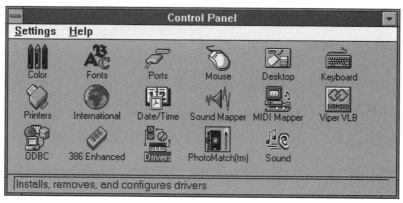

Figure 31.6 *The Control Panel's Drivers icon.*

When you double-click your mouse on the Drivers icon, Windows will display the Drivers dialog box, as shown in Figure 31.7.

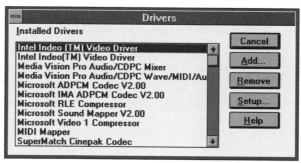

Figure 31.7 *The Drivers dialog box.*

The Drivers dialog box lists the sound and video player drivers currently installed on your system. To add a new driver, select the Add button. Windows will display the Add dialog box, as shown in Figure 31.8.

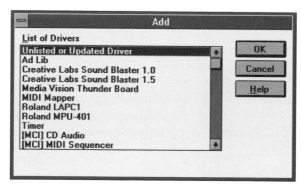

Figure 31.8 *The Add dialog box.*

If an option matches your new hardware, highlight the option and choose OK. Windows may then display a dialog box that prompts you to insert one of your Windows floppy disks. Insert the correct floppy and press ENTER. If you do not find a matching device, select the Unlisted or Updated Driver option. Windows will display a dialog box prompting you to insert into drive A, the floppy disk that came with your hardware. Insert the disk and press ENTER.

WHAT YOU MUST KNOW

When you install new hardware, there will be times when you must inform Windows. In this lesson, you have learned how to inform Windows 95 and 98 of your hardware changes using the Add New Hardware Wizard. In addition, if you are using Windows 3.1, you learned how to use the Windows Setup and Control Panel programs to inform Windows of your new hardware.

Much of this book's discussion has focused on installing new hardware components. As it turns out, many users have a more difficult time installing new software programs. Lesson 32, "Installing New Software" examines the steps that are common to most software installations. Before you continue with Lesson 32, however, make sure that you understand the following key concepts:

- ✓ When you install new hardware, there may be times when you must inform Windows.

- ✓ If you are using Windows 95 or 98, the easiest way to install software support for your new hardware is to use the Add New Hardware Wizard.

- ✓ If you are using Windows 3.1, you can use the Windows Setup program to inform Windows of a change to your video, keyboard, mouse, or network.

- ✓ If you are using Windows 3.1, you can use the Control Panel Drivers icon to install a device driver for a sound card or video player.

Lesson 32

Installing New Software

By reading this book, you have taken a big step and have begun performing your own hardware upgrades. As you have learned so far, upgrade operations are actually quite easy. Equally as important is your ability to install your own software. As you will find, software installations are normally very straightforward. After you get one or two software installations under your belt, you will be well on your way to controlling your software.

This lesson examines the steps you should perform to install software on your disk. By the time you finish this lesson, you will understand the following key concepts:

- You cannot break your computer by installing software.

- You should always back up your disk before performing a major software upgrade.

- Most software programs use a program named SETUP to perform the installation.

- Using Windows 95 or 98, you can use the Add/Remove Software Wizard to simplify software upgrades.

- Removing software from your disk is harder than installing the software.

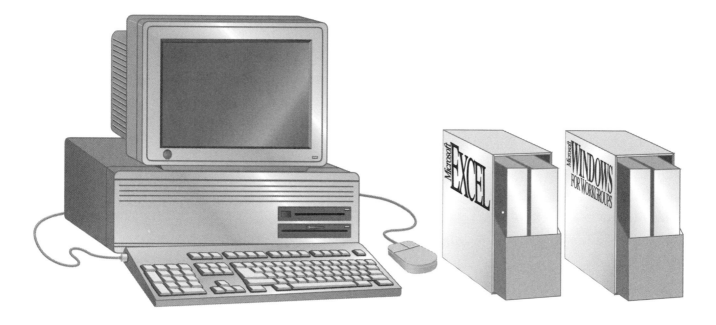

STARTING AN INSTALLATION

Before you begin a software installation, it is important to understand that you cannot break your computer by installing software onto your computer's disk. In the very worst case, the software will not work, and you will need a more experienced user either help you determine why and help you fix the error, or to remove the software from your disk. As a rule, do not make your first software installation a major program, such as Windows 98 or Office 2000, or the Internet software you must use everyday. If you must install such a program, have an experienced user help you.

Note: Never install a major software program such as Windows 98, or an upgrade to a program you use every day without first backing up your hard disk. In this way, should an error occur, you can quickly restore your disk to its previous contents.

Do not start a software installation without first looking through the installation instructions that accompanied your software. If you are performing your first software installation, you may find the installation a little confusing. What you are looking for is the name of the installation program. Normally, installation programs use a name such as SETUP or INSTALL. Next, depending on whether you are working from Windows or MS-DOS, the steps you will perform to run the installation program will differ. As you perform the software installation, keep the manual by your side.

INSTALLING A PROGRAM FROM WITHIN WINDOWS 95 OR 98

To simplify your software installation, Windows 95 and 98 provides special software called the Add/Remove Programs Wizard that uses dialog boxes to walk you through the installation process. To install software using the Wizard, perform these steps:

1. Select the Start menu Settings option and choose Control Panel. Windows, in turn, will open the Control Panel window.

2. Within the Control Panel window, double-click your mouse on the Add/Remove Programs icon. Windows, in turn, will start the Wizard, displaying the Add/Remove Programs Properties dialog box as shown in Figure 32.1.

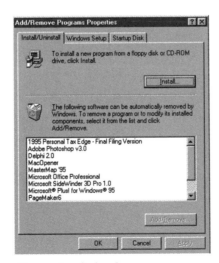

Figure 32.1 The Add/Remove Programs Properties dialog box.

3. Click your mouse on the Install button. The Wizard, in turn, will prompt you to insert the floppy or CD-ROM that contains the program you are installing.

4. Insert the floppy or CD-ROM and click your mouse on Next. The Wizard, in turn, will search the floppy disk or CD-ROM for an installation program. If the Wizard locates the installation program, the Wizard will display a dialog box that contains the installation program name. Otherwise, if the Wizard cannot find an installation program, the Wizard will display a dialog box that prompts you to type in the installation program name.

5. If the Wizard's dialog box is displaying the correct program name, click your mouse on the Finish button to start the installation. Otherwise, type in the correct program name and then select Finish. The Wizard, in turn, will start the program's installation.

INSTALLING A PROGRAM FROM WINDOWS 3.1

If you are installing a Windows-based program, you should perform the software installation from within Windows. In fact, many programs force you to be running Windows. After starting Windows, select the File menu, as shown in Figure 32.2.

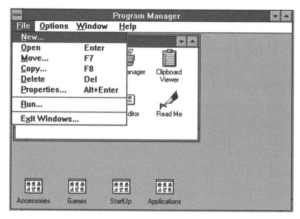

Figure 32.2 *The Windows File menu.*

Select the Run option. Windows will display the Run dialog box. Assuming you are running the SETUP program that resides in drive A, you would type in the program name **A:\SETUP**, as shown in Figure 32.3. After the installation completes, you can run the program by double-clicking the program's icon. If the program provides a tutorial, stop and run it. The time you spend within the tutorial will save you much time and effort in the future.

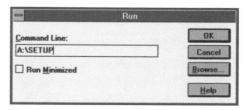

Figure 32.3 *The Windows Run dialog box.*

INSTALLING A PROGRAM FROM DOS

To install an MS-DOS-based program, insert the first installation disk in drive A or B. Next, to start the installation, you normally type in the name of the installation program, preceded by the appropriate drive letter and a colon. For example, assuming the installation program is named SETUP and your installation disk resides in drive A, you would start the installation as follows:

```
C:\> A:SETUP   <ENTER>
```

Most software programs ask you to respond to one or more questions. To simplify the installation, the programs normally provide default answers. In most cases, you can simply use the default responses. After the installation program completes, you might have to restart your computer. In some cases, the installation program will restart your system for you automatically. After the installation is complete, you can run the program by typing its name at the MS-DOS prompt and pressing ENTER. The documentation that accompanied your software will specify the correct command name you should use. If, when you type the program name, MS-DOS displays an error message instead of running the program, MS-DOS most likely could not find the program:

```
C:\> NEWPROG   <ENTER>
Bad command or filename
```

Should this error message occur, double-check that you are using the correct command name and that you are spelling the command name correctly. Next, verify that the program resides in the current directory. If the program resides in a different directory, use the CHDIR command to select that directory. If you have problems running a program that resides in a different directory, you might want to place the program's directory name into the PATH command defined in your *AutoExec.BAT*. For more information on the PATH command, turn to the MS-DOS documentation that accompanied your PC.

BROWSING THE README FILE

Producing software documentation is an expensive and time-consuming process. As a result, almost every software program you install provides a file on disk that contains information that did not get included in the product's documentation. Normally, the file has a name like *ReadMe.TXT*, *Read.Me*, or *ReadMe.DOC*. Search the first installation disk for such a file. Using your word processor, you can normally open the file and print its contents.

REMOVING A PROGRAM FROM YOUR DISK

Over time, there may be times when you want to remove a program file from your disk, normally because you no longer use the program and you now need the disk space. Unfortunately, removing a program can be much harder than installing the program. Often, to remove a program from your disk, you need working knowledge of MS-DOS or Windows.

Note: Always back up the files on your disk before you remove a program. In this way, should you make an error or later wish you had not removed the files, you can quickly restore them.

REMOVING A PROGRAM FROM WITHIN WINDOWS 95 OR 98

To simplify program removal from your disk, many newer programs now provide software that will uninstall the program. In fact, just as Windows 95 and 98 provide a Wizard to help you install a program, Windows provides a Wizard to help you remove progams. Unfortunately, not all programs provide such uninstall capabilities. When you start the Uninstall Wizard, the Wizard will display a list of the programs you uninstall. To start the Uninstall Wizard, perform these steps:

1. Select the Start menu Settings option and choose Control Panel. Windows, in turn, will open the Control Panel window.

2. Within the Control Panel, double-click your mouse on the Add/Remove Programs icon. Windows 95, in turn, will display the Add/Remove Programs Properties dialog box, as shown in Figure 32.4. Within the dialog box, you will find a list of programs you can use the Wizard to uninstall from your system.

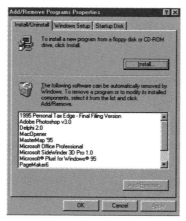

Figure 32.4 *The Add/Remove Programs Properties dialog box.*

3. Within the list of programs, click your mouse on the program you want to uninstall.

4. Click your mouse on the Add/Remove button. The Wizard, in turn, may display one or more dialog boxes asking you to confirm the program removal.

PROGRAMS RESIDE IN DIRECTORIES

When you install a program on your disk, the program is usually placed in its own directory. The best way to visualize a directory is as a filing cabinet drawer, within which only the files related to the program are placed. To remove a program from your disk, you must remove the directory that contains the program files. Before you can delete program files, you must identify the program's directory name. As a general rule, if you do not know how to determine the program's directory name, you should have a more experienced user assist you.

REMOVING A PROGRAM FROM WITHIN WINDOWS 3.1

Removing a program from within Windows 3.1 is a two-step process. To begin, you delete the program icon from within the Program Manager. Second, you must delete the program files and directories from within the File Manager. To delete a program or group icon, single-click (do not double-click) your mouse on the icon to select the icon. Next, press the DEL key. Windows will display a Delete dialog box, similar to that shown in Figure 32.5, asking you to verify that you want to delete the icon. When the dialog box appears, click your mouse on the Yes option to delete the icon.

Figure 32.5 *The Delete dialog box.*

Note: *To delete a program group icon (a program group is a window that holds several program icons), minimize the group window to an icon, highlight the icon, and press **DEL**.*

To delete a program directory from within Windows, run the File Manager, as shown in Figure 32.6.

Figure 32.6 *The Windows File Manager.*

Within the File Manager directory tree, single-click (do not double-click) your mouse on the program's directory. Next, press the DEL key. Windows will display a Delete dialog box similar to that shown in Figure 32.7.

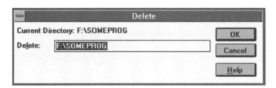

Figure 32.7 *The Delete dialog box.*

Select the OK option. Windows, in turn, will display the Confirm Directory Delete dialog box shown in Figure 32.8. Select the Yes to All button. When the delete operation completes, use the File menu to exit the File Manager.

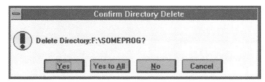

Figure 32.8*The Confirm Directory Delete dialog box.*

REMOVING A PROGRAM FROM YOUR DISK IN DOS

If you are using DOS 6 or later, removing a program's directory from your hard disk is relatively easy. To begin, use the CHDIR command to select the root directory as the current directory:

```
C:\> CHDIR  \   <ENTER>
```

Next, use the DELTREE command to remove the directory. Assuming, for example, that you are deleting a directory named SOMEPROG, you would use the following DELTREE command:

```
C:\> DELTREE  SOMEPROG   <ENTER>
```

If you are not using DOS 6 or later, removing a program from your disk can be more challenging. In fact, you will want an experienced user to assist you. To begin, use the CHDIR command to select the program's directory. In the case of the directory SOMEPROG, use CHDIR as follows:

```
C:\> CHDIR   \SOMEPROG    <ENTER>
C:\SOMEPROG>
```

Make sure that your DOS prompt now shows the name of the directory that you intend to delete. Next, use the DEL command to delete the files each directory contains:

```
C:\SOMEPROG> DEL  *.*  <ENTER>
```

The *.* (pronounced "asterisk dot asterisk" or "star dot star") in the DEL command tells DOS to delete all the files within the directory. Because an errant DEL command that uses *.* can have devastating results, DEL will ask you to verify the operation by displaying the following prompt:

```
All files in directory will be deleted!
Are you sure (Y/N)?
```

If you are sure that the directory is correct, press **Y** to delete the files. Next, use the DIR command to display the directory's contents:

```
C:\SOMEPROG> DIR   <ENTER>
```

If you have successfully deleted all the files the directory contains, your directory listing will appear as follows:

```
C:\SOMEPROG> DIR   <ENTER>

 Volume in drive C has no label
 Volume Serial Number is 1DD2-2667
 Directory of C:\SOMEPROG

.             <DIR>        05-22-96    3:57p
..            <DIR>        05-22-96    3:57p
      2 file(s)              0 bytes
                    87,949,312 bytes free
```

The two entries (. and ..) that appear in the directory listing appear in all subdirectories, whether the subdirectory contains other files or not. If your directory listing only displays these two entries, the directory is empty.

After the directory is empty, use the CHDIR command with two dots (..) to move up one level in the directory tree:

```
C:\SOMEPROG> CHDIR ..  <ENTER>
```

Next, use the RMDIR command to remove the directory:

```
C:\> RMDIR  SOMEPROG  <ENTER>
```

To improve their own file organization, many programs will use additional levels of directories. When you perform a directory listing for such a program, your directory listing will reveal additional entries such as those shown here:

```
C:\SOMEPROG>  DIR    <ENTER>

 Volume in drive C has no label
 Volume Serial Number is 1DD2-2667
 Directory of C:\SOMEPROG

.                 <DIR>         05-22-96    3:57p
..                <DIR>         05-22-96    3:57p
PROGRAMS          <DIR>         05-22-96    3:57p
DATA              <DIR>         05-22-96    3:57p
        4 file(s)              0 bytes
                      87,916,544 bytes free
```

In such cases, you must perform the following steps for each directory listed (as well as lower-level directories contained within each directory):

1. Select the directory using the CHDIR command.

2. Use the DEL command to delete the directory's files.

3. Use the DIR command to display the directory's contents.

4. If the directory is empty, move up one level using the CHDIR command and then use the RMDIR command to remove the directory.

5. If the directory contains additional subdirectories, perform Steps 1 through 5 for each.

What You Must Know

With software changing and being improved so frequently, it is important to know how to upgrade your computer's software. In this lesson, you have learned how to install and remove software from within both Windows and MS-DOS.

One of the easiest ways to improve your system's performance is to install special software called a disk cache, which speeds up many disk operations. Lesson 33, "Improving Disk Performance Using a Disk Cache," examines the steps you must perform to install a disk cache. Before you continue with Lesson 33, however, make sure that you have learned the following key concepts:

✓ You cannot break your computer by installing software. In the worst case, the software will not work, and you must simply remove the software from your disk.

✓ If you are upgrading a program to a new version, you can normally simply install the new software without first removing the previous version.

✓ Most software programs use a program named SETUP or INSTALL to perform the installation. The documentation that accompanied your software will specify the commands you should run to install the software.

✓ In many cases, the latest documentation about a program does not make it into the printed manual. Most software developers, therefore, will include additional information about the product on disk. You can often find help text about a program in a *ReadMe* file that resides on the installation disk.

✓ Removing software from your disk is harder than installing the software. The first time you remove software from your disk, you will want an experienced user to assist you. Make sure you back up the software you are removing before you remove it.

Lesson 33

Improving Disk Performance with a Disk Cache

As you have learned, disks are mechanical devices (with moving parts), which makes them much slower than their electronic counterparts (such as RAM). As several of the lessons in this book have discussed, one of the best ways to improve your system performance is to reduce the number of slow disk read-and-write operations your system must perform. In this lesson, you will learn how to set aside part of your PC's fast random-access memory (RAM) as a disk cache which, in turn, reduces disk operations. By the time you finish this lesson, you will understand the following key concepts:

- Programs read information from disk into your computer's random-access memory

- When a program records information, the program writes the information from memory to disk

- A disk cache is a large buffer in memory that the operating system (Windows or MS-DOS) uses to reduce slow disk operations

- Windows 95 and 98 provides built-in disk caching software

- Using MS-DOS, you can create a disk cache using the SMARTDRV command

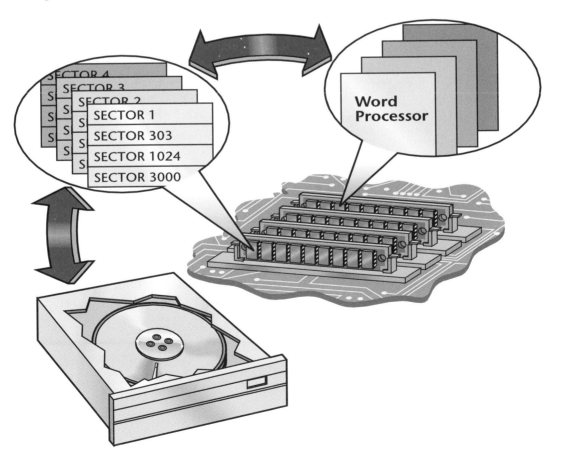

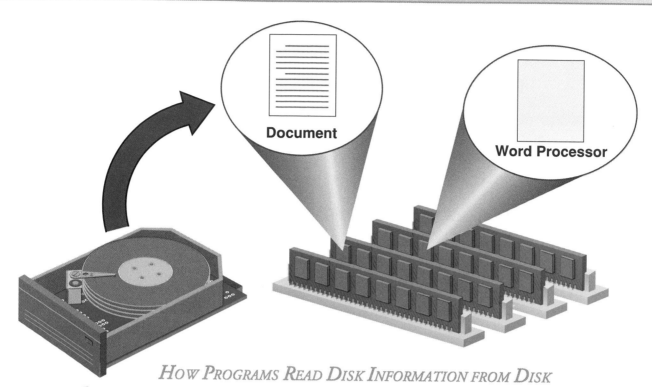

How Programs Read Disk Information from Disk

Document File

As you know, files let you store information from one computer session to the next. To use the information a file contains, programs must read the information from disk into your computer's random-access memory. For example, assume you are editing a file that contains a memo. To do so, your word processor would first read the memo from disk into your PC's RAM. After the data (in this case, the memo document) resides in memory, the program can access it.

When programs read information from disk, they normally only read the information one sector at a time, as the information is needed. If your file resides in four sectors, for example, your word processor might perform four slow disk-read operations.

Programs Read Information into Memory

Before your programs can use information stored on disk, your programs must read the information into your computer's random-access memory. Disks store information in storage locations, called *sectors*. When your programs read data from disk, they read the data one disk sector at a time.

Because disks are mechanical devices, they are much slower than their electronic counterparts. Thus, one way to improve your system performance is to reduce the number of slow disk I/O operations your system must perform. A disk cache provides an easy way to reduce disk I/O operations.

UNDERSTANDING A DISK CACHE

A *cache* is simply a storage location. Before winter, for example, squirrels store their nuts in a cache. A *disk cache* is simply a storage location in your computer's random-access memory into which the operating system reads and stores disk sectors.

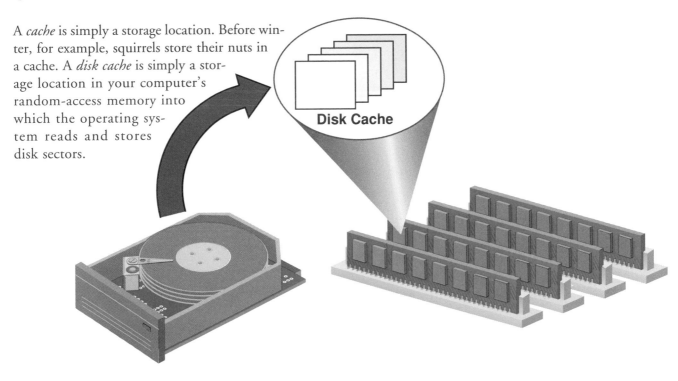

Disk Cache

As you have learned, files are stored on disk within sectors. Normally, programs will read data into memory one sector at a time—a slow process.

When you use a disk cache, the operating system will read extra sectors into the cache during each read operation. When a program needs information stored in subsequent sectors, the operating system might very likely find the information within the disk cache.

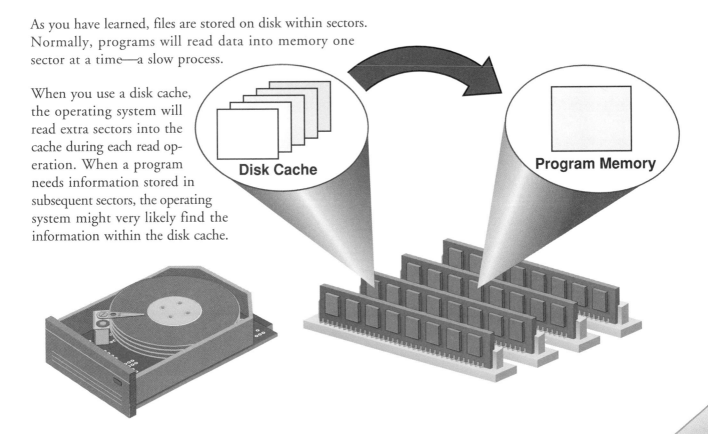

Disk Cache

Program Memory

If the data the program requests resides within the cache, the operating system can quickly access the data from the computer's fast memory, eliminating the need for the slow disk-read operation. If the data is not in the cache, the operating system will read the data from disk.

Some programs, such as a database, may reread the same information from disk. In many cases, such programs will find the data they need within the disk cache. As a result, the programs eliminate slow disk-read operations. If the desired information is not found within the cache, the information is simply read from disk.

USING A DISK CACHE WITHIN WINDOWS 95 OR 98

Windows 95 and 98 make using a disk cache very easy; both build cache support into the operating system itself. Under Windows 95 or 98, you do not have run any other software programs to install a disk cache (MS-DOS, for example, requires that you run the SMARTDRV command to enable caching).

Within both Windows 95 and 98, however, you can control the disk cache settings by performing these steps:

1. Select the Start menu Settings option and choose Control Panel. Windows, in turn, will display the Control Panel window.

2. Within the Control Panel window, double-click your mouse on the System icon. Windows will display the System Properties dialog box.

3. Select the Performance tab. Windows will display the Performance status page.

4. Select the File System button. Windows, in turn, will display the File System Properties dialog box as shown in Figure 33.1.

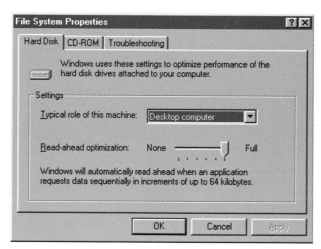

Figure 33.1 *The Windows File System Properties dialog box.*

5. Open the Typical role of this machine pull-down list and select the setting that best describes your computer. Windows will allocate cache settings based on your selection.

6. Using your mouse, drag the Read-ahead optimization slider to select the size of the buffer Windows uses for a disk read-ahead buffer. In general, the faster your PC and hard disk, the larger read-ahead buffer you desire. Likewise, if you work with large files on a regular basis, such as a large database, select a larger read-ahead buffer. Each time you direct Windows to read data from disk, Windows will fill the read-ahead buffer with extra data. Later, when your program needs more information from a file on disk, Windows may find the data in the read-ahead buffer, which eliminates the need for a slow disk-read operation. If you are using a slow system or a slow hard disk, you may want to reduce the disk-buffer size. Otherwise, Windows may spend considerable time doing nothing but reading your disk to keep the buffer full.

7. Click your mouse on the OK button to put your changes into effect.

DISK CACHING UNDER MS-DOS

If you are using MS-DOS, you create a disk cache using a special software program. Several third-party software companies offer disk caching software. However, the most commonly used caching software is the SMARTDRV program, provided free with DOS. To use SMARTDRV, your computer must contain extended memory (see Lesson 35, "Installing MS-DOS-based Memory Management Software"). Most users place the SMARTDRV command in their AUTOEXEC.BAT file to ensure that MS-DOS uses the SMARTDRV disk cache each time their systems start.

When you use SMARTDRV, you consume extended memory to hold the disk buffer. If you are using Windows 3.1, there may be times when Windows can put your PC's extended memory to better use than for a disk cache. As such, SMARTDRV uses two buffer sizes—one buffer size specifies the initial cache size and the second specifies the minimum size to which Windows can reduce the cache, in order to use memory better. Depending upon how much extended memory your system contains, the size of the SMARTDRV cache will differ. Table 31 lists the default cache sizes for different extended memory amounts.

Extended Memory	Initial Cache Size Size	Minimum Cache
1Mb	All	0Kb
2Mb	1Mb	256Kb
4Mb	1Mb	512Kb
6Mb	2Mb	1Mb
>6Mb	2Mb	2Mb

Table 31 Default SMARTDRV disk cache sizes.

In most cases, you can use SMARTDRV's default settings. However, when you invoke SMARTDRV, you can specify different buffer sizes. For more information on SMARTDRV settings, invoke the SMARTDRV command from the DOS prompt using the question mark switch (/?):

```
C:\> SMARTDRV /?      <ENTER>

Installs and configures the SMARTDrive disk-caching utility.

smartdrv [[/E:elementsize] [/B:buffersize] [drive [+]|[-]] [size]
[winsize]]...

drive letter  Specifies the letter of the disk drive to cache.
              (drive letter alone specifies read caching only)
+             Enables write-behind caching for the specified drive.
-             Disables all caching for the specified drive.
size          Specifies the amount of XMS memory (KB) used by the
              cache.
winsize       Specifies the amount of XMS memory (KB) used in
              Windows.
/E:element size    Specifies the size of the cache elements
              (in bytes).
/B:buffer size     Specifies the size of the read buffer.
/C            Writes all write-behind information to the hard disk.
/R            Clears the contents of existing cache and restarts
              SMARTDrive.
/L            Loads SMARTDrive into low memory.
/Q            Prevents the display of SMARTDrive information on
              your screen.
/S            Displays additional information about the status of
              SMARTDrive.
```

IF WINDOWS 3.1 WILL NOT RUN

If, after you install a SMARTDRV disk cache, Windows 3.1 will not run, you may need to use SMARTDRV's double-buffering capabilities. Some disk controllers (the electronics that operate the disk drive) will not work with SMARTDRV when Windows runs in 386 Enhanced mode. In such cases, you simply must install the SMARTDRV device driver in your CONFIG.SYS using the /DOUBLE_BUFFER switch, as shown here:

DEVICE=C:\DOS\SMARTDRV.EXE   /DOUBLE_BUFFER

You must use the /DOUBLE_BUFFER switch only when Windows does not run after you install SMARTDRV. Normally, such errors occur when you are using the EMM386 memory manager.

*Note: When you place a device entry in your CONFIG.SYS file for SMARTDRV, you still invoke the SMARTDRV command from within AUTOEXEC.BAT. In other words, the CONFIG.SYS device driver entry is used **in addition to** the SMARTDRV command, not instead of it.*

BE AWARE OF WRITE-BEHIND CACHING

In addition to performing caching for read operations, caching can also be used for disk write operations. When write caching is used, the operating system places the information your programs write to disk into the cache. In this way, should the program need to read the information a second time, it will find the latest information contained within the cache. In addition, the operating system can later perform the disk-write operation at a time which may be more convenient, depending on your current processing.

In other words, to improve your system performance, write caching employs a technique called *write-behind caching*. Using this technique, the operating system places the information a program writes to disk first to the cache and not to the disk. In this way, the program can continue without having to wait for the slow disk operation to complete. Later (within a few-seconds delay), the operating system writes the information to disk.

Unfortunately, if the PC loses power or the PC is restarted before the operating system writes the cached information to disk, the information in the cache is lost and never recorded on your disk. When you use write caching, you maximize your system performance. However, you also expose yourself to possible data loss. If you cannot afford possible data loss, disable write caching.

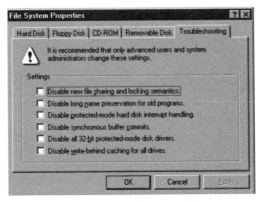

To eliminate this window of possible data loss, many users will disable write caching, trading increased data security for a loss of performance. To disable write-behind caching, within Windows 95 or 98, you can use the File System Properties dialog box Troubleshooting sheet, shown in Figure 33.2.

Figure 33.2 *The File System Properties dialog box Troubleshooting sheet.*

To disable write-behind caching with SMARTDRV, invoke SMARTDRV using the /X swtich:

```
SMARTDRV   /X
```

To determine if your system is using write caching, invoke SMARTDRV from the MS-DOS prompt, as shown here:

```
C:\> SMARTDRV   <ENTER>
Microsoft SMARTDrive Disk Cache version 5.0
Copyright 1991,1993 Microsoft Corp.

Cache size:  2,097,152 bytes
Cache size while running Windows:  2,097,152 bytes

               Disk Caching Status
  drive    read cache    write cache    buffering
_____

   A:         yes            no            no
   B:         yes            no            no
   C:         yes            no            no


For help, type "Smartdrv /?".
```

If you are using write caching, you can get SMARTDRV to *flush* (write) all of the information in the buffer to disk immediately by using the /C switch, as follows:

```
C:\> SMARTDRV   /C   <ENTER>
```

WHAT YOU MOST KNOW

A disk drive, even a hard drive, is very slow compared with the computer's fast electronic memory. In this lesson, you have learned how to install and use a disk cache to speed up your disk operations.

No matter how you use your computer, if you are like most users, you must constantly search for ways to find available space on your disk. In Lesson 34, "Doubling Your Disk's Storage Capacity," you will learn how you can double your disk's storage capacity using disk compression software. Before you continue with Lesson 34, however, make sure that you have learned the following key concepts:

✓ A disk cache is a large buffer the operating system sets aside within your computer's random-access memory into which it reads and stores disk sectors.

✓ Before the operating system reads the disk for a specific sector (a slow operation), the operating system first checks to see if the sector resides in the cache (a fast operation). If the sector is in the cache, the operating system can quickly retrieve and use the sector. If the sector is not in the cache, the operating system can read the sector from disk.

✓ Windows 95 and 98 provide built-in disk-caching software. Using the File System Properties dialog box, you can control your cache settings.

✓ If you are using MS-DOS, you can use the SMARTDRV command to create a disk cache.

Lesson 34

Doubling Your Disk's Storage Capacity

No matter how they use their computers, most users can quickly consume their hard disk's available disk space. As the price of hard disks continues to drop, many users now replace their hard disks with larger ones, or possibly even add a second hard disk. Unfortunately, as fast as users add disk space, they are often able to use it up. As it turns out, one of the most cost-effective ways to increase your available disk space is not by purchasing a new hard disk, but rather, to use software to double your existing disk's storage capacity.

This lesson examines how you can use the Windows DriveSpace program or the MS-DOS DBLSPACE command to double your disk's storage capacity. The programs this lesson presents are not the only software program you can use to increase your disk's capacity. Several third-party software manufacturers offer disk-compression software. However, because these programs are free (one ships with Windows and the other with MS-DOS), this lesson will examine their use. By the time you finish this lesson, you will understand the following key concepts:

- How disk compression software doubles your disk storage capacity

- If you are using Windows 95 or 98 you can double your disk storage capacity using the DriveSpace program

- If you are using MS-DOS, you can double your disk storage capacity using the DBLSPACE command

UNDERSTANDING DISK COMPRESSION

As you know, the PC works in terms of ones and zeros (binary digits). When your disk records information, the disk too represents data using ones and zeros. If you were to examine these ones and zeros on disk, you would find many long sequences of either all ones or all zeros.

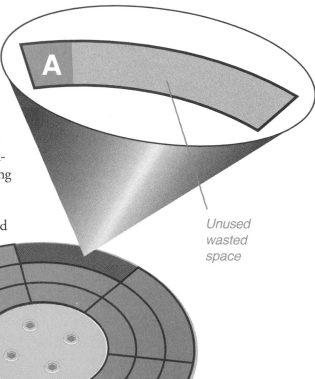

Unused wasted space

Assume, for example, that a file contains 100 zeros followed by 50 ones. These values would normally consume 150 bits of disk space. Disk compression software replaces such repetitive digit sequences with a small code that states that 100 zeros follow or 50 ones follow. Using these compact codes, compression software can free up tremendous amounts of disk space.

As you have learned, disks normally store files in one or more sectors. The smallest amount of disk space a file can consume is a disk sector. Even a file that contains only a single character (one byte) still consumes a disk sector. In the case of a 512-byte sector, 511 bytes would be wasted for the one-byte file.

Disk compression software transparently combines all the files on your disk into one large file—which eliminates such wasted disk space. To the user, you see no difference. A directory listing of the compressed disk will display each of the files. Behind the scenes, however, the disk compression software manages this large file.

By eliminating wasted disk space and by replacing digit sequences with a more compact code, disk compression software recovers large amounts of disk space—often doubling the disk's storage capacity.

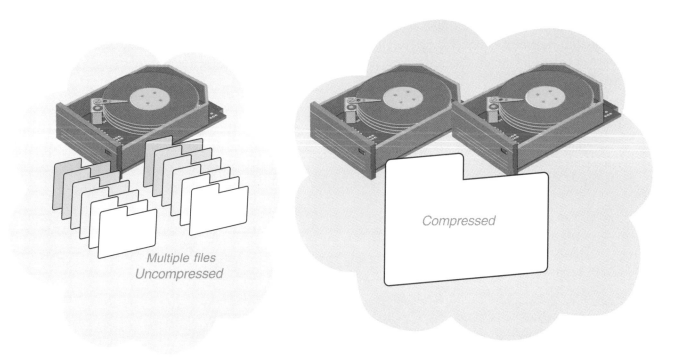

Multiple files
Uncompressed

Compressed

COMPRESSING YOUR DISK UNDER WINDOWS 95 OR 98

If you are using Windows 95 or 98, you can compress your disk using the DriveSpace System Tool that Windows provides with its accessory programs. To compress your disk using the DriveSpace program, perform these steps:

1. Select the Start menu Programs option and choose Accessories. Windows, in turn, will display the Accessories menu.

2. Within the Accessories menu, select the System Tools menu and choose DriveSpace. Windows 95, in turn, will display a window similar to that shown in Figure 34.1 that lists your available drives.

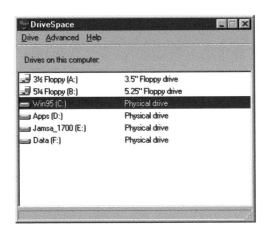

Figure 34.1 *Selecting the drive you want to compress.*

3. Within the dialog box, click your mouse on the drive you want to compress. Then, select the File menu Compress option. DriveSpace, in turn, will display a dialog box that summarizes how much disk space you can gain by compressing the selected drive.

4. Within the dialog box, select Start. DriveSpace, in turn, will display a dialog box asking you to verify the operation.

5. Select Compress Now. DriveSpace will first check your disk for errors. If no errors exist, DriveSpace will compress your disk. Otherwise, DriveSpace will display a dialog box telling you to use the Scandisk program to correct the errors. If DriveSpace successfully compresses your disk, it will display the Compress a Drive dialog box, as shown in Figure 34.2, that summarizes the operation.

6. Within the Compress a Drive dialog box, choose Close.

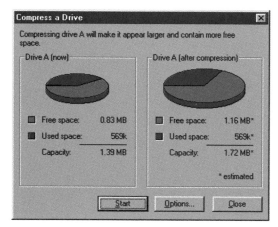

Figure 34.2 *The Compress a Drive dialog box.*

After DriveSpace has finished, start the Windows Explorer and examine the folders on your disk. You will find, there are no logical changes to your folders. In fact, you might not be able to tell that your files have been compressed—with the exception that you should now have considerable free disk space. Behind the scenes, however, DriveSpace has indeed compressed the files on your disk.

WHERE DID THE NEW DISK DRIVE COME FROM?

If, after you compress your disk, you run the Windows Explorer, you should notice a new disk drive—possibly a drive named H. As it turns out, disk compression leads to two disk drives—a compressed drive and a small uncompressed drive. The compressed disk drive contains the files on your disk that DBLSPACE just compressed. The uncompressed drive contains the files that Windows needs to start.

As you have read in this lesson, disk compression software compresses all the files on your disk, combining the compressed files into one larger file. When you start Windows after compressing your disk, Windows mounts this file as if the file were a disk. Physically, you still have only one disk. Logically to Windows, however, you have two disks—one compressed and one not. The DriveSpace command oversees the disk operations behind the scenes. For more information on the DriveSpace command, refer to the book *1001 Windows 98 Tips*, Jamsa Press, 1998.

PERFORMING FILE OPERATIONS

After you compress a disk, Windows (behind the scenes) will also compress the files you create on that disk, automatically. If you copy a file from the compressed disk to an uncompressed drive, such as a floppy disk, for example, Windows will copy the file in an uncompressed format, letting you can easily exchange files with another user, even when your disk is compressed.

USING THE MS-DOS DBLSPACE COMMAND TO DOUBLE YOUR DISK'S CAPACITY

If you are using MS-DOS, as opposed to Windows 95 or 98, you can use the DBLSPACE command, provided with most versions of MS-DOS 6 (or later), to compress the files on your disk. Unfortunately, legal disputes between STAC Electronics (the maker of STACKER) and Microsoft (the maker of DBLSPACE) led Microsoft to remove DBLSPACE from some versions of MS-DOS. Thus, your system may not have the DBLSPACE command.

BACKUP YOUR DISK BEFORE YOU COMPRESS

No matter which disk compression software you choose—never run a disk compression program without first making a complete backup of the files on your disk. Disk compression software makes extreme changes to the information stored on your disk. Should an error occur in this process, the information stored on your disk might be lost.

If you have successfully backed up the files on your hard disk, invoke the DBLSPACE command with the /COMPRESS switch and your hard-disk drive-letter, as shown here:

```
C:\> DBLSPACE   /COMPRESS  C:  <ENTER>
```

The DBLSPACE command will start, first examining your disk's contents and surface, and displaying a screen similar to that shown in Figure 34.3.

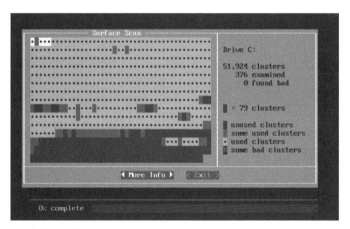

Figure 34.3 The DBLSPACE disk surface examination.

After the disk surface scan completes, DBLSPACE will start compressing your files, displaying a status screen similar to that shown in Figure 34.4.

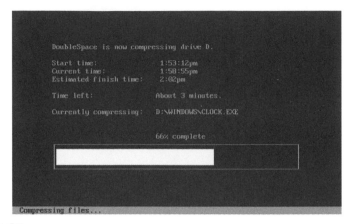

Figure 34.4 *The DBLSPACE status screen.*

WHAT YOU MUST KNOW

If you are like most users, you can never have enough disk space. In this lesson, you have learned how you can double your disk space without buying a new disk drive.

In Lesson 35, "Installing MS-DOS-based Memory Management Software," you will learn how to configure DOS to make the best use of your system's memory. Before you continue with Lesson 35, however, make sure that you have learned the following key concepts:

- ✓ One of the easiest ways to increase your disk's capacity is to use disk-compression software.

- ✓ Disk compression software increases your disk storage capacity by storing files in a more compact way, in one large file.

- ✓ After you compress a disk, you use the disk just as you always have in the past. The disk drive letter, the directory structure, and even the files will seem unchanged.

- ✓ If you are using Windows 95 or 98, you can compress the files on your disk using the DriveSpace utility.

- ✓ If you are using MS-DOS 6 (or later), you can compress the files on your disk using the DBLSPACE command.

- ✓ Never compress a disk without first backing up the disk's current contents.

Lesson 35

Installing MS-DOS-based Memory Management Software

Most users will agree that although MS-DOS has earned its place in the Operating System Hall of Fame, users should no longer be running MS-DOS-based systems. Unfortunately, a suprising number of systems still run MS-DOS or MS-DOS-based programs. To make the most of these systems, you must know how to perform MS-DOS-based memory-management operations. This lesson examines various memory types and the steps you must perform to access the memory using MS-DOS.

By the time you finish this lesson, you will understand the following key concepts:

- The differences between conventional, extended, expanded, high, and upper memory
- How to install an extended-memory device driver
- How to load MS-DOS into the high-memory area in order to make more room for programs in conventional memory
- How to load device drivers and memory-resident programs into the upper-memory area

Because of the different PC memory types, memory management can be a difficult subject. If you are using Windows 95, the only time you need to use the memory-management techniques this chapter presents is when you run Windows 95 in MS-DOS mode or when you run a MS-DOS-based program within a window. Windows 95 and 98 use their own built-in memory-management software for Windows-based programs. For more information on Windows memory management, turn to the book *1001 Windows 98 Tips*, Jamsa Press, 1998.

UNDERSTANDING CONVENTIONAL MEMORY

When the original IBM PC was first released in 1981, the PC supported 1MB of memory, called *conventional memory*. Part of the conventional memory (640KB) is available for program use, and part (384KB) is reserved for use by your video display and other hardware devices. When you start your computer, the computer loads MS-DOS into the lower portion of conventional memory. When you later run programs, MS-DOS loads these programs from disk into memory.

Every PC, be it an 8088, 80286, 386, 486, or even a Pentium, uses the 1MB conventional memory. No matter how much memory your computer has, MS-DOS-based programs always run within the 640KB conventional memory program space. If a program cannot fit within the 640KB memory region, MS-DOS cannot run the program. As you will learn, however, your programs can store their data in extended and expanded memory, making more room in the 640KB region for program instructions. When users perform memory management within MS-DOS, their goal is to free up as much of the 640KB region as possible for use by their programs.

UNDERSTANDING EXTENDED MEMORY

4 Gb
Extended
Memory
1 Mb
Conventional
Memory
0

As programs have become more powerful, they have grown substantially in size, to the point that many programs cannot hold their instructions and data in the 640KB program area. Beginning with the 286 processor, the PC can use a second memory type called *extended memory*. Depending on the model, PCs can hold several hundred megabytes of extended memory. MS-DOS-based programs can use extended memory to hold their data, such as a spreadsheet or large word processing document. MS-DOS-based programs cannot store program instructions within the extended memory. When you turn on your PC's power, the PC will display a count of your computer's working memory. By examining the value displayed, you can determine how much extended memory your computer holds. For example, assume your computer screen displays the value 8192 (8MB). If you subtract the 1MB of conventional memory, you will find that your computer holds 7MB of extended memory.

When you purchase a PC, the PC will normally come with 8 to 16MB of memory. The first 1MB of this memory is your PC's conventional memory area. As you learned in Lesson 12, "Adding Memory to Your PC," when you add memory to your computer, you will normally purchase memory chips called SIMMs or DIMMs, which you install on your system's motherboard within your PC's system unit.

INSTALLING AN EXTENDED MEMORY DEVICE DRIVER

Before MS-DOS can use extended memory, you must install the *HIMEM.SYS* device driver in your *CONFIG.SYS* file using an entry similar to that shown here:

```
DEVICE=C:\DOS\HIMEM.SYS
```

You can use the MS-DOS EDIT command to edit the *CONFIG.SYS* file. After you place the *HIMEM.SYS* entry in your *CONFIG.SYS* file, you must restart your system for the device driver to take effect. To restart your system, exit all programs and press the CTRL-ALT-DEL keyboard combination.

VIEWING YOUR EXTENDED MEMORY USE WITH MEM

Within MS-DOS, the MEM command lets you display your system's memory use. For example, the following MEM command displays the amount of extended memory your system contains:

```
C:\> MEM   <ENTER>
```

PUTTING EXTENDED MEMORY TO USE

Not all software programs can take advantage of extended memory. Thus, most users will use a portion of their extended memory for a SMARTDRV cache. Lesson 33, "Improving Disk Performance with a Disk Cache," discussed the SMARTDRV disk-caching software in detail. At that time, you learned that you can improve your system performance by using some of your extended memory as a large disk buffer.

UNDERSTANDING HIGH MEMORY

If you are using a 386-based computer (or higher) and your computer has extended memory as just discussed, you can take advantage of the first 64KB of extended memory, called the *high-memory area,* to hold MS-DOS. As you have read, MS-DOS is normally loaded into the 640KB program space. In this way, MS-DOS itself consumes memory that could be used by your programs. By moving MS-DOS into the high-memory area, you free up more of the 640KB region for your program use.

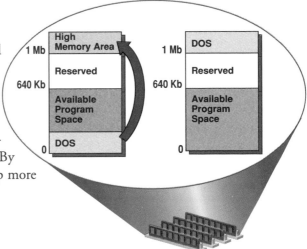

Note: To determine whether your computer has extended memory, watch the amount of memory the computer displays on your screen when you turn on the PC's power. If your computer displays a memory count higher than 1024, your PC contains extended memory, and you can use the steps discussed next to take advantage of the high-emory area.

LOADING MS-DOS INTO THE HIGH-MEMORY AREA

To load MS-DOS into the high-memory area, you simply edit your *CONFIG.SYS* file and add the following two entries:

```
DEVICE=C:\DOS\HIMEM.SYS
DOS=HIGH
```

To begin, use the CHDIR command to select the root directory and then use the EDIT command to edit the *CONFIG.SYS* file, as shown here:

```
C:\> EDIT   CONFIG.SYS    <ENTER>
```

Examine your *CONFIG.SYS* entries closely to ensure that the file does not already contain these entries or a similar entry (that contains DOS=):

```
DEVICE=C:\DOS\HIMEM.SYS
DOS=HIGH,UMB
```

If your *CONFIG.SYS* file does not contain the entry previously shown, add the entries to the file. Next, press ALT-F to select EDIT's File menu. Select the Save option. Select the File menu a second time and choose Exit. Next, restart your system by pressing the CTRL-ALT-DEL keyboard combination.

UNDERSTANDING EXPANDED MEMORY

When the IBM PC was first released in 1981, the PC could only support 1MB of memory. If you placed more than 1MB of memory into your computer, the 8088 processor simply could not use it. The PC could not address (access) memory locations whose addresses were above 1MB. Unfortunately, spreadsheet programs such as Lotus 1-2-3 quickly consumed the PC's available memory. To provide the PC with more memory, hardware developers came up with *expanded memory*, a way to trick the PC into using memory beyond 1MB. Today, however, expanded memory is rarely used. Therefore, this lesson will not discuss its use. If you need information on expanded memory, turn to your MS-DOS documentation.

UNDERSTANDING UPPER MEMORY

The PC reserves the top 384KB of conventional memory for use by the video display and other hardware devices. Parts of this 384KB region, called the *upper-memory area*, are not used. Therefore, MS-DOS lets you load device drivers and memory-resident programs into these unused areas (called upper-memory blocks). Normally, MS-DOS loads device drivers and memory-resident programs into the 640KB program space. By moving these programs to the upper-memory area, you free up more of the 640KB program space for use by your programs.

The upper-memory area is the 384KB block of memory between 640KB and 1MB. Much of the upper-memory area is reserved for use by the PC's video display. When your computer displays letters on the screen, your PC must first place the letters into the video memory. The video memory, however, only consumes part of the upper-memory area, leaving part of the memory available for your program use.

A *memory-resident* program is a program that remains in your computer's memory after you run it. The MS-DOS PRINT command, for example, remains in memory to print files while you issue other commands from the MS-DOS prompt. Likewise, as you have learned, some device drivers, such as *MOUSE.COM*, remain in memory to let MS-DOS use the driver to access a specific device. Memory-resident programs and device drivers normally reside within the 640KB program space.

You can load memory-resident programs and device drivers into the upper-memory area, freeing up more of the 640KB region for your program use.

DIRECTING MS-DOS TO SUPPORT THE UPPER-MEMORY AREA

Before you can use the upper-memory area, you must tell MS-MS-DOS to support it. To begin, place the *EMM386.EXE* device driver in your *CONFIG.SYS* file, as shown here:

```
DEVICE=C:\DOS\EMM386.EXE      NOEMS
```

The *EMM386.EXE* device driver lets you allocate extended memory for use as expanded memory. In this case, the NOEMS parameter tells MS-DOS that you do not want to use expanded memory. Instead, you are simply using the device driver to provide support for the upper-memory area. Next, you must place a DOS entry similar to the following in your *CONFIG.SYS* file:

```
DOS=HIGH,UMB
```

UMB is an abbreviation for *upper-memory block*. An upper-memory block is a section of memory within the upper-memory area. When you load a device driver or memory-resident program into the upper-memory area, MS-DOS will allocate an upper memory block to hold the program. After you place these entries in your *CONFIG.SYS* file, you must restart your system for the change to take effect.

PUTTING THE UPPER-MEMORY REGION TO USE

After you provide upper-memory support, you can direct MS-DOS to load device drivers and memory-resident programs into the upper-memory area. In Lesson 30, "Understanding Device Drivers," you learned that to install a device driver you place a DEVICE entry in your *CONFIG.SYS* file. To install a device driver into the upper-memory area, use the DEVICEHIGH entry, as shown here:

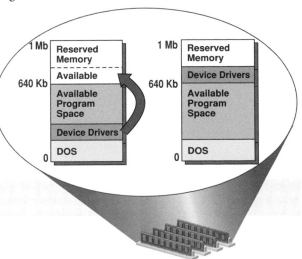

```
DEVICEHIGH=C:\DOS\ANSI.SYS
```

When MS-DOS encounters a DEVICEHIGH entry in your *CONFIG.SYS* file, it first tries to load the device driver into the upper-memory area. If there is not enough memory in the upper-memory area to hold the driver, MS-DOS will load the driver into the 640KB memory region, just as if you had used the DEVICE entry. You cannot use the DEVICEHIGH entry until you have installed upper-memory support. Thus, you cannot use DEVICEHIGH for the *HIMEM.SYS* or *EMM386.EXE* device drivers. The following entries illustrate how you might use DEVICEHIGH within your *CONFIG.SYS* file:

```
DEVICE=C:\DOS\HIMEM.SYS
DEVICE=C:\DOS\EMM386.EXE    NOEMS
DOS=HIGH,UMB
DEVICEHIGH=C:\DOS\ANSI.SYS
```

You can do a similar thing with memory-resident programs. By default, when you load a memory-resident program, such as PRINT, MS-DOS will place the program in the 640KB program area. With support for the upper-memory area, however, you can use the LOADHIGH command to place such programs into the upper-memory area. For example, the following LOADHIGH command directs MS-DOS to load the PRINT command into upper memory:

```
LOADHIGH C:\DOS\PRINT.COM
```

Note: LOADHIGH is a command, not a CONFIG.SYS entry. You might use LOADHIGH within your AUTOEXEC.BAT file. Because of its frequency of use, MS-DOS lets you abbreviate LOADHIGH as simply LH.

WHAT YOU MUST KNOW

If you are using or managing an older MS-DOS-based system, you must make full use of the MS-DOS memory-management techniques. In this lesson, you learned about the various memory types and how to configure them within MS-DOS. If you are using Windows, the only time you must worry about MS-DOS settings is if you run MS-DOS-based programs or work within an MS-DOS window. Windows manages its own memory in a much different way.

In Lesson 36, "Defragmenting Your Disk," you will learn how to improve your system's performance by defragmenting your disk. Before you continue with Lesson 34, however, make sure that you have learned the following key concepts:

✓ Your computer's electronic memory (or RAM) may consist of conventional, extended, expanded, upper, and high memory.

✓ All PCs have a 1MB conventional memory area. Conventional memory consists of two parts: a 640KB program space that holds MS-DOS and other programs you run, and a 384KB region that is reserved for your video display and other hardware devices. Extended memory is the memory beyond the PC's 1MB conventional memory.

✓ Before MS-DOS can use extended memory, you must place the *HIMEM.SYS* device driver in your *CONFIG.SYS* file. MS-DOS-based program instructions must reside in your computer's conventional memory. However, many programs let their data reside in extended memory.

✓ If you are using a 286-based computer (or higher) that contains extended memory, you can load MS-DOS into a special memory region called the high memory area. By placing MS-DOS into the high memory area, you free up conventional memory for your program use.

✓ The upper-memory area is the 384KB region between 640KB and 1MB. Much of the upper-memory area is reserved for use by the PC's video. However, part of the upper-memory area is available for use by MS-DOS. To use the upper-memory area, you must be using a 386-based computer or higher. By placing memory-resident programs and device drivers in the upper-memory area, you free up the 640KB program area for use by your programs.

✓ Before you can use the upper-memory area, you must first install the *EMM386.EXE* device driver and place a DOS=UMB entry in your *CONFIG.SYS* file.

✓ To load a device driver in the upper-memory area, use the DEVICEHIGH entry. If MS-DOS is unable to fit the device driver into the available upper memory, MS-DOS will load the driver into the 640KB program area.

✓ To load a memory-resident program into the upper-memory area, use the LOADHIGH command. If MS-DOS is unable to fit the command into the available upper memory, MS-DOS will load the program into the 640KB program area.

Lesson 36

Defragmenting Your Hard Disk

If programs start slowly when you double-click on the program icon from within Windows or when you type the program name at the MS-DOS prompt, files on your hard disk may be fragmented. To store information, disks record information in storage locations, called sectors. A file is *fragmented* when its sectors are dispersed across your disk. In contrast, a contiguous (non-fragmented) file resides in consecutive sector locations on your disk. As you will learn in this lesson, it takes the disk drive longer to read or write fragmented files, which makes your programs load slower. Files become fragmented as a natural result of creating, editing, and deleting files. Fortunately, there are many different software programs you can run that *defragment* your disk. If you are concerned about system performance, you should run such programs on a regular basis. If you are using Windows 95 or 98, you can use the Disk Defragmenter program. If you are using DOS version 6, or later, you can use the DEFRAG command to defragment your disk. By the time you finish this lesson, you will understand the following concepts:

- How your disk drive reads and writes files

- How fragmented files decrease your system performance

- How files become fragmented

- How to correct fragmented files

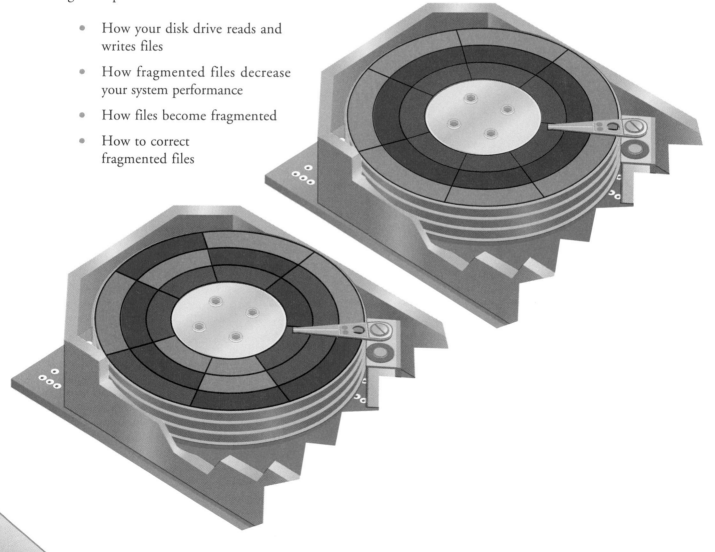

How a Disk Reads and Writes Information

To store information, your disk records information in storage locations on the disk's surface, called *sectors*. As you can see, a disk contains rows of concentric circles, called *tracks*. Each track is further divided into fixed-sized sectors. A disk sector typically stores 512 bytes (characters) of data.

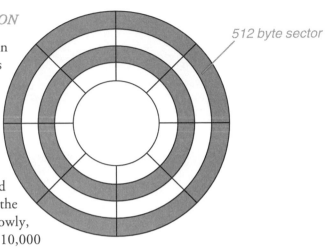

512 byte sector

To read or record information, the disk drive uses a read/write head, which is similar to a needle used by old record players. Like a record album, the disk spins past the read/write head. Unlike an album that rotates very slowly, your hard disk spins very quickly (from 3,600 to over 10,000 revolutions per minute, depending on your disk drive type).

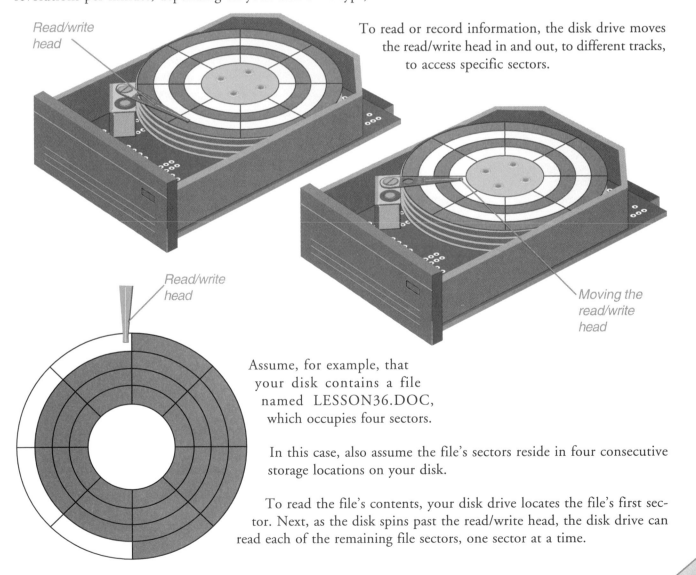

Read/write head

To read or record information, the disk drive moves the read/write head in and out, to different tracks, to access specific sectors.

Moving the read/write head

Read/write head

Assume, for example, that your disk contains a file named LESSON36.DOC, which occupies four sectors.

In this case, also assume the file's sectors reside in four consecutive storage locations on your disk.

To read the file's contents, your disk drive locates the file's first sector. Next, as the disk spins past the read/write head, the disk drive can read each of the remaining file sectors, one sector at a time.

HOW FRAGMENTED FILES DECREASE YOUR SYSTEM PERFORMANCE

As you just learned, to read a file's contents, the disk drive must read the file's sectors as they spin past the disk read/write head. In the previous example, the file's sectors resided in consecutive sectors. Files whose sectors reside in consecutive locations are *contiguous*.

On the other hand, files whose sectors do not reside in consecutive storage locations are *fragmented*.

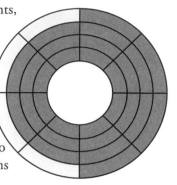

Contiguous file

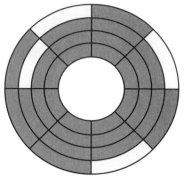

Fragmented file

Unlike your computer's fast electronic parts, such as memory or the CPU, a disk drive is a mechanical device—the disk spins within the drive and the read/write head must move in and out to access sectors that reside in different tracks. Because the disk drive is mechanical, it is much slower than its electronic counterparts. An easy way to improve system performance is to reduce the number of slow disk operations your computer must perform. Correcting fragmented files does just that. Assume, for example, that the file LESSON36.DOC, just discussed, resides in sectors that are dispersed across your disk. To read the file's contents, the disk drive locates the file's first sector. After reading the first sector, the disk drive must wait (over half a revolution) for the second sector to spin past the read/write head.

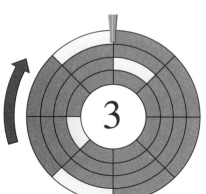

Next, to read the third sector, the disk drive must first move the read/write head to the correct track, then wait for that sector to spin past the head.

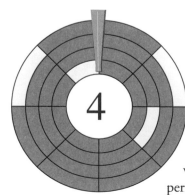

Finally, to read the last sector, the disk drive must again move the read/write head, then wait for the sector to spin past. To read the fragmented file, the disk drive had to repeatedly wait for the sector to spin past the read/write head.

Such rotational delays add up, increasing the amount of time it takes to read a file which, in turn, decreases your system performance.

How Files Become Fragmented

Files become fragmented naturally as you create, edit, and delete files. You are not doing anything wrong if your disk becomes fragmented. In most cases, you cannot prevent fragmented files—instead, you simply correct them. Assume, for example, that you start a letter to a friend. When you save the file to disk, your disk drive records the information within a disk sector.

Next, assume that as you are working on the letter, you have to stop typing so that you can type an office memo. When you save the memo to a file on disk, your drive will store the file in one or more sectors on your disk.

When the memo is complete, you might resume your work on the letter you previously saved to disk. As the length of your letter grows, the letter might require several disk sectors.

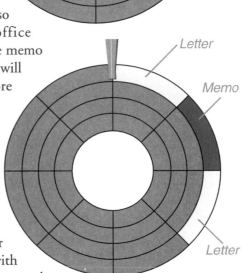

In this case, when your drive records the rest of the letter to disk, your drive will place the additional data in a sector that is not consecutive with the previous sector. As a result, the file containing your letter is now fragmented.

Recognizing the Symptoms

As you have learned, fragmented files decrease your system performance by increasing the amount of time it takes the disk drive to read the file on your disk. If, when you run a program from within Windows or from the MS-DOS, the program seems to load slowly, your disk might be fragmented. Fragmented files occur naturally, simply by creating, editing, and deleting files on your disk. You cannot prevent fragmentation; instead, you correct it when the symptoms become present.

Correcting Fragmented Files

To correct fragmented files, you run a special software program that moves the information your files contain, placing the information into consecutive sectors on your disk. There are several third-party software programs you can use to defragment your disk. In addition, if you are using Windows 95 or 98, you can defragment your disk using the Disk Defragmenter accessory program to defragment your disk. If you are using DOS 6 (or later), you can use the DEFRAG command to correct fragmented files.

DEFRAGMENTING YOUR DISK UNDER WINDOWS 95 OR 98

If you are using Windows 95 or 98, you can use the Disk Defragmenter program to defragment your disk. To run the Disk Defragmenter program, perform these steps:

1. Select the Start menu Programs option and choose Accessories. Windows, in turn, will display the Accessories menu.

2. Within the Accessories menu, choose the System Tools menu and choose Disk Defragmenter. Windows will display the Select Drive dialog box.

3. Within the Select Drive dialog box, use the Drives pull-down list to select the drive letter of the disk you want to defragment, and then select OK. The Disk Defragmenter program may display a dialog box that tells you how much of your disk is fragmented.

4. Within the dialog box, select Start. The Disk Defragmenter program, in turn, will begin defragmenting your disk, displaying a dialog box similar to that shown in Figure 36.1 that tells you how much of the disk it has defragmented.

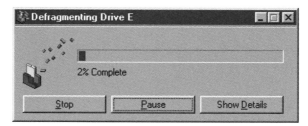

Figure 36.1 *The Disk Defragmenter status information.*

If you click your mouse on the Show Details button, the Disk Defragmenter program will display a screen similar to that shown in Figure 36.2 with which you can watch the program's processing.

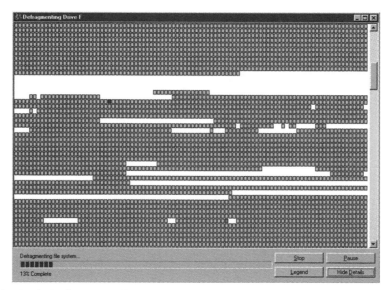

Figure 36.2 *Viewing the Disk Defragmenter's processing.*

DEFRAGMENTING YOUR DISK DOES NOT RECOVER DISK SPACE

When you defragment files, you essentially move the files so that each file's contents reside in consecutive storage locations. By defragmenting files, you do not free up additional disk space. Instead, you simply make better use of the disk space that has already been consumed.

DEFRAGMENTING YOUR DISK UNDER MS-DOS

If you are using MS-DOS, you can defragment your files using the DEFRAG command. To issue the DEFRAG command, you must be at the MS-DOS prompt. If you are currently running Windows 3.1, use the Program Manager's File menu Exit Windows option to end your Windows session. Next, from the DOS prompt (C:\>), type DEFRAG and press ENTER:

```
C:\> DEFRAG   <ENTER>
```

The DEFRAG command will run, examining your disk's contents. Next, DEFRAG will display its Recommendation dialog box, as shown in Figure 36.3.

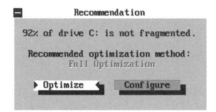

Figure 36.3 *DEFRAG's Recommendation dialog box.*

Select the Optimize option and press ENTER. DEFRAG will start defragmenting your disk, displaying a screen similar to the one shown in Figure 36.4.

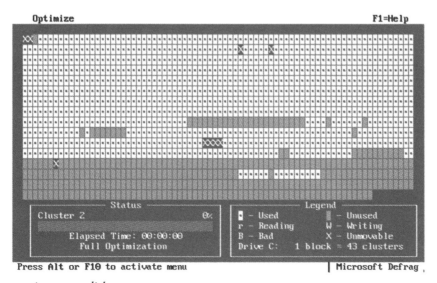

Figure 36.4 *Defragmenting your disk.*

Depending on your disk's size, the amount of time DEFRAG requires will differ. When DEFRAG completes, it will display a dialog box asking you if you want to defragment another drive or if you want to exit. Select the Exit option to return to DOS.

Note: If you are using disk compression software, such as DBLSPACE (discussed in Lesson 34, "Doubling Your Disk's Storage Capacity," DEFRAG will defragment both your compressed and uncompressed drives.

WHAT YOU MUST KNOW

As you store, edit, and resave files on your disk, your files will eventually become fragmented. If you find that your programs are taking longer to run or your documents longer to load, your files may be fragmented. In this lesson, you learned how files become fragmented and how to repair them, thus improving your system performance.

In Lesson 37, "Fine-Tuning Windows Memory Use," you will learn how to fine-tune several key Windows memory settings and how to speed up disk I/O operations within Windows. Before you continue with Lesson 37, however, make sure that you have learned the following key concepts:

✓ A fragmented file is a file whose contents are dispersed across your disk. A contiguous (or nonfragmented) file, on the other hand, resides in consecutive disk locations.

✓ Fragmented files decrease your system performance because it takes longer for the slow (mechanical) disk drive to access them.

✓ Files become fragmented naturally, when you create, edit, and delete files.

✓ Using software such as the Windows Disk Defragmenter or the MS-DOS DEFRAG command, you can defragment your files and improve your system performance.

Lesson 37

Fine-Tuning Windows Memory Use

In Lesson 12, "Adding Memory to Your PC," you learned how to add random-access memory (RAM) to your PC. As you have read, after you add memory to your PC, you normally improve Windows performance instantly. For Windows to run a program, the program must reside within the computer's memory. If Windows is running multiple programs, each program must reside in memory. The more memory your PC holds, the more programs Windows can load into memory at one time.

If your PC does not have unlimited memory (which no PC does), however, Windows periodically moves one program out of memory to disk to make room for other programs. This lesson examines ways you can "fine-tune" Windows performance under Windows 95 and 98 as well as Windows 3.1.

By the time you finish this lesson, you will understand the following key concepts:

- How Windows uses "virtual memory" to give your programs the illusion that your PC has more memory than it does

- How to display and set virtual memory use within Windows 95 or 98

- How to display and set virtual memory use within Windows 3.1

- How to improve Windows performance by speeding up disk operations

UNDERSTANDING WINDOWS VIRTUAL MEMORY USE

In Lesson 12, you examined your PC's random access memory (RAM). Today, most PCs sold have at least 16MB of RAM. Those users who want the best performance within Windows should use 32 to 64MB (or more) of RAM. The RAM that resides in your computer is *physical memory*; you can see it, and touch it, and when programs run, they reside within it.

As you know, Windows lets you run multiple programs at the same time. Depending on the number of programs you run, Windows and the programs can quickly use up your computer's physical memory. Thus, Windows uses a technique called *virtual memory* to trick the programs into thinking your computer has more memory than the physical RAM. Virtual memory combines your computer's RAM chips with a large *swap file* on your disk.

For a program to run, the program must reside in your computer's physical memory (RAM). When you run multiple programs at the same time, Windows moves inactive programs from physical memory to the swap file on disk, to make room in RAM for other programs. Should you select the program's window for use, Windows will move the program back into memory, possibly swapping a different program out to the swap file on disk. Because your programs think your computer has more memory than is actually present, the nonexistent memory is called *virtual* memory. The amount of virtual memory available to Windows controls the number of programs you can run at one time.

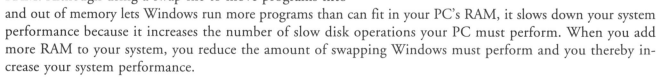

Virtual Memory

As you have learned throughout this book, your disk, because it is a mechanical device, is much slower than your PC's electronic components, such as RAM. Although using a swap file to move programs into and out of memory lets Windows run more programs than can fit in your PC's RAM, it slows down your system performance because it increases the number of slow disk operations your PC must perform. When you add more RAM to your system, you reduce the amount of swapping Windows must perform and you thereby increase your system performance.

CONTROLLING WINDOWS 95 OR 98 VIRTUAL-MEMORY USE

Unless you are a very experienced user, you should not change the Windows virtual-memory settings. Instead, you should let Windows configure its virtual memory based on your PC's available memory and disk space. If, however, you are an experienced user and you want to experiment with the Windows virtual-memory settings, perform these steps:

1. Select the Start menu Settings option and choose Control Panel. Windows, in turn, will open the Control Panel window.

2. Within the Control Panel window, double-click your mouse on the System icon. Windows will display the System Properties dialog box.

3. Click your mouse on the Performance tab. Windows, in turn, will display the Performance tab, as shown in Figure 37.1.

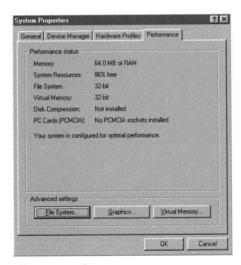

Figure 37.1 *The System Properties Performance tab.*

4. Click your mouse on the Virtual Memory button. Windows, in turn, will display the Virtual Memory dialog box, as shown in Figure 37.2.

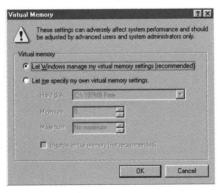

Figure 37.2 *The Windows Virtual Memory dialog box.*

5. After you make your changes to the virtual-memory settings, choose OK.

USING A TEMPORARY OR PERMANENT SWAP FILE

Like Windows 95 and 98, Windows 3.1 can use a permanent or temporary swap file. If you use a permanent swap file, Windows will consume a large part of your disk to hold the file. However, provided the file is large enough, the permanent swap file often improves Windows performance. If you use a temporary swap file, you can reduce the amount of hard disk space Windows consumes, but your performance may suffer.

If you have a reasonable amount of RAM (16MB or more) and you have sufficient free disk space (100Mb or more), Windows 95 and 98 users should let Windows itself, manage the swap file (leaving the swap file as a temporary file). If you are low on disk space, you may want to temporarily change your swap file settings. If you are using Windows 3.1, you should use a permanent swap file to improve your system performance.

CONTROLLING WINDOWS 3.1 VIRTUAL MEMORY USE

To change your swap file settings, within Windows 3.1, open the Control Panel and double-click your mouse on the the 386 Enhanced icon. Windows, in turn, will display the 386 Enhanced dialog box, as shown in Figure 37.3.

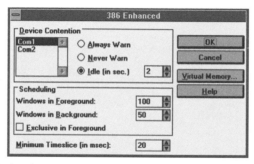

Figure 37.3 *The 386 Enhanced dialog box in Windows 3.1.*

Within the 386 Enhance dialog box, select the Virtual Memory button. Windows will display the Virtual Memory dialog box shown in Figure 37.4. Within the Virtual Memory dialog box, see the Type field to determine whether you are using a permanent or a temporary swap file.

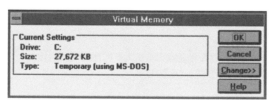

Figure 37.4 *The Virtual Memory dialog box in Windows 3.1.*

If you are already using a permanent swap file, select the Cancel option to close the dialog box. If you are using a temporary swap file, you can improve your system performance by clicking on the Change button to select a permanent swap file. Windows will expand the Virtual Memory dialog box, as shown in Figure 37.5. Within the dialog box, note the New Settings field. The field lets you select the disk on which you want Windows to create the permanent swap file, as well as the swap-file size. Normally, Windows specifies a swap-file size that is much larger than you require. You might want to specify a swap-file size that is 2/3 of the size shown. To specify a new swap-file size, click on the New Size field using your mouse and type in the desired size. Next, select the

OK option. Windows will display a dialog box asking you to verify your changes. Select Yes. Next, Windows will display a dialog box asking you if you want to restart your computer. Select the Restart Now option. When Windows restarts, it will use your new permanent swap file.

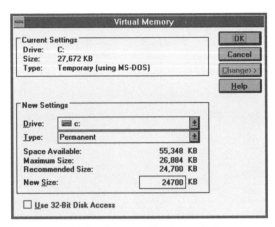

Figure 37.5 *The expanded Virtual Memory dialog box in Windows 3.1.*

SPEEDING UP DISK OPERATIONS

Because Windows lets you run multiple programs at the same time, Windows must protect one program from another. If two programs print at the same time, Windows must intercept the printouts to ensure that the program that asked for the printer first prints first, and two printouts are not garbled. To help Windows protect one program from another, Windows uses a special capability of the PC called *protected mode*. When programs run in protected mode, they cannot directly access a device or the computer memory in use by a second program. Unfortunately, MS-DOS and many older BIOS chip, which oversee disk input and output operations, run in the computer's *real mode*.

In the past, to perform a disk read or write operation, Windows 3.1 would change from protected mode to real mode and then ask the BIOS chip to perform the operation. When the operation completed, Windows would change back to protected mode. Unfortunately, the constant switching between protected and real mode is very time consuming and slows down your system performance. Fortunately, most disk drives support 32-bit protected mode operations. When you use these operations, you let Windows perform the disk input and output operations normally performed in real mode by the BIOS. In this way, your system performance increases tremendously because you eliminate the constant switching between real and protected mode.

CONTROLLING WINDOWS 95 OR 98 USE OF 32-BIT DISK ACCESS

If you are using Windows 95 or 98, your system will use 32-bit disk operations by default. So, normally, you can ignore the disk settings. That is, unless, you have an older disk that does not support the 32-bit protected-mode operations. In such a case, you must direct Windows not to use 32-bit disk operations, but instead, to use slower 16-bit (or real-mode) disk operations. To control Windows support for 32-bit disk access, perform these steps:

1. Select the Start menu Settings option and choose Control Panel. Windows, in turn, will open the Control Panel window.

2. Within the Control Panel window, double-click your mouse on the System icon. Windows will display the System Properties dialog box.

3. Select the File System tab. Windows will display the File System page.

4. Click your mouse on the Troubleshooting tab. Windows will display the Troubleshooting page as shown in Figure 37.6.

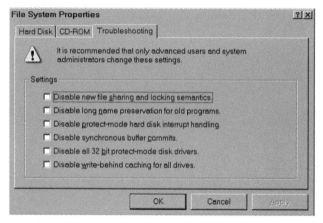

Figure 37.6 *The System Properties Troubleshooting page.*

5. To turn off 32-bit disk access, click your mouse on the Disable all 32 bit protected-mode disk drives checkbox, placing a checkmark within the box.

6. Choose OK.

CONTROLLING WINDOWS 3.1 USE OF 32-BIT DISK ACCESS

To select 32-bit disk operations within Windows 3.1, select the Control Panel and double-click your mouse on the 386 Enhanced icon. Windows will display the 386 Enhanced dialog box, previously shown in Figure 37.3. Within the 386 Enhanced dialog box, click your mouse on the Virtual Memory button. Windows will display the Virtual Memory dialog box, previously shown in Figure 37.4. Within the Virtual Memory dialog box, see the Type field to determine how Windows is accessing your disk:

> **Type:**   **Permanent (using BIOS)**
>
> **Type:**   **Permanent (using 32-bit access)**

If you are currently using 32-bit disk access operations, close the dialog box. If you are using a battery-powered laptop computer, check with your computer manufacturer to determine if your computer supports 32-bit disk access before continuing.

If your system is currently using BIOS disk access, click your mouse on the Change button. Windows will expand the Virtual Memory dialog box, displaying addition fields. Within the dialog box, note the small checkbox that appears at the bottom of the dialog box:

> ☐ **Use 32-Bit Disk Access**

To enable 32-bit disk access, click your mouse on the check box, placing an X in the box. Next, select the OK option. Windows will display a dialog box asking you to verify your changes. Select Yes. Next, Windows will display the Warning dialog box shown in Figure 37.7 that states 32-bit disk access may be unreliable on some battery powered computers.

Figure 37.7 Windows 32-bit disk warning dialog box.

If you are not using a battery-powered laptop computer or if you have verified with your computer manufacturer that 32-bit disk access is supported, select Yes. Windows will then display a dialog box asking you if you want to restart your computer now or to continue working. Within the dialog box, select the Restart Now option to restart Windows and put your changes into use. When Windows restarts, it will use the faster 32-bit protected mode disk access.

Note: Should Windows fail to start after you select 32-bit disk access, your disk controller does not support 32-bit operations. In such cases, edit the file SYSTEM.INI, which resides in the WINDOWS directory, using an editor such as EDIT, provided with DOS. Within the file, locate the 32BitDiskAccess entry and change it to Off, as shown here:

```
32BitDiskAccess=Off
```

Save your file change to disk and restart Windows.

WHAT YOU MUST KNOW

When you run many programs at the same time within Windows, you can use up all your PC's RAM. In this lesson, you learned how Windows manages memory and how you fine-tune Windows for your memory requirements. In Lesson 38, "Troubleshooting with MSD," you will learn how to use the MS-DOS MSD command to display key information about your system. As you will learn, MSD is a very valuable troubleshooting tool. Before you continue with Lesson 38, however, make sure that you have learned the following key concepts:

✓ Windows uses virtual memory to give programs the illusion that they have more memory than is physically installed in their system. Virtual memory combines your computer's RAM with a swap file on disk. Windows moves inactive programs to the swap file to free up memory for the active programs.

✓ You can improve Windows 3.1 performance (at the cost of disk space) by selecting a permanent swap file. To select a permanent swap file, use the Control Panel 386 Enhanced icon.

✓ If you are using Windows 95 or 98, you should not modify the virtual-memory settings unless you are a very experienced user. In fact, most users have no reason to change the settings.

✓ Windows lets you improve the speed of disk read and write operations by selecting 32-bit disk access. To control 32-bit disk access under Windows 3.1, use the Control Panel 386 Enhanced icon. To control 32-bit disk access under Windows 95 or 98, use the Control Panel System icon.

Lesson 38

Cleaning Up Your Existing Disk Space

In Lesson 15, "Installing a New Hard Drive," you learned how to install or attach a new hard drive to your PC. With the cost of large hard drives becoming quite affordable, many users will choose to upgrade their hard drives. Unfortunately, as fast as a user can add disk space, many users have the ability to use it up. In Lesson 34, "Doubling Your Disk's Storage Capacity," you learned how to compress the files on your disk to double your disk's storage capacity. Before you upgrade or compress your hard disk, you should perform the steps this lesson presents to remove unnecessary files from your disk. By deleting files from your disk, you free up the disk space the files consumed so that Windows can reuse the space to store other files. By the time you finish this lesson, you will understand the following key concepts:

- To clean up your disk, you should delete files from your disk that you no longer need or move files you may not need to a floppy disk.

- When you delete a file, Windows does not actually remove the file from your disk. Instead, Windows moves the file into the Recycle Bin folder. To actually remove a file from your disk, you must delete the file from the Recycle Bin or flush the Recycle Bin's contents.

- Many Windows-based programs create temporary files that they store within the *Windows\Temp* folder or the *TEMP* folder. You should examine these two folders on a regular basis and discard any files the folder contains.

- Windows 98 provides the Disk Cleanup Wizard you can use discard temporary files, flush the Recycle Bin, and to delete temporary files your browser may have downloaded from across the Web.

DETERMINING A DISK'S FREE SPACE

This lesson focuses on ways you can clean up a disk to free up space that Windows can use to store other files. To determine the amount of free space your disk currently contains, you can use the Windows Explorer (under Windows 95 and 98) to perform these steps:

1. Click your mouse on the Start button. Windows, in turn, will display the Start menu.

2. Within the Start menu, click your mouse on the Programs option. Windows will display the Programs submenu.

3. Within the Programs submenu, click your mouse on the Windows Explorer option. Windows will open an Explorer window.

4. Within the Explorer window, right-click your mouse on the disk drive whose free space you desire. Windows, in turn, will display a small pop-up menu.

5. Within the pop-up menu, click your mouse on the Properties option. Windows will display the Disk Properties dialog box, as shown in Figure 38.1.

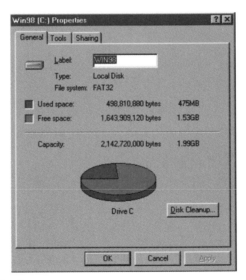

Figure 38.1 *The Disk Properties dialog box.*

6. Within the Disk Properties dialog box, you can see the disk's current free space. To close the dialog box, click your mouse on the OK button.

MANAGING YOUR OWN FILES

Within an office, workers discard paper files they no longer need on a regular basis. Workers often move papers they may or may not need at some time in the future into long-term storage. In a similar way, users must manage the files they store on their disks. In other words, when you no longer need a file's contents, you should delete the file.

If you think that you may need a file's contents at some point in the future, but you do not need the file now, you may want to move the file from your hard disk onto a floppy or Zip disk that you then store in a safe location. In general, you should clean up (delete or move unnecessary files from within) your own folders at least once a month.

FLUSHING THE WINDOWS RECYCLE BIN

When you delete a file, Windows does not actually erase the file's contents from your disk. Instead, Windows moves the file into a special folder on your disk called the *Recycle Bin*. Windows provides the Recycle Bin folder to help users "undelete" one or more inadvertently deleted files. If, after a user deletes a file (or files) the user decides he or she needs the file's contents, the user may be able to move the file from the Recycle Bin folder back to the file's original location on the user's disk. Although the Recycle Bin can be very useful when you must "undelete" one or more files, Windows use of the Recycle Bin means your system does not immediately free up disk space when you delete one or more files. Assume, for example, that you must free up disk space, so you delete a 50MB file named *BigReport.DOC* from your disk . After you delete the file, however, you find that your disk does not have an additional 50MB of space. In fact, you find that your disk's free space has not increased at all!

The reason that deleting the file from your disk did not free up additional space is that Windows did not actually delete the 50MB file from your disk. Instead, Windows moved the file into the Recycle Bin. To recover the disk space, you must remove the file from the Recycle Bin. To empty the Recycle Bin (which users refer to as *flushing the Recycle Bin*), you have two choices. First, you can discard all the files in the bin, or second, you can remove a specific file. To empty the entire bin, perform these steps:

1. Within the Windows Desktop, double-click your mouse on the Recycle Bin icon. Windows, in turn, will open the Recycle Bin folder.

2. Within the Recycle Bin folder, select the File menu Empty Recycle Bin option. Windows will display a dialog box asking you to confirm that you want to discard the bin's contents. Click your mouse on the Yes option.

3. To close the Recycle Bin folder, click your mouse on the folder's Close button.

CLEANING UP THE TEMP FOLDER

When you run programs within Windows, there will be many times when a program will create one or more temporary files. For example, in Lesson 25, "Upgrading Your Printer," you learned that when you print a document, Windows does not send the document to your printer, but rather, Windows makes a copy of the document on your disk. Windows then uses the copy to print the document. Likewise, when you edit a document, many word processing programs will create a temporary backup copy of your file on disk. Normally, when such programs finish their processing, they discard the temporary file. Unfortunately, there are times when a program, for some reason, does not delete its temporary files. As a result, over time, what started out as temporary files, are now consuming considerable space on your disk.

Most Windows-based programs create their temporary files within the *Windows\Temp* folder. You should get into the habit of cleaning out the *Windows\Temp* folder at least once a week, and more frequently, if you are low on disk space. To clean out the *Windows\Temp* folder, you will use the Windows Explorer to delete the files that the folder contains by performing these steps:

1. Click your mouse on the Start button. Windows, in turn, will display the Start menu.

2. Within the Start menu, click your mouse on the Programs option. Windows will display the Programs submenu.

3. Within the Programs submenu, click your mouse on the Windows Explorer option. Windows will open an Explorer window.

4. Within the Explorer window, select the Windows folder and then select the Temp subfolder. The Explorer, in turn, will display a list of the files the folder contains.

5. After you have selected the *\Windows\Temp* folder, click your mouse on the Explorer Edit menu and choose the Select All option. The Explorer, in turn, will highlight the folder's file list in reverse video. Next, click your mouse on the Delete button or press the DEL key. The Explorer will display a dialog box asking you to confirm that you want to move the files to the Recycle Bin. Select Yes.

6. To close the Explorer window, click your mouse on the window's Close button.

*Note: If your disk's root directory has a TEMP folder, you should also periodically check that folder's contents for unnecessary files as well. Some older programs, will create their temporary files within the TEMP folder as opposed to **Windows****Temp**.*

UNDERSTANDING HOW INTERNET FILES AND YOUR E-MAIL MESSAGES CONSUME DISK SPACE

When you view a Web site's contents, your browser must download the site's text and graphics files to your PC before it can display them. When use your browser to move from one site to another, your browser does not immediately discard the previous site's files. Instead, your browser lets the files remain on your disk in case you should choose to revisit the site. That way, rather than forcing you to wait once again for the files to download, your browser can display the files it previously downloaded. As you might guess, over time your browser could build up a collection of such temporary files, which consume a considerable amount of disk space. To discard your temporary Internet files, you can use Internet Properties dialog box, shown in Figure 38.2 . To display the Internet Properties dialog box, double-click your mouse on the Control Panel's Internet icon.

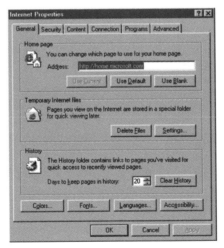

Figure 38.2 *The Internet Properties dialog box.*

As you know, when you receive electronic-mail messages from other users, your e-mail software places the messages into your Inbox folder. Over time, the number of messages within your Inbox can become quite large and difficult to manage. Most e-mail programs, therefore let you organize your messages within other message folders. As rule, you will periodically want to clean out your e-mail folders by deleting messages you no longer require. As is the case when you delete files within Windows, when you delete a message, your e-mail software normally does not remove the message from your disk, but rather, the e-mail software moves the message into a Deleted Messages folder (that works much like the Windows Recycle Bin, letting you later undelete the message should need the message's contents). If you are getting low on disk space, you should direct your e-mail software to discard the messages that your Deleted Messages folder contains. Depending on the e-mail software you are using, the steps you must perform to discard the Deleted Messages folder's contents will vary. If you receive messages with attached documents, your e-mail messages can quickly consume considerable disk space.

USING THE WINDOWS 98 DISK CLEANUP WIZARD

If you are using Windows 98, you can direct Windows to flush the Recycle Bin's contents, discard your temporary files, and even to delete files you have downloaded from across the Web, in one step, using the Disk Cleanup Wizard. To start the Disk Cleanup Wizard, perform these steps:

1. Click your mouse on the Start menu. Windows, in turn, will display the Start menu.

2. Within the Start menu, click your mouse on the Programs menu and choose Accessories. Windows will display the Accessories submenu.

3. Within the Accessories submenu, click your mouse on the System Tools option and choose Disk Cleanup. Windows, in turn, will display the Select Drive dialog box, as shown in Figure 38.3, that prompts you to select the drive you want to clean up.

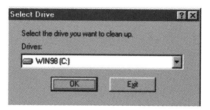

Figure 38.3 *The Select Drive dialog box.*

4. Within the Select Drive dialog box, use the pull-down list to select the drive you desire and then click your mouse on the OK button. Windows, in turn, will display the Disk Cleanup dialog box that lets you select the folders you want Windows to empty, as shown in Figure 38.4.

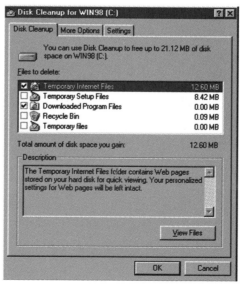

Figure 38.4 *The Disk Cleanup dialog box.*

5. Within the Disk Cleanup dialog box, place a checkmark next to each folder whose contents you want Windows to discard, and then click your mouse on the OK button. Windows, in turn, will display a dialog box asking you to confirm that you really want to delete the files. Select Yes.

WHAT YOU MUST KNOW

Although the prices for large hard disks have become quite affordable, you may find that by cleaning up your disk you can put off having to buy a new hard disk, at least for a while. In this lesson, you learned several operations you can perform (at least once a month) to clean up your hard disk. In Lesson 39, you will learn how to use the MS-DOS-based MSD command to identify various PC settings, such as IRQ assignments. Before you continue with Lesson 39, however, make sure that you understand the following key concepts:

✓ By taking time to clean out the files in your disk, you can normally recover considerable disk space.

✓ To clean up your disk, delete files you no longer need or move files you may not need to a floppy or Zip disk.

✓ When you delete a file, Windows moves the file into the Recycle Bin. If you want to free up the disk space that the file consumed, you must delete the file from the Recycle Bin or flush the Recycle Bin's contents.

✓ Using the Windows Explorer, you should examine the *Windows\\Temp* folder (and the root-directory *TEMP* folder, if one exists on your disk) on a regular basis and discard any files the folder contains.

✓ If you send and receive a lot of e-mail messages, your e-mail folders may be consuming considerable disk space. As a rule, you should clean up your e-mail folders at least once a month.

✓ To help you manage your disks, Windows 98 provides the Disk Cleanup Wizard, software that will help you delete temporary files and empty the Recycle Bin.

Lesson 39

Troubleshooting with MSD

MSD is a utility program provided with DOS and Windows 3.1 that you can use to examine your system configuration. MSD is an acronym for *Microsoft Diagnostic*. Using MSD, you can display information about your computer's memory use, port and IRQ settings, and much more. This lesson examines the MSD command in detail. If you are using Windows 95 or 98, turn to Lesson 40, "Using the Windows Device Manager," which discusses the Windows Device Manager. MSD is a very powerful program. Using MSD you can detect and avoid possible hardware conflicts, which reduces future troubleshooting nightmares. By the time you finish this lesson, you will understand the following key concepts:

- How to use MSD to display key system settings

- How to print an MSD report ideal for use with technical support personnel

- How to browse through the PC's current memory use

STARTING *MSD*

MSD is a utility program that you run from the DOS prompt. Do not run MSD with Windows active—you will not get correct results. Instead, exit Windows and start MSD from the DOS prompt, as shown here:

```
C:\> MSD   <ENTER>
```

MSD will start, displaying its main menu, as shown in Figure 39.1. From MSD's main menu, you can determine specifics about your hardware, as discussed next.

Note: *If you are using Windows 95, but you have the MSD command on your disk, start Windows 95 in DOS mode to run MSD. To start Windows 95 in DOS mode, select the Start menu Shutdown option. Windows 95, in turn, will display its Shutdown menu. Select the Restart the computer in MS-DOS mode option. After you run MSD, restart Windows 95 by typing* **WIN** *at the DOS prompt and pressing* ENTER.

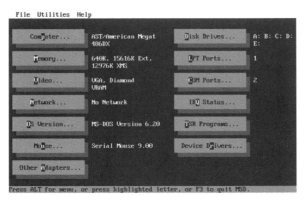

Figure 39.1 *MSD's main menu.*

DISPLAYING COMPUTER SPECIFICS

The MSD Computer option lets you display information about your processor, BIOS, and bus types. To display this information, press **P** at the MSD main menu. MSD, in turn, will display the Computer dialog box, as shown in Figure 39.2. To return to the MSD main menu, press ENTER.

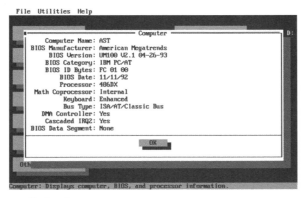

Figure 39.2 *The MSD Computer dialog box.*

Note: *You do not have to memorize the shortcut key for each option—they are visibly highlighted on the screen.*

DISPLAYING MEMORY SPECIFICS

The MSD Memory option lets you display information about your system memory use, such as the amount of conventional and extended memory, as well as your current use of the upper-memory area. To display this memory information, press **M** at the MSD main menu. MSD, in turn, will display the Memory dialog box, as shown in Figure 39.3.

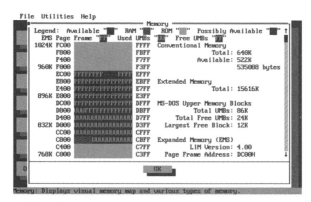

Figure 39.3 *The MSD Memory dialog box.*

If you press your keyboard's UP ARROW and DOWN ARROW keys, you can scroll through additional information. Use the legend that appears at the top of your screen to understand your memory use.

DISPLAYING VIDEO SPECIFICS

The MSD Video option lets you display specifics about your system's video capabilities, such as the display type, presence of a local bus, and the current video mode. To display the video specifics, press **V** at the MSD main menu. MSD, in turn, will display the Video display dialog box, as shown in Figure 39.4.

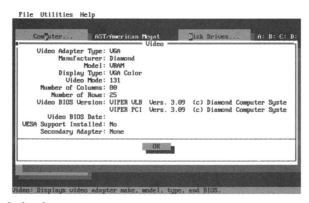

Figure 39.4 *The MSD Video dialog box.*

Video cards support several different text and graphics modes. Different text modes normally control the number of colors your screen can display and the number of character rows and columns. Normally, the PC displays 25 rows with no more than 80 characters on each row. When you work from the DOS prompt, you can normally ignore the video mode. Windows users, on the other hand, might want to experiment with different video modes (as discussed in Lesson 20, "Upgrading Your Video Card") to determine the number of colors and resolution that best meets their needs. To return to the MSD main menu, press ENTER.

DISPLAYING NETWORK SPECIFICS

The MSD Network option lets you display specifics about your system's network, such as the network name, network BIOS, and so on. To display the network specifics, press **N** at MSD's main menu. MSD, in turn, will display the Network dialog box, as shown in Figure 39.5. To return to the MSD main menu, press ENTER.

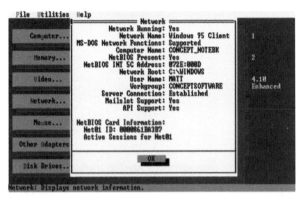

Figure 39.5 *The MSD Network dialog box.*

DISPLAYING OPERATING SYSTEM SPECIFICS

The MSD Operating System option lets you display specifics about the current operating system, such as current version number, boot disk, and DOS location (conventional or high-memory area). To display the operating system specifics, press **O** at the MSD main menu. MSD, in turn, will display the OS Version dialog box, as shown in Figure 39.6. To return to the MSD main menu, press ENTER.

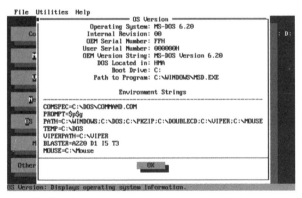

Figure 39.6 *The MSD OS Version dialog box.*

DISPLAYING MOUSE SPECIFICS

The MSD Mouse option lets you display specifics about your mouse, such as the mouse driver type and version, the mouse IRQ, and mouse sensitivity. To display the mouse settings, press **U** at MSD's main menu. MSD, in turn, will display the Mouse dialog box, as shown in Figure 39.7. To return to the MSD main menu, press ENTER.

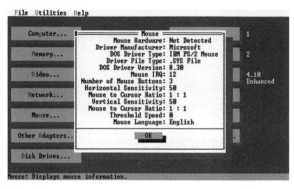

Figure 39.7 *The MSD Mouse dialog box.*

DISPLAYING ADAPTER SPECIFICS

The MSD Other Adapters option lets you display specifics about other hardware adapters, such as a joystick. To display adapter specifics, press **A** at the MSD main menu. MSD, in turn, will display the Other Adapters dialog box, as shown in Figure 39.8. To return to MSD's main menu, press ENTER.

Figure 39.8 *The MSD Other Adapters dialog box.*

DISPLAYING DISK DRIVE SPECIFICS

The MSD Disk Drives option lets you display specifics about your disk drives, such as the type, size, available space, and layout. To display the disk drive specifics, press **D** at MSD's main menu. MSD, in turn, will display the Disk Drive dialog box, as shown in Figure 39.9. If the disk drive settings shown are not correct, you will very likely need to update your computer's CMOS settings. To return to the MSD main menu, press ENTER.

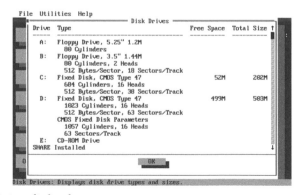

Figure 39.9 *The MSD Disk Drive dialog box.*

DISPLAYING LPT PRINTER PORT SPECIFICS

The MSD LPT Ports option lets you display specifics about your LPT printer ports, such as the port address and whether or not the computer sees a printer attached to the port. To display printer port specifics, press **L** at the MSD main menu. MSD, in turn, will display the LPT Ports dialog box, as shown in Figure 39.10.

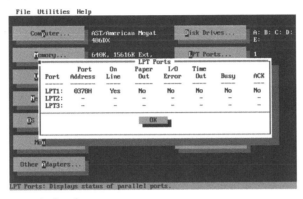

Figure 39.10 *The MSD LPT Ports dialog box.*

If you are having trouble with a printer, use MSD to make sure the computer sees the printer. To return to the MSD main menu, press ENTER.

DISPLAYING SERIAL PORT SETTINGS

The MSD COM Ports option lets you display specifics about your system's serial ports, such as their current port address and data communication settings. To display the serial port settings, type **C** at the MSD main menu. MSD, in turn, will display the COM Ports dialog box, as shown in Figure 39.11.

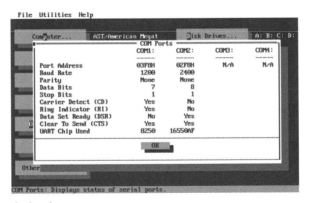

Figure 39.11 *The COM Ports dialog box.*

If you experience conflicts between serial port devices, such as a modem and mouse, use the COM Ports dialog box to verify that two devices are not using the same port address. Likewise, if you have trouble printing to a printer connected to a serial port, use this dialog box to examine the current port settings. The documentation that accompanied your printer will specify the settings the port must match. To return to the MSD main menu, press ENTER.

DISPLAYING IRQ SPECIFICS

As you read in Lesson 8, "Understanding Common Conflicts," IRQ is an acronym for interrupt request. As you install different hardware cards, you need to be aware of each card's interrupt-request line. Each card uses a unique IRQ line to signal the processor (to interrupt the processor) to request processing. For example, each time you move the mouse, the mouse interrupts the processor to tell it about the move. To display your PC's current IRQ settings, press **Q** at the MSD main menu. MSD, in turn, will display the IRQ Settings dialog box, as shown in Figure 39.12.

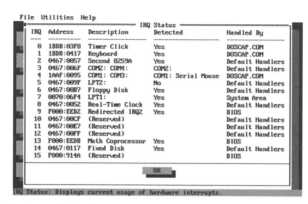

Figure 39.12 *The MSD IRQ Settings dialog box.*

If you are using an older PC based on an 8-bit bus (see Lesson 4), your system will support 8 IRQ lines, numbered 0 through 7. Table 39.1 lists the devices that normally correspond to these IRQ lines.

IRQ Number	Device
0	Timer
1	Keyboard
2	Available
3	COM2
4	COM1
5	Hard disk controller
6	Floppy disk controller
7	LPT1

Table 39.1 *Devices that normally correspond to IRQ 0 through 7 on an 8-bit bus.*

If you are using a 286-based PC or higher, your system will use 16 IRQ lines, numbered 0 through 15. Table 39.2 lists the devices normally assigned to these IRQ lines.

To support the 16 IRQ levels, your PC uses two special chips called *interrupt controllers*. The first controller chip corresponds to interrupts 0 through 7 and the second to interrupts 8 through 15. To access this second set of interrupts, your PC actually steals the line for IRQ 2 and uses it for a special purpose. To activate one of the interrupts on the second controller, the PC sends a signal on IRQ 2. In this way, IRQ 2 is said to be "cascaded." When a signal is sent on IRQ 2, the second interrupt controller jumps into action. Thus, your PC really only supports 15 interrupt-request lines.

IRQ Number	Device	IRQ Number	Device
0	Timer	8	Real time clock
1	Keyboard	9	Redirected as IRQ2
2	Cascaded	10	Available
3	COM2	11	Available
4	COM1	12	Available
5	LPT2	13	Math coprocessor
6	Floppy disk controller	14	Hard disk controller
7	LPT1	15	Available

Table 39.2 *Devices normally associated with IRQ 0 though 15.*

If you examine different hardware cards, such as a modem or a mouse, for example, you might find that the card's default setting is IRQ 2. As you just learned, however, IRQ 2 is not really used. When you set a card to IRQ 2, the signal is transparently routed to IRQ 9. If you examine the previous MSD IRQ Status dialog box, things should make more sense. As you can see, MSD lists 16 IRQs. IRQ 2 is set to something called Second 8259A—that's the second interrupt controller. If you examine IRQ 9, you will see that it corresponds to the Redirected IRQ 2.

When you need to assign an IRQ to a new device, search the MSD screen for a (Reserved) entry. These entries are available for use.

QUICKLY LOCATING AVAILABLE IRQs

When you install a new hardware card, you might need to assign an IRQ (interrupt request) line to the card. Each card in your system must have a unique IRQ. To determine an available IRQ, perform these steps:

1. Invoke the MSD command from the DOS prompt.

2. Press **Q** to select the IRQ Settings option.

3. From the list of IRQs, search for a (Reserved) entry. These entries are available for use.

DISPLAYING INFORMATION ON MEMORY-RESIDENT PROGRAMS

A memory-resident program is a program that remains active in your computer's memory until you restart your system. Many device drivers, for example, are implemented as memory-resident programs. Memory-resident programs are sometimes called *TSR* or terminate-and-stay-resident (in-memory) programs. The MSD TSR

Programs option lets you display specifics about memory-resident programs. To display specifics on memory-resident programs, press **T** at the MSD main menu. MSD, in turn, will display the TSR Programs dialog box, as shown in Figure 39.13.

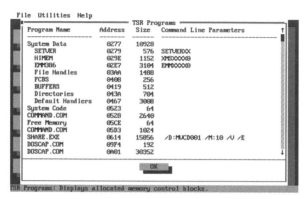

Figure 39.13 The MSD TSR Programs dialog box.

If you press your keyboard's UP ARROW and DOWN ARROW keys, you can scroll through the list of memory-resident programs. To return to the MSD main menu, press ENTER.

DISPLAYING DEVICE DRIVER SPECIFICS

A device driver is special software that lets your computer use a hardware device. Lesson 28 examines device drivers in detail. The MSD Device Drivers option lets you display device driver specifics such as the corresponding filename, the number of the devices the driver controls, the segment and offset address of the driver's header, and device attributes. To display device driver specifics, press **R** at MSD's main menu. MSD, in turn, will display the Device Driver dialog box, as shown in Figure 39.14.

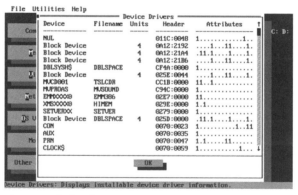

Figure 39.14 The MSD Device Drivers dialog box.

If a device driver does not specify a filename, the device driver is built into DOS. The filenames listed correspond to the device driver files that were installed from your CONFIG.SYS file when your system booted. The attributes specify different device characteristics. Table 39.3 lists the meanings of the different device attributes. To return to the MSD main menu, press ENTER.

Attribute Bit	Meaning If Set
0	This character device corresponds to the standard input device
1	This character device corresponds to the standard output device
2	This character device is the NUL device
3	This device is the CLOCK$ device
4	This character device supports fast I/O operations through Int 29H
6	This block device supports logical drive mapping and generic functions
7	This device supports IOCTL services
11	This device supports driver functions 0DH, 0EH, and 0FH
13	This device supports driver functions 10H and 02H
15	This device is a character device

Table 39.3 *Meaning of device driver files.*

PRINTING MSD REPORTS

Before you call a company's technical support, you should first to do some of your own homework. One of the best places to start is to print a copy of your MSD settings. To do so, press the ALT-F keyboard combination to select MSD's File menu, as shown in Figure 39.15. Select the Print option.

Figure 39.15 *The MSD File menu.*

If the company's technical support asks you for specific system settings, you will very likely find the settings within your MSD reports. In fact, you might even want to fax the reports to the technical support person.

GETTING MORE FROM MSD

If you are an experienced user, take time to examine the tools provided on MSD's Utilities menu. Using these tools, you can examine your system's memory use in detail, test the printer connections, and change various CONFIG.SYS and AUTOEXEC.BAT settings.

EXITING MSD

To exit the MSD program back to DOS, press the F3 function key or press the ALT-F keyboard combination to select the File menu. From the File menu, choose Exit.

WHAT YOU MUST KNOW

If you are about to install new hardware or if you are trying to troubleshoot a hardware conflict, you will find the MSD command very convenient. In Lesson 40, "Using the Windows Device Manager," you will learn other tips you should follow as you troubleshoot computer problems. Before you continue with Lesson 40, however, make sure that you have learned the following key concepts:

✓ The MSD command provided with DOS and Windows 3.1 can provide you with specifics about your computer's current hardware use.

✓ Using MSD, for example, you can determine which interrupt request (IRQ) lines are currently in use and avoid having to troubleshoot time-consuming IRQ conflicts.

✓ Before you call a company's technical support, you should print a copy of MSD's current settings. In many cases, you might want to fax the printout to the technical support personnel.

Lesson 40

Using the Windows Device Manager

In Lesson 40, "Troubleshooting with MSD," you learned how to use the MSD command under MS-DOS to display low-level hardware settings, such as your system's IRQ use. If you are using Windows 95 or 98, you can use the Windows Device Manager to examine, and, in some cases, change your system's low-level settings. This lesson examines the Device Manager in detail. By the time you finish this lesson, you will understand the following key concepts:

- The Windows Device Manager lets you display information about your hardware similar to that of the DOS-based MSD command

- Using the Windows Device Manager, you can detect hardware conflicts

- Depending on the hardware device, you may be able to change device settings using the Device Manager

DISPLAYING SYSTEM SETTINGS

To help you resolve hardware conflicts, Windows 95 and 98 provide the Device Manager. Using the Device Manager, you can view hardware settings, display information about hardware conflicts, remove software support for a device, and even change device settings. To start the Device Manager, perform these steps:

1. Select the Start menu Settings option and choose Control Panel. Windows 95, in turn, will open the Control Panel window.

2. Within the Control Panel window, double-click your mouse on the System icon. Windows will display the System Properties dialog box

3. Select the Device Manager tab. Windows, in turn, will display the Device Manager sheet, as shown in Figure 40.1.

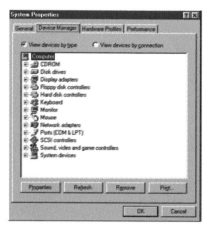

Figure 40.1 *The Windows Device Manager page.*

The Device Manager presents your system devices using a tree-like structure that is similar to a directory tree. If you examine Figure 40.1, you will find that the Device Manager precedes entries with a box that contains a small plus sign. If you click your mouse on the plus sign, the Device Manager will display the next level of devices. For example, if you click your mouse on the box that precedes the Disk drives entry, the Device Manager will expand the branch to display each of your disk-drive types, as shown in Figure 40.2.

Figure 40.2 *Using the Device Manager to display disk-drive types.*

When you expand a device branch, the Device Manager changes the plus sign that appeared in the small box to a minus sign. To collapse the branch, click your mouse on the small minus sign.

PRINTING YOUR DEVICE SETTINGS

Before you continue, take time now to print the Device Manager's hardware settings. Next, examine your print-out to better understand your system's hardware. After you examine your system settings, place the printout in a safe location. If you ever need to restore the settings for a specific device, you can use the printout as your guide. To print your system settings from within the Device Manager, perform these steps:

1. Click your mouse on the Device Manager Print button. The Device Manager will display the Print dialog box, as shown in Figure 40.3.

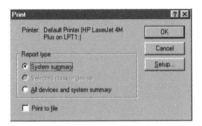

Figure 40.3 *The Device Manager Print dialog box.*

2. Within the Report type field, select the All devices and system summary option.

3. Choose OK.

USING THE DEVICE MANAGER TO RECOGNIZE HARDWARE CONFLICTS

When you install a hardware device, Windows tries to determine the device's IRQ and base-address. If Windows realizes that the new device's settings conflict with another device, the Device Manager will display a red X on top of the device name that appears within the Device Manager hardware list. To resolve a hardware conflict for an older (non plug-and-play) device, you may have to remove the card and change jumper or DIP switch settings. Then, you must tell Windows the new settings you have assigned to the card using the Device Manager, as discussed next.

USING THE DEVICE MANAGER TO SPECIFY NEW DEVICE SETTINGS

Using the Device Manager, you can display and change device settings. Depending on the corresponding de-vice-driver software (the software which lets Windows communicate with the device), the device settings you can change may differ. To get a better feel for how you might change device settings, double-click your mouse on the Mouse entry within the Device Manager list.

When the Device Manager expands the Mouse branch to display your mouse type, double-click on the icon that corresponds to the current mouse. The Device Manager, in turn, will display a Properties dialog box similar to the one shown in Figure 40.4.

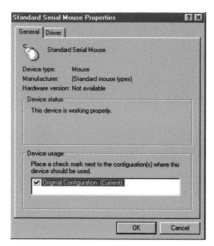

Figure 40.4 *The Mouse Properties dialog box.*

Within the Mouse Properties dialog box, you can display information about the mouse device driver, as well as the mouse hardware settings. For example, to display the mouse IRQ setting, select the Resource tab. The Device Manager, in turn, will display the Resource page, as shown in Figure 40.5.

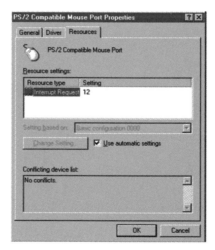

Figure 40.5 *The Mouse Properties Resource page.*

As you can see, the Resource page lists the mouse IRQ. For the devices that reserve a range of memory addresses, the Resource page will list the corresponding base (or starting address). Note that at the bottom of the Resource page, the Device Manager lists devices whose settings conflict with those of the mouse (which, in this case, is no devices). If the Device Manager recognizes a conflict, you can use this list to troubleshoot the error.

Note: Depending on your mouse type, your Mouse Properties Resource page may not display an IRQ setting. For example, if you are using a serial mouse, you connect your mouse to a serial port such as COM1 or COM2. In that case, your mouse IRQ corresponds to that of the serial port. Using the Device Manager, select the Properties button for the corresponding serial port to learn the mouse IRQ.

CHANGING DEVICE SETTINGS

To use the Device Manager to change a device setting, first click your mouse on the Use automatic settings checkbox that appears on the Resource page. When the box contains a checkmark, Windows will choose the device settings automatically. To manually override the Windows settings, you must first remove the checkmark. Next, click your mouse on the Change Setting button. Depending on your device type, Windows will display a dialog box within which you can change settings. Some devices, however, do not have settings you can change using the Device Manager.

REMOVING A DEVICE

If you remove a device from your system, and the device still appears within the Device Manager list, you can use the Device Manager to remove the device from the list. Likewise, should you assign an errant value to a device setting within the Device Manager and you cannot get the device to work, you can remove the device and then reinstall the device software. To remove a device from your system, perform these steps:

1. Within the Device Manager list, expand the branch that contains the device you want to remove.

2. Click your mouse on the device and choose Remove. The Device Manager, in turn, will display a dialog box warning you that you are about to remove the device.

3. Choose OK.

If you immediately want Windows to reinstall software support for the device (assuming you had removed the device due to a setting error), click your mouse on the Device Manager Refresh button. Windows, in turn, will examine your system for unknown devices and will install software for each device it finds.

WHAT YOU MUST KNOW

Newer hardware cards, such as modems and sound cards, support plug-and-play which lets the cards determine the settings other hardware in your PC is using, so the card can use different settings. In this way, plug-and-play hardware is very easy to install and to get working. Unfortunately, many users still have older cards that do not support plug-and-play. In such cases, the user must determine the proper settings. Using the Windows Device Manager, users can view the current system settings in order to find settings that are unused. Also, should a hardware conflict arise, the Device Manager may identify the conflict for the user, which reduces the user's troubleshooting time. This lesson examined the Windows Device Manager and how you use it to identify and resolve hardware conflicts. In Chapter 41, "Monitoring Windows Performance," you will learn how to use the Windows System Monitor to identify bottlenecks within your PC. Before you continue with Chapter 20, however, make sure you have learned the following key concepts:

✓   When you install new hardware, you need to ensure you do not use settings that are in use for another device. If such conflicts arise, the hardware or your system may not work.

✓   Windows supports plug-and-play hardware and software which reduces hardware conflicts.

✓   Older hardware devices do not support plug-and-play.

✓   Using the Device Manager, you can view hardware settings and resolve hardware conflicts.

✓   Some hardware devices have settings you can change using the Device Manager.

Lesson 41

Monitoring Windows Performance

If your system is responding slowly, you may quickly determine that you must upgrade something. Your challenge, however, may be to determine what hardware device to upgrade. If you are using Windows 95 or 98, you can take advantage of the System Monitor program to help you locate your system bottlenecks (those areas that are slowing down your system performance, such as having insufficient RAM). Using the System Monitor, you chart the activities that Windows normally performs behind the scenes. By watching charts over a period of time and during a variety of events, you can better understand your system and the processing it performs. This lesson will get you started with the Windows System Monitor. By the time you finish this lesson, you will understand the following key concepts:

- Using the System Monitor, you chart events within your system that influence your system performance.

- The System Monitor lets you chart activities within the Windows 95 kernel, file system, and virtual memory.

- To use the System Monitor effectively, you must observe its charts over an extended period of time and while you perform common operations.

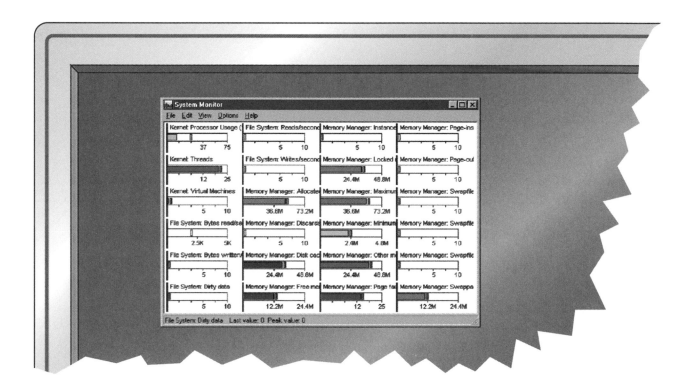

BOTTLENECKS DECREASE YOUR SYSTEM PERFORMANCE

When you think about upgrading your PC, start with the items that are slowing your system down. Users often refer to these "performance stealers" as bottlenecks. The most common places bottlenecks can occur within your system include:

- Within the processor (the CPU)

- Within the computer's RAM (or due to insufficient RAM)

- Within the video card

- Across a network or modem connection

- Within a disk drive (due to a slow drive or fragmented files)

UNDERSTANDING HERTZ AND MEGAHERTZ (MHz)

If you have shopped for a new computer, you have probably encountered a wide variety of systems and speeds. You can buy PCs with 166MHz (166 megahertz) Pentium chips, 266MHz chips, and even 450MHz chips. As you have learned, the higher a processor's megahertz, the faster the system. Within the CPU is a small clock that coordinates your computer's processing. The processor's speed tells you how many times per second the clock ticks. A processor whose clock ticks 1 million times per second has a speed of 1MHz. A 333MHz Pentium, therefore, is a processor whose clock ticks 333 million times per second! Each time the processor's clock ticks, the processor performs one and sometimes two instructions! Therefore, one of the fastest ways to improve your system's speed is to upgrade to a faster processor. As the price of computers continues to drop, those users who insist on top performance should plan to purchase a new PC every 18 months.

MEASURING YOUR SYSTEM BOTTLENECKS

As you work, there will be times when the bottlenecks in your system are obvious. For example, if your system is slow to start programs or to access files, your disk has very likely become fragmented. Likewise, if you are continually sitting in front of your PC waiting for your modem to download information from the Internet, a slow modem may be your bottleneck. Unfortunately, at other times, your bottlenecks may not be obvious. In such cases, however, you can use the Windows System Monitor to help you determine potential problems. To start the Windows System Monitor, perform these steps:

1. Select the Start menu Programs option and choose Accessories.

2. Within the Accessories menu, choose the System Tools menu and choose System Monitor. Windows, in turn, will display the System Monitor, as shown in Figure 41.1.

Figure 41.1 *The Windows System Monitor window.*

Using the System Monitor window, you can chart different system events. Within the System Monitor, you select the items you want to watch. Specifically, you can monitor the Windows file system, operating-system kernel (the key software within the operating system that Windows uses to manage hardware and programs), and Windows virtual-memory use. Also, depending on your network software, the System Monitor may let you track different items. To chart an item using the System Monitor, perform these steps:

1. Select the Edit menu Add Item option. The System Monitor, in turn, will display the Add Item dialog box, as shown in Figure 41.2.

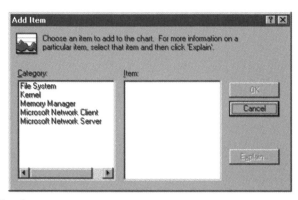

Figure 41.2 *The Add Item dialog box.*

2. Click your mouse on the category you desire. In this case, click your mouse on the File System category. The System Monitor will display a list of category items within the right-hand side of the Add Item dialog box, as shown in Figure 41.3.

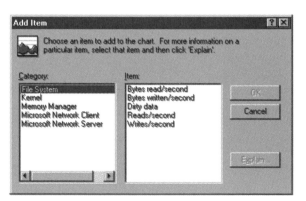

Figure 41.3 *Displaying category items you can monitor.*

3. Within the item list, you can select one item or you can hold down your keyboard's CTRL key as you click your mouse to select multiple items.

4. Choose OK. The System Monitor will display a chart for each item, as shown in Figure 41.4.

Note: *Before you add an item for charting, you can use the Add Item dialog box to display information about an item (the item's purpose). To display item specifics, select the item and click your mouse on the Explain button. The System Monitor, in turn, will display a pop-up window that briefly describes the item.*

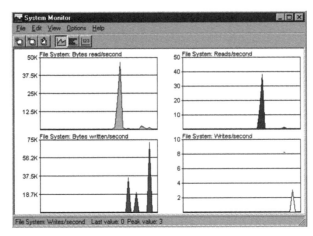

Figure 41.4 *Using the System Monitor to track multiple items.*

REMOVING AN ITEM FROM YOUR MONITOR LIST

Over time, you may find you no longer need to monitor a specific item. To remove an item from your monitor list, perform these steps:

1. Select the Edit menu Remove Item option. The System Monitor will display the Remove Item dialog box.

2. Within the item list, select the item you want to remove and choose OK.

CHANGING THE SYSTEM MONITOR'S CHART DISPLAY

As you watch items, the System Monitor lets you change the type of chart it displays. For example, Figure 41.5 displays system information using bar charts. Likewise, Figure 41.6 uses line charts to display similar information. Lastly, Figure 41.7 displays information using numbers only. To select the System Monitor chart type, select the View menu and choose the option that corresponds to the chart type you desire.

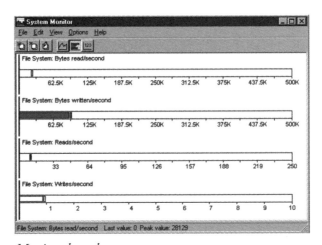

Figure 41.5 *Displaying System Monitor bar charts.*

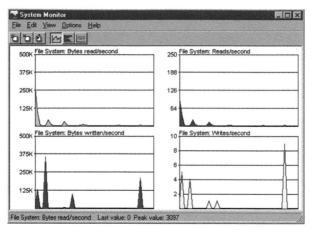

Figure 41.6 *Displaying System Monitor line charts.*

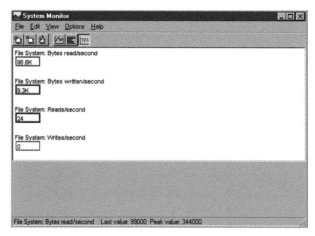

Figure 41.7 *Displaying System Monitor numeric values.*

WHAT YOU MUST KNOW

As your programs become more powerful and more complex, they demand more system resources, such as a fast CPU and sufficient random access memory. In this lesson, you learned how to use the System Monitor to help you detect potential bottlenecks within your system. Using the System Monitor, you can determine where your system is spending most of its processing time and then you can upgrade that part of your system first. In Lesson 42, "Basic Troubleshooting Techniques," you will learn steps you should perform to resolve common PC errors. Before you continue on your journey, make sure you have learned the following key concepts:

✓ The Windows System Monitor helps you detect bottlenecks within your system that decrease your system performance.

✓ The System Monitor lets you monitor your system's Kernel operations, the file system, and its memory use.

✓ To make the best use of the System Monitor, you need to observe the System Monitor's output over an extended period of time.

Lesson 42

Basic Troubleshooting Tips

Several of the lessons presented throughout this book have told you ways you can correct different PC problems. Unfortunately, you may not always know where you should look to find solutions for an error. This lesson examines several common PC problems and the steps you should take to correct them. By the time you finish this lesson, you will know where to turn when you encounter common system errors.

YOUR PC DOES NOT START, AND YOU DO NOT HEAR THE PC FAN WHIR

If, when you turn on your PC's power, the PC does not start, and you do not hear the PC's fan whir, perform the following steps:

- Make sure the PC's power plugs are plugged in correctly. If your PC has a small power light, and it comes on but nothing else happens, you know, at least, your computer is plugged in.

- Make sure the wall outlets you are using work—for example, plug a lamp into the socket and see if the lamp comes on.

- Verify that your surge suppresser is working correctly and that its breaker has not been tripped—for example, plug a lamp into the surge suppresser.

If each of the above is in working order, you might have to replace your PC's power supply, as discussed in Lesson 22, "Replacing the PC's Power Supply."

Your System Displays a Message about Invalid System Settings

As you learned in Lesson 6, "Understanding Your Computer's CMOS Memory," when your PC is not powered on, it uses a small battery-powered memory (called the CMOS memory) to keep track of specific settings, such as your disk types, system memory, keyboard types, and so on. Like all batteries, the CMOS batteries will eventually fail. When your battery fails, your system will display an error message, similar to the following, when your system starts:

```
Invalid System Settings Run Setup
```

This message can also appear after you add different hardware to your system unit, such as a new disk drive. Each time your system starts, it examines the available hardware, comparing it to your CMOS settings. If your hardware settings do not match your CMOS settings, your system will display the error message. Should this message appear, you must reset your CMOS settings, as discussed in Lesson 6. If your CMOS battery has died, you will need to replace the battery, as discussed in Lesson 7, "Replacing Your PC's CMOS Battery."

Your System Displays the Message "Non-System disk or disk error"

This message normally occurs when you leave a nonbootable floppy disk in drive A when you start your computer. Should this error message occur, remove the floppy disk and press any key to start your system. If your floppy drive does not contain a disk, try restarting your system by powering off and then powering back on your PC. If your system still displays the error, your hard disk may have become damaged.

In such a case, start your system using a bootable floppy disk. Examine your hard disk to determine whether it is readable. If you can access the hard disk, turn to a book on MS-DOS and examine the SYS command that lets you transfer operating system files from a bootable disk to another disk. In this case, you may have to transfer the files from a bootable floppy disk back to your hard disk. If you cannot access the hard disk, you will very likely need to reformat the disk using the MS-DOS FORMAT command.

Take time now to create a bootable floppy disk that you store in a safe location. If you are using Windows 98, double-click your mouse on the Control Panel Add/Remove Programs. Windows, in turn, will display the Add/Remove Programs Properties dialog box, within which you can use the Startup Disk sheet to create your bootable disk.

Your System Displays the Message "No such drive"

If, after you install a new hard drive, your system displays the message "No such drive" when you try to access the drive, perform these steps:

- Examine your system's CMOS settings, as discussed in Lesson 6, "Understanding Your Computer's CMOS Memory," to ensure that the CMOS sees the drive.

- If you have not already done so, you must partition the hard disk, as discussed in Lesson 15, "Installing a New Hard Drive."

Your System Displays the Message "Bad or missing Command Interpreter"

If your system displays the message "Bad or missing Command Interpreter," the file *COMMAND.COM* is missing from your disk's root directory. If this error message occurs, start your PC using a bootable floppy disk. Next, copy the file *COMMAND.COM* to your disk's root directory. Examine the root directory file *CONFIG.SYS* and examine the COMSPEC entry, which tells DOS where to locate the *COMMAND.COM* file. Make sure the entry points to the file's correct location on your disk. The file *COMMAND.COM* is responsible for displaying the MS-DOS prompt and processing the commands you type.

Your System Displays the Message "Bad command or file name"

If, when you type in a MS-DOS command, your screen displays the message "Bad command or file name," you may have mistyped the command. Or, the command's program file may not reside on your disk or in the current directory path. To start, double-check your command spelling and ensure that you are using the correct command name. Next, ensure that the command's program file resides in the current directory or a directory defined in the MS-DOS command PATH. For more information on the MS-DOS command PATH, refer to the MS-DOS documentation that accompanied your system.

Your System Displays the Message "Not ready reading drive" or "Drive is not Accessible"

If your system displays the message "Not ready reading drive," or if Windows displays the message "Drive is not Accessible" you are probably trying to access a floppy, Zip, or CD-ROM drive that does not contain a disk. If this error message occurs, abort the current operation or place a floppy disk into the drive and retry the command.

Your System Displays the Message "Insufficient Disk Space"

If, when you run a program, your system displays the message "Insufficient disk space," your computer's disk does not have enough empty space to hold the operation's result. If this message occurs, the current command will fail. If possible, delete unnecessary files to free up sufficient disk space, as discussed in Lesson 38, "Cleaning Up Your Existing Disk Space." Otherwise, you might consider using disk-compression software, as discussed in Lesson 34,"Doubling Your Disk's Storage Capacity," to increase your disk capacity. Finally, you may have to upgrade to a larger disk, as discussed in Lesson 15, "Installing a New Hard Drive."

Your System Displays the Message "Insufficient memory"

If, when you run a command, your system displays the message "Insufficient memory," you have very likely invoked too many memory-resident programs or device drivers. Most PCs today have sufficient memory for common operations. If this error message appears, turn to Lesson 33, which covers memory management, to determine ways you can better use your system memory. If Windows claims to have insufficient memory, exit Windows and restart your computer. Over time, if not restarted, errors in Windows programs will consume Windows available memory. Next, turn to Lesson 35 and ensure that you are getting the most from your Windows memory use.

Your System Displays the Message "Internal stack overflow, system halted"

If, while you are working within MS-DOS or Windows 3.1, your system displays the message "Internal stack overflow, system halted," a device is interrupting your processor so rapidly that your processor has run out of stack space (the memory where the processor temporarily sets aside its current work). If this error message occurs, power your PC off and on. When your system starts, edit the CONFIG.SYS file and add the following entry:

```
STACKS=8,512
```

After you save the file's new contents, restart your system using the **CTRL-ALT-DEL** keyboard combination.

YOUR SYSTEM JUST SEEMS TO BE RUNNING SLOWLY

If your system just does not seem as responsive as it used to, perform these steps:

- Clean up the files on your disk to free up additional disk space, as discussed in Lesson 38, "Cleaning Up Your Existing Disk Space."

- Defragment your disk, as discussed in Lesson 36, "Defragmenting Your Hard Disk."

- Run the ScanDisk program to examine your disk. You can start ScanDisk from the Accessory menu System Tools submenu.

- Add more RAM, as discussed in Lesson 12, "Adding Memory to Your PC."

YOUR SYSTEM DISPLAYS THE MESSAGE "GENERAL FAILURE READING (WRITING) DRIVE"

If, when you try to access a drive, your system displays the message "General failure reading (writing) drive," the drive has very likely not yet been formatted. Before Windows or MS-DOS can store information on a disk, you must first format the disk for use. To format a disk, you must use the MS-DOS FORMAT command, as discussed in Lesson 15, "Installing a New Hard Disk." If your drive contains a formatted disk, run the ScanDisk program to test the disk for errors.

YOUR MOUSE OR MODEM QUITS WORKING WHEN YOU USE THE OTHER

If, when you use your mouse, your modem stops working, or vice versa, your computer has an IRQ conflict. If such errors occur, turn to Lesson 39, "Troubleshooting with MSD" or Lesson 40, "Using the Windows Device Manager," to determine the cause of the IRQ conflict. The, select a different IRQ setting for either your mouse or modem. Depending on your hardware devices, you will then assign the IRQ setting using jumpers, DIP switches, or software, as discussed in Lesson 8, "Understanding Common Conflicts."

YOUR MOUSE DOES NOT RESPOND

If you are using an older MS-DOS-based program, the program may simply not support the mouse. If a Windows-based program does not respond to your mouse, perform these steps:

- Ensure that you are using the correct driver for your mouse, as discussed in Lesson 30, "Understanding Device Drivers."

- Test whether or not other programs, such as Windows, are responding to your mouse.

- Double-check your mouse-cable connection to ensure that it is secure.

- If you recently installed other hardware, use the MSD command or Windows Device Manager to determine if you have an IRQ conflict.

Because a mouse is a mechanical device, a mouse can fail over time. Likewise, it is also possible for a mouse cable to go bad (try wiggling the wire while moving the mouse). Also, you may want to clean your mouse by turning the mouse over, opening the small plastic holder that keeps the mouse ball in place and then using an aerosol blower to clean out dust from inside the mouse. You may even want to clean the mouse roller and ball using a cloth that you dampen with rubbing alcohol.

YOUR PRINTER DOES NOT PRINT

If, when you try to print, nothing happens, perform these steps:

- Make sure the printer is plugged in and powered on.

- Make sure the printer cable is securely connected to the printer and your PC.

- If you are using Windows, make sure Windows is configured to use the correct printer port. Also, make sure you are using the correct printer driver.

- Within the Windows Printer folder (which you can access from the Start menu Settings submenu), right-click your mouse on the printer icon. Windows will display a pop-up menu. Within the menu, choose Properties. Windows will display the printer's Properties dialog box. Within the dialog box, you can print a test page to the printer. If the page does not print correctly, Windows will start a Troubleshooting Wizard to help you determine the cause of the error.

If your printer will print for some programs, but not for others, you must tell the programs to use the Printer, which you can normally do within the program's Print dialog box.

It is possible for a printer cable, parallel port, or printer electronics to go bad. Many printers contain their own diagnostic programs—if yours does not or the diagnostic shows nothing wrong, have your printer tested by your computer retailer or service shop.

YOUR KEYBOARD DOES NOT RESPOND

If you type, and your PC ignores your keystrokes, double-check your keyboard cabling to ensure that the cable is securely in place. If your PC still ignores your keystrokes, power off your system, unplug and plug in your keyboard cables, and then restart your PC. In most cases, an entire keyboard will normally not fail. If you have keyboard problems, it is normally a stuck key or a single key that your PC is ignoring. Should your PC ignore a specific key, your keyboard very likely needs cleaning. In such cases, purchase a small aerosol blower from your computer retailer and use it to blow out the dust that surrounds the keys.

YOUR PC DOES NOT DISPLAY VIDEO

If you turn on your PC, and no video appears, perform these steps:

- Make sure your monitor is plugged in, powered on, and its cables are securely in place. Ensure that your monitor's power light illuminates.

- Make sure your monitor is securely connected to the video card.

- If necessary, unplug your system unit, remove the system unit cover, and ensure that the video card is securely in place within its expansion slot.

- If possible, test the video card by connecting a different monitor.

A Word on Cleaning

Ideally, you should keep your computer in a smoke- and dust-free environment. As a rule, you can keep your PC very clean simply by dusting it with a cloth. Never dust, clean, or spray a cleaner on your PC while the PC is powered on or plugged in. To keep your PC clean, all you really need is a lint-free cloth, some Q-tips, a little rubbing alcohol, and an aerosol blower. In general, if you keep your PC dust- and smoke-free, you will greatly reduce your chance of disk errors, stuck keys, and overheated PC components.

Windows 95 or 98 Will Not Start

If Windows 95 fails to start when you turn on your PC, turn your computer's power off and back on. When your screen displays the message Starting Windows 95 . . ., press the F8 function key. Windows 95, in turn, will display a menu of options similar to that shown here:

```
Microsoft Windows 95 Startup Menu

=====================================

     1. Normal

     2. Logged (\BOOTLOG.TXT)

     3. Safe mode

     4. Safe mode with network support

     5. Step-by-step confirmation

     6. Command prompt only

     7. Safe mode command prompt only

Enter a choice:
```

Within the Startup menu, select the Safe mode option which directs Windows 95 to load only key software it needs to start. In other words, Windows 95 will not load network software or nonstandard device drivers. Next, if your system starts in safe mode, examine the Windows 95 error-log files discussed next. To start Windows 98 in safe mode, hold down your keyboard CTRL key as your system starts.

Using the Windows Boot Log

Each time Windows 95 or 98 starts, Windows creates a file in your root directory, named *BootLog.TXT*, within which Windows details each step of its startup process. By reading the *BootLog.TXT* file's contents, you can determine quickly which device drivers Windows has loaded into memory and possibly the driver that is causing your error. You may then be able to replace or update the device-driver file. The following listing, for example, illustrates partial contents of the file *BootLog.TXT*:

```
[001114FE] Loading Device = C:\WINDOWS\HIMEM.SYS
[00111501] LoadSuccess   = C:\WINDOWS\HIMEM.SYS
[00111502] Loading Device = C:\WINDOWS\EMM386.EXE
[0011150E] LoadSuccess   = C:\WINDOWS\EMM386.EXE
[00111512] Loading Device = C:\WINDOWS\MOUSE.SYS
[00111526] LoadSuccess   = C:\WINDOWS\MOUSE.SYS
(Logo disabled)
[001115FD] Loading Vxd = CONFIGMG
[001115FF] LoadSuccess = CONFIGMG
Initializing KERNEL
LoadStart = system.drv
LoadSuccess = system.drv
LoadStart = keyboard.drv
LoadSuccess = keyboard.drv
LoadStart = mouse.drv
LoadSuccess = mouse.drv
LoadStart = gdi.exe
LoadStart = C:\WINDOWS\SYSTEM\GDI32.DLL
LoadSuccess = C:\WINDOWS\SYSTEM\GDI32.DLL
```

USING THE WINDOWS 98 SYSTEM CONFIGURATION UTILITY

If you are using Windows 98, you should take advantage of the System Configuration Utility, shown in Figure 42.1, to help you troubleshoot system errors. Using the System Configuration Utility, you can run a diagnostic startup operation which directs Windows to interact with you before it performs specific operations. In addition, you can perform a selective startup opeartion to control which files (such as *System.INI*) that Windows processes and which programs Windows starts.

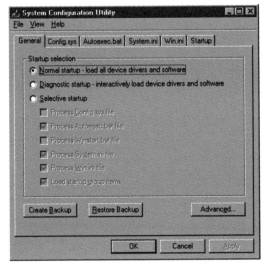

Figure 42.1 *The Windows 98 System Configuration Utility.*

To run the System Configuration Utility, perform these steps:

1. Click your mouse on the Start button. Windows, in turn, will display the Start menu.

2. Within the Start menu, select the Programs menu Accessories option. Windows will display the Accessories submenu.

3. Within the Accessories submenu, select the System Tools option and choose System Information. Windows, in turn, will display the System Information window, as shown in Figure 42.2, which you can use to display specifics about your system.

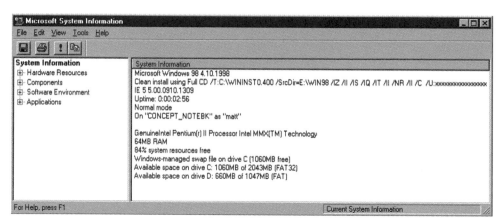

Figure 42.2 *The System Information window.*

4. Within the System Information window, select the Tools menu System Configuration Utility option.

Using the Windows 98 Troubleshooting Wizards

If you are using Windows 98, you can take advantage of several troubleshooting Wizards that Windows 98 provides within its online Help facility. As you have learned, a Wizard is a software program that helps you perform a specific task. In this case, the Wizards may help you resolve a modem or printer error. To start the troubleshooting Wizards, start Windows online Help facility and then search for **troubleshoot**. The Help system, in turn, will display a list of its Wizards.

WHAT YOU MUST KNOW

In this lesson, you have learned how to deal with many of the more common errors you might encounter when you work with your PC. Many of the error messages you will encounter while you work with your computer are application errors, generated by such programs as Windows, MS-DOS, or even your word processor. When your screen displays an error message after your PC has been running for some time, turn to the documentation that accompanied the application that was running when the error occurred. In most cases, the documentation will provide you with steps you should perform to correct the error.

For the past 41 lessons, you have examined a variety of PC hardware and software issues. Before you continue on your way, make sure you understand the following key concepts:

✓ When you are troubleshooting your system, start with the easiest and least expensive fix first and work your way gradually toward the most difficult and expensive. For example, check the plug before you dismantle your power supply.

✓ Before you change your PC's system settings, make sure you record the original values. Likewise, before you remove or change any physical switches or parts, either take notes or a Polaroid photo. That way, you will have the original settings should you need them in the future.

✓ Read the manual. You just might find your exact problem and its solution described in detail.

✓ Fix one problem at a time. If your fix does not work, put your PC back the way it was and try another fix. You can lose control of your status if you try too many things at once.

✓ Think functionally and sequentially. Operations within the computer all follow basic rules of physics—although it might seem like it, there are no computer gremlins. If you think about the order of the process, the place to locate the problem might become apparent.

✓ Ask a user group in your area for technical support. Sometimes an apparently catastrophic error is common or has a common fix.